The Queen Mother's Family Story

BY THE SAME AUTHOR

King George V, as a sportsman
H.R.H. Princess Marina, Duchess of Kent
The Life of Lady Houston
The Life of Sir Malcolm Campbell

The Modern Shooter
Farming Adventure
Sporting Adventure
Newfoundland—The Fortress Isle
Poison on the Land
Wild Wings

JAMES WENTWORTH DAY

The Queen Mother's Family Story

ROBERT HALE · LONDON

First published in Great Britain 1967

Second Edition 1979

ISBN 0 7091 7342 3

Robert Hale Ltd
Clerkenwell House
Clerkenwell Green
London EC1R 0HT

PRINTED IN GREAT BRITAIN
BY LOWE & BRYDONE LTD., THETFORD, NORFOLK

CONTENTS

ILLUSTRATIONS

ACKNOWLEDGEMENTS

I desire to acknowledge my gratitude, for invaluable help, to the Earl of Strathmore who gave free access to family papers in the Charter Room at Glamis Castle; to the Dowager Countess Granville for her personal reminiscences of Glamis and its legends; to the late Sir David Bowes-Lyon for much help; to Mr. J. F. Kemp, Factor of the Glamis Estates; to Mr. George Fairweather, former Head Keeper at Glamis for many lively memories; to Mrs. C. Beckwith who worked closely with the late Miss Lilian Bowes-Lyon whose heroic work in the East End at the height of the bombing of London will endure for ever as an epic of personal sacrifice; to Sir Shane Leslie for a shaft of new light on the problem of the "Monster"; to an old friend Mrs. Mary How (formerly Viscountess Lymington); and to Mr. Ralph Arnold for permission to consult and quote from his invaluable book *The Unhappy Countess* (Constable, 1957), without which it would have been impossible to have given so full an account of the incredible plots and intrigues of the blackguardly Stoney Bowes, surely the greatest cad of recent centuries.

Lady Elphinstone's guide to Glamis was of enormous help, whilst I owe a bow of thanks across the grave to the Rev. John Stirton, Senior Minister of Crathie and a Chaplain to the late King George VI, who was an outstanding authority on the ecclesiastical history of Glamis, and to the late Mr. A. H. Millar for his scholarly notes on Earl Patrick's "Book of Record" which, in itself, is an unique work.

I am grateful to the librarians of the *Daily Mail* and of the Chelmsford Library for their assistance in many directions, and to my private secretaries, Miss Janet Clark for her research work, and Mrs. B. H. Hayward for having typed the manuscript in almost record time.

Ingatestone, Essex. J.W.D.

PREFACE TO THE SECOND EDITION

SINCE this book was first written in 1967 certain changes have inevitably taken place. Timothy Patrick, sixteenth Earl of Strathmore, has died and been succeeded by the present Earl, Fergus, who is dedicated to the castle and its unique family heritage, and to whom I owe a deep dept of gratitude for his help with this edition.

Mr. Kemp, the previous Factor, who Lord Strathmore says did an immense amount of work for the family and for the Estate during what had been difficult times, died in 1977. His son, now a lawyer in Edinburgh, preserves the family name but alas the working link with Glamis is broken. Messrs. Arthur Young McLelland Moores & Company are the present Factors to the Estate which has expanded its agricultural activities to 1,500 acres of arable land and 1,000 acres of hill pastures. Mixed farming is carried on, with the emphasis on malting barley and potatoes.

The castle is open to visitors and their numbers swell each year. Last year, 1977, no less than 65,000 people paid to walk within the walls of history. As in so many other stately homes, their desire for personal mementoes of the house is catered for by a shop which also sells books and postcards relating to the place.

J.W.D.

INTRODUCTION

"The first to fight in war, the last to quarrel in peace.
The first to help anyone in trouble."

HER Majesty Queen Elizabeth, the Queen Mother, is the supreme mother-figure today in a world tortured by fear, rootless, disillusioned, largely bereft of beliefs. In this bleak era of shaken values she remains the wise, calm, smiling epitome of motherhood. The national symbol of unselfish love. She typifies Christian values.

What, then, do we know of the family background, the upbringing and the home which produced one who is perhaps the universal image of the ideal mother today?

If one were to ask the average person how much they know of the Queen Mother's family, the Bowes-Lyons, the answer would probably be a vague picture of a grim Scottish castle called Glamis, terribly haunted by a family "Monster" who puts Dracula in the shade.

Middle-aged people recall magazines which chilled their youthful blood with stories of the monster at Glamis. He was said to be a certain Lord Glamis, born a hideous monstrosity two hundred years or so ago, who lived to an incredible age. Imprisoned in a secret cell cut in the 15-feet thick castle walls, this dreadful creature was seen only by each succeeding earl,—who was confronted with it on his twenty-first birthday—the family lawyer, and the estate agent or factor, as he is known in Scotland. One assumes that the Monster was, in fact, the rightful heir and had been so through the lives of several succeeding earls.

The Monster was never spoken of in the family, but constantly written about. He was Britain's most fearful family skeleton.

And by no means the only horror to haunt the embattled castle of the medieval Thanes of Glamis.

The Bowes-Lyon story took a prettier turn when the late King, as Duke of York, fell in love with a girl with cornflower blue eyes in a Hertfordshire park and married her—the Queen Mother. And the rest of England said, with a grateful sigh: "Thank God for a drop of good Scots blood at last".

There is, however, vastly more in the Bowes-Lyon story than a haunted castle and a royal romance. Few people know this because the Bowes-Lyons have never sought publicity. They prefer the country to London. They shun television and broadcasting. They do not strut in politics. They do not prink themselves publicly in uniform. They preach no popular gospels. They lead no flamboyant crusades. Yet, for 600 years, they have produced a succession of men and women to whom kindliness, self-sacrifice and a deep sense of public duty is almost a legend. When fame and power are forced upon them they invest them with a unique quality of embracing friendliness.

The Queen Mother, the Queen and Princess Margaret are the supreme examples. Their secret surely lies in one phrase, spoken to me quite casually over a drawing-room tea table by the Dowager Lady Granville, the Queen Mother's sister. "You know, we Lyons are not a clan", she said, rather thoughtfully. "We never were a clan. We were always a family".

Go to Glamis village, with its little grey stone houses and austere church, sprawling along either side of a burn, under the shelter of the great park wall of the castle, and this sense of "the family" almost hits you.

Everyone in Glamis takes it for granted that "the family" means, not only the Earl in his castle, but themselves in their cottages. And those three royal ladies, far away in London.

That is why they speak of the Queen Mother as "our ain little Leddie Elizabeth". You note the possessive sense. She belongs to them. So does Princess Margaret. After all, she was born at Glamis; she is a local girl. They remember her, and Princess Elizabeth, running down the village street to buy their two penn'orth of sweets at Mr. Buchanan's shop.

Go away from the almost feudal village of Glamis, into the distant market towns of Forfar or Kirriemuir, or the great seaport of Dundee, and what do you find? Exactly the same possessive attitude. The same fierce pride in the Lyons of Glamis.

The truth is that the Queen Mother's family is not merely respected. It is loved. One might almost say it is *owned*.

Here, then, is some inkling of the secret power which, quite unconsciously and utterly unaffectedly, the Bowes-Lyon family exercise. At home in Angus they are an essential, friendly part of the background of life. They belong to the scene as much as the far-off, snow-whitened tops of the Grampian Mountains or the old Scots pines, red-trunked in sunlight on the hills. They are "the family—the neighbours at the castle".

"The Glamis family are the first to fight in war. The last to quarrel in peace. The first to help anyone in trouble." That is how Wullie Savage, taxi-driver of Kirriemuir, summed up the Bowes-Lyons as he drove me on my first visit to Glamis. And he added: "One of the best presents that Buckingham Palace ever had came from Glamis."

Today, the Commonwealth echoes that proud, local boast. And Wullie Savage, be it noted, is not and never was, a tenant on the Glamis Estate; he is just a typical, local Scot who takes an immense pride in the local family, which has more than made good on the greatest stage in history.

Let us look further into this long tale of the Bowes-Lyons, the Bowes who brought their fortune into the family, and the Lyons who were at Glamis for centuries before.

Glamis, at first sight, is unforgettable. I came on a sharp day of champagne sunlight and saw suddenly the soaring pile of keep and tower, pepperpot turrets and battlements, rise, splendidly unreal, pinky-grey against a winter sunset of orange and green. Far off the snowy line of the Grampians were a backcloth of unearthly beauty. The flag of the Lyons flew stiffly in the wind.

It was a castle not of this world, but of the world of Hans Andersen. A castle of ghosts, and Queens, reaching to the stars. This air of ethereal unreality impresses one instantly. It does not awe. Glamis has not that overmastering sense of brutish power and dark cruelty which so many Norman castles, even in ruin, emanate. Too often the dungeon and the rack, the thumbscrew and the press, have left their foreign mark of Latin cruelty.

Glamis has, rather, the sense of a family stronghold, a place of succour and security for its Lord and his people. And so, indeed, it was when rings of fortified walls with successive embattled gateways surrounded it. Yet it has more dark secrets than perhaps any castle in Britain. Not least, that macabre fresco of violent death outlined on the wooden floor of an upper room. There, not many years ago, the Queen Mother's great-aunt remembered seeing, stained in the floorboards, the outline of a dead body where, as Lady Elphinstone says, "a man had lain outstretched and blood had run practically all round him."

I think of a prettier little cameo of memory—an evening of frosty light when, by the corner of the kitchen-garden wall, where the trees in Bents Wood were magical with snow, a couple of woodcock, chasing each other with the speed of snipe, nearly flew smack into my bottom waistcoat button. That, somehow, does not happen to one on ordinary days in humdrum places.

I spent a week in the castle. It has nine ghosts, more or less. Some, like the "family monster", have faded out altogether. None the less, the place is haunted. I sat, almost alone, in it on a dark winter's night, a blinding snowstorm outside. Suddenly the vast, towering pile with its gilded State Rooms, its haunted chapel, secret passages, stone vaulted halls, dungeons and crypt, was plunged into utter blackness by a power cut.

In those dark minutes I knew, as never before in any haunted house, that this was the castle of ghosts. Too many grown-up members of the family, whose word I respect, have seen too much to leave one in any doubt. The gentlest ghost, and that most often seen, is the "Grey Lady". She appears in the chapel. No one quite knows who she is—this gentle, forgotten Lyon who says her prayers in the sunlight.

Few families are older than the Lyon family, for centuries Thanes of Glamis. They had their own army more than 600 years ago. Their private hangman more recently than that. The Hangman's Chamber at Glamis, white-walled, bare of furniture, is not a room one would choose to sleep in.

They kept a hangman, not because they were tyrants, but because the Scottish kings gave them, as Thanes of Glamis, the responsibility of maintaining justice, law and order throughout the wide lands of Angus. That power was never abused.

"There was never yet an arrogant Lyon", said a local farmer to me. "Always guid men an' gentle leddies." Pomposity has never been their middle name. How many great families can claim the same?

This inheritance of ruling power, through Royal blood, gave the family its sense of duty. It also gave the Lyons that innate modesty and open-hearted friendliness which is the secret of the Queen Mother's power over the hearts of men and women.

A woman brought the first royal blood into the family in 1372 when Sir John Lyon, tall and fair, nicknamed "The White Lyon". married Princess Joanna, daughter of King Robert II of Scotland. She brought him the castle and lands of Glamis and the title and powers of Thane of Glamis, a king with power of life and death.

That was the beginning of the family at Glamis. Today the castle stands, a grey-pink, soaring pile of towers, battlements and chimneys, in a great park, between the Grampian Mountains and the heathery skyline of the Sidlaw Hills. It is said to be the most haunted house in all Britain.

King Malcolm II of Scotland was murdered there. His ghost may open your bedroom door. Shakespeare placed the murder of Duncan, by Macbeth, in the stone-floored, vaulted Duncan's Hall of the castle, and when the Queen Mother was a child this was the one room through which she and her sisters always scuttled at top speed.

No family has had more fantastic ups and downs. A Lady Glamis was burnt as a witch by James V, yet a few years later, Mary, Queen of Scots, dined with the family and stayed the night.

In recent years they have produced two great illegitimacy cases at Law. Before that, the most sensational abduction scandal on record. One of the family won the Derby four times, but was happier on the Left Bank in Paris than on Newmarket Heath. He left as his memorial the most fantastic museum of art in Britain.

Another Bowes-Lyon should have been given the V.C. in the last war. He was burnt in effigy instead.

In 1924 an Aberdeen shop-girl named Connie Bain, fired by the newspaper stories of the Queen Mother's own romance, took her claim for legitimacy to the Edinburgh Court. They admitted her right to be recognized as a Bowes-Lyon and a cousin of the Royal Family. Yet another, a young and dashing soldier, shot himself at midnight in a thunderstorm a few years ago. His was a tragedy of love fit for a Victorian novel.

Another member of the family, a woman, was not only rich in her own right, but an outstanding poetess, devoted to country life, peace and beauty. Yet she gave her life to the people of Bow and Stepney during the nightly horrors of the blitz on London when East End streets were an inferno of flames, dead and dying. Thereby she earned the title of "The Florence Nightingale of the East End". Her story alone is one of the minor epics of the Second World War.

That is not all the tale. The family once were worth millions in money. They owned a principality in land, three castles and six lesser mansions.

Until a few years ago they dwelt in splendour. They owned 65,000 acres. Now 12,000 acres have been sold to satisfy that most immoral of all taxes, death duties. The gilt is rubbed off and the splendour is a memory. Forty servants at Glamis have fallen to four. Fifty rooms are bare of furniture. When I visited him, Lord Strathmore was living a spartan life in a few small rooms, in his towering, haunted castle. He had one motor-car only.

Streatlam Castle, the Durham seat, is flat to the ground and Gibside, that once splendid mansion, is a roofless ruin.

The town house has gone. Castle Lyon, outside Dundee, is a home for Borstal boys, or something equally unattractive. The family goes on.

It ranges from the Queen Mother to blue-blooded girl secretaries and an heiress who lost legs and hands and finally, her life, working for the slum children of Stepney in the last war. The Bowes-Lyons are like that. Warriors in war. Utterly unselfish in peace.

PART ONE

THE BOWES STORY

I

MARY ELEANOR—COUNTESS OF TRAGEDY

THE most fantastic and pathetic figure in the Bowes-Lyon family story is Mary Eleanor Bowes, ninth Countess of Strathmore. She brought to the Lyons of Glamis, in 1767, the Bowes wealth worth millions. She inherited 43,000 acres in land, £21,000 in rents, coal mines and ironworks, Streatlam Castle and Gibside in Durham. Like many Scottish noble families the Lyons were powerful but poor. Mary Eleanor's riches put them on a level with the wealthiest English nobility.

The Bowes family descended from Sir Adam Bowes, a fourteenth-century lawyer who amassed a fortune and married the heiress of the Trayne family of Streatlam Castle in the County Palatine of Durham. Sir J. Bowes was Queen Elizabeth I's ambassador to Russia in 1583 and went on many important missions for his Sovereign. In 1691 Sir William Bowes, grandfather of the unfortunate Mary Eleanor, married the heiress of the Blakiston family of Gibside near Gateshead and thereby added that large property to his already wide lands.

George Bowes, father of Mary Eleanor, was a far-sighted forceful man of affairs. He was one of the early coal-owners and a pioneer of many improvements. He founded a coal trade company or partnership called the Grand Allies. He also went in for price cutting in a big way which annoyed other coal-owners, but added vastly to his own fortune. He succeeded to the estates when he was only twenty-one years old, remarkably handsome and extremely wild. He settled down when responsibility fell on his shoulders.

His first wife was Eleanor Verney, the only child of the Hon

Thomas Verney, whom he married when she was only fourteen. She was a remarkably well-educated child of encyclopaedic knowledge, "the most accomplished of her sex", as he wrote when she died a year later.

For twenty-two years George Bowes was a childless widower devoted to his estates and his coal mines, eminently successful, a great sportsman and a man with a real appreciation of beauty in art, architecture and nature.

He was the first man to start a pack of foxhounds in Durham, which he did with nineteen couple of hounds, bought in 1738 from Sir William Middleton of Belsay Castle in Northumberland. A few years later, in 1745, he bought a famous pack of fox-hounds from Thomas Fownes of Steepleton Iwerne in Dorset. It was said to be "the first pack of English hounds to be entered solely to fox".

He also bred a good many racehorses. His father, incidentally, had owned the famous Byerly Turk mare, one of the foundation mares of the best bloodstock today.

George Bowes preferred Gibside to Streatlam and there he laid out and planted the park and gardens with notable good taste. He engaged James Paine as his architect and carried out an extensive building programme, part Gothic and part classical, which was impressive. There is no doubt that George Bowes had very real talent as an artist, an amateur architect, a landscape gardener, and as a connoisseur of pictures and furniture. He gave fifteen hundred guineas for the famous painting of Rubens' wife *enceinte*, in a fruit shop.

Added to all this he was Member of Parliament for Durham, a devoted Whig and had great personal charm.

Twenty-two years after his child-wife died he married Mary Gilbert, whose father owned St. Pauls Walden in Hertfordshire. Thus that estate came into the Bowes-Lyon family and it was there, in the grounds, two hundred years later, that the Duke of York proposed to Lady Elizabeth Bowes-Lyon, now the Queen Mother.

George and Mary Bowes had one child only, Mary Eleanor. She was born on 24th February, 1749. Her father was devoted to her. She inherited his charm, his artistic instinct and love of beauty, his zest for living and for knowledge, but her father forgot to teach her the value of religion.

Her life was one of riches, tragedy and misery. It is easy to condemn her, but far more just to regard her as a clever, spoilt woman who was a bad judge of men, as clever women often are, and who, because of her enormous wealth, was the target for every adventurer in England.

She wrote a pathetic little book called *Confessions* in which she laid bare her love affairs, one of which at least was touchingly idealistic, and in doing so laid bare her own soul:

> I am convinced that a want of a proper sense of religion has been the original cause of all my errors; all the grounds of this mischief were laid before my father died, and then I was only between eleven and twelve years old. . . . As he was uncommon handsome and a great rake in his youth, he grew very pious in his advanced years, and having felt the want of education and study he was (as I have heard him say) determined his heir should not feel the same inconveniences. Accordingly he brought me up with a view to my being as accomplished at thirteen as his favourite first wife was at that age, in every kind of learning except Latin.
>
> At four years old I could read uncommonly well and was kept tight to it, made to get many things off by heart. I read the Bible, but at the same time equal or greater pains were taken to instruct me in the mythology of every heathen nation that ever existed; and my father, who was a real patriot and a brave man, was continually expatiating on the patriotic virtues and shining merits of the ancient philosophers and heroes. My mind was so puzzled with such a variety of religions that, except the firm belief of a God, I knew not which of all the modes of worship to adopt from real conviction, as to the weak judgment of a child all appeared equally supported by tradition. However, I saw my father was a christian and a protestant, therefore I called and believed myself one too. . . .
>
> One other misfortune for me was that, though my father did not applaud suicide and revenge in general terms, by their names, I have often hear him speak highly of men who have been guilty of them, Cato for one instance. My father's whole care and attention was bestowed in the improvement of my knowledge in whatever I

showed a genius for, and in acquiring me a good stock of health, hardening and strengthening my constitution by every possible means, often the most rigid ones. My father was continually talking of, and endeavouring to inculcate into me, sentiments of generosity, gratitude, fortitude and duty to himself; and an insatiable thirst for all kinds of knowledge. But I never heard him once say, to the best of my recollection, that chastity, patience and forgiveness of injuries were virtues; and he was very passionate.

A touchingly pathetic confession which sheds revealing light on the background, upbringing, traditions and muddled religious values of this highly intelligent girl.

When she was only thirteen she had her first childish love affair. At a children's ball she met a boy of fifteen, Campbell Scott, younger brother of the Duke of Buccleuch. He was intelligent, and one imagines good-looking. Mary Eleanor wrote: "Mr. Campbell Scott liked my conversation and as he was smart and clever I liked his." This boy and girl affair was given a fillip by her cousin, a young Liddell, who was at Eton with Campbell Scott and "teazed us into a belief that we were in love with each other. Mr. Scott told me he had a tender affection for me and liked my company better than any other girl's; at which I was not displeased; but, in return, I particularly remember that I made use of the words 'tender esteem for him'."

Later, they exchanged rings. "When Mr. Scott gave me the blue ring, I gave him one my father had given me, exactly the same, by which means nobody perceived I had got a new ring and thus no one knew but ourselves."

Young Scott went abroad with his regiment and died a year later of smallpox. Mary Eleanor was cut to the heart. She wore his blue ring for years afterwards.

Another childhood admirer was Charles James Fox, who was then at Eton with Campbell Scott. She records primly. "The present Mr. Fox had a great liking for me, and followed me, but he had too much pride to tell me so directly, as he saw I preferred Mr. Scott. For which reason, I know, he abused us both. But, like Mr. Scott, he was clever."

Mary Eleanor's mother was shy and reserved whereas the daughter was high-spirited. None the less she referred all her many suitors to her mother's judgement. All were turned down.

Then came John Lyon, eldest son of Thomas Lyon, eighth Earl of Strathmore, whose wife was the co-heiress of James Nicholson of West Rainton in County Durham. He was born in County Durham and much of his boyhood was spent there.

He was so handsome that he was known in later life as "the beautiful Lord Strathmore". On the face of it he seemed an ideal match. Her mother, however, did not regard him as such and her governess, Mrs. Parish, was dead against him. None the less they became engaged. She frankly admitted later that she was captivated by "Lord Strathmore's beauty which was then very great and a dream, or rather a vision to which I was foolish enough to give more credit than it deserved".

Whilst the negotiations for the marriage settlement were going on—and they took a year and a half—poor little Mary Eleanor came to the conclusion that she had decided to marry the wrong man. She wrote: "I found our tempers, dispositions and turns differed, I wished to retract (and would [have] if I dursed have consulted with my mother) but my pride and sometimes my weakness would not let me."

In the end they married. Jesse Foot, author of *Lives of Andrew Robinson Bowes, Esq. and the Countess of Strathmore*, says of him, "the late Earl of Strathmore was not exactly calculated to make even a good, learned woman a pleasing husband. His Lordship's pursuits were always innocent and without the smallest guile, but they were not those of science or any other splendid quality. A sincere friend, a hearty Scotchman and a good bottle companion were parts of his character. He would rather suffer himself than sour the Countess by imposing any restraint upon her."

They were married at St. George's, Hanover Square, on her eighteenth birthday, 24th February, 1767, and spent the honeymoon at St. Pauls Walden. Lord Strathmore, who was thirty, had agreed to "take and use the surname of Bowes next, before and in addition to his titles of honour", and had further agreed that any children "should use the surname of Bowes in addition to any title or honour to which they might have right".

This marriage lasted nine years and there were five children—John, born in 1769, George in 1771, Thomas in 1773, Maria Jane in 1768 and Anna Maria in 1770.

In her *Confessions* Lady Strathmore wrote: "I had by him [Lord Strathmore] all my five children; and during that time never had one thought, did one action, or said one word which Heaven might not know without blaming me, or indeed himself; except the dislike I had but too much cause to entertain for Mr. Lyon [the hon. Thomas Lyon, Lord Strathmore's brother]."

Her mother had prophesied from the start that the rest of the Lyon family would not take to her. There seems to have been a good deal of truth in this.

The fact that her father had left £600,000 in trust for her and that she was due to inherit the St. Pauls Walden estate and highly valuable freeholds in Middlesex from her mother made no difference. It is difficult to see precisely what they did object to. She declares in her *Confessions*:

> Thomas Lyon publicly and causelessly, as many can witness, insulted me in the public rooms in Edinburgh when I was with him and Mrs. Lyon, who was just married, all the race week without Lord Strathmore, during which time he behaved in such a manner as scandalized the whole town of Edinburgh, who at that time hated him as much as they liked and pitied me. I complained mildly to Lord Strathmore about his brother, but it was an unfortunate and most prejudiced rule with him that Mr. Lyon could not err; so I got no other redress than his saying that though he was hasty he had a good heart and never meant to offend. I never complained to my mother on any occasion of Lord Strathmore or his family; but on the contrary expressed an uncommon regard for both, of which she was jealous, and [I] made her believe they used me extremely well; for as I had married him against her advice, my pride would not let me complain had they used me ten times worse.

There is no doubt that Mary Eleanor and her husband were ill-suited. There may have been no violent clashes between them, but temperamentally they were not in sympathy; more important, she was not in love with him, although she behaved as a dutiful wife, except for a mild flirtation with James Graham, brother of the Laird of Fintry, and her liaison with a smooth scoundrel, George Grey, a man of obscure antecedents who had made some little fortune in India and had bought land in Scotland. Her affair with him was the first major step on the downward path which was to lead her to unutterable misery.

During the early part of her marriage to Strathmore she gave a lot of time to botany and wrote a poetical drama in five acts entitled *The Siege of Jerusalem*. Strathmore was interested in neither.

Then, in 1772, she met James Graham of Fintry, the youngest of three brothers. The elder brother had been strongly attracted by her during the time he had been factor at Glamis where he had "full powers to kill the game, to hunt and to fish".

Mary Eleanor hated Glamis but when Robert Graham's advances became too marked she snubbed him "as was proper and which, from my foolish flirting with him, I daresay he did not expect. He went from Glamis in a pet and, being a man of violent resentments . . . he directly proposed to Miss Peggy Mylne, who always had a penchant for him but whom he had taken every opportunity both in public and private to abuse in a most groundless and baseless manner."

James, the youngest brother, was a very different kettle of fish. "He was", she records, "quite a boy, but a very extraordinary one, and I must confess much too forward for his years, and too conscious of those shining talents which no heart can in some degree, without difficulty, be proof against when he chooses to exert his arts."

This young man not only got his foot well inside the door at Glamis, but managed to stay a fortnight and, as Mary Eleanor records:

> . . . during which time he did everything to ingratiate himself, and succeeded so well that he could not help perceiving the progress he had made; and indeed, when he pressed me to it, I partly confessed it. Luckily his sister was staying, therefore we were never

alone. But us three, walking a whole morning to the amount of several miles measured in the great hall of Glamis, every turn he marked with a pencil. I had my hand on a piece of paper he pinned up at the end of the hall, which paper and pencil—unluckily a very remarkable one—he told me he would preserve with his life; but I hope he has lost it. I am not sure, but I have reason to think he got some of my hair from his sister.

The whole affair was charmingly childish, more than a little adolescent, and quite innocent. When James had to join his regiment in London, Mary Eleanor and James's sister contrived a code of initials by which they could correspond. Lady Strathmore records:

> I received one letter only from him which I burnt to ashes, and drank them up for fear of any accident. I never wrote to him but once, which was in a feigned hand and which none but himself could understand. This was in a cover of his sister's letter, which reached him all torn to pieces and long after the time it ought, so that it was quite unintelligible; and I never after that wrote to him except once, all before he left London. We often sent such messages as we could with safety, through his sister's means, who all the time protested that she would not do such a thing, and made Mrs. Parish [Mary Eleanor's old governess] believe all the affection was on my side and that she wished to dissuade me from such thoughts and refused to write any messages . . . actually the reverse of her character. Nothing would have induced me to keep up a correspondence or the least acquaintance with her, but my passion for her brother and the use she was to me in it.

Finally, the affair developed into something much less innocent and far more involved. The second Graham brother, Robert, also fell for her to such a degree that "when he spoke of me his eyes used to dart fire and sparkle like diamonds. . . . But I was so taken up with James that I paid no attention to him".

Later, after admitting to less innocent *affaires*, she says:

> Mr. James Graham was the only one besides who could have stood the least chance of succeeding in such an attempt. Yet, violent

> as my passion for him was, I do sincerely think that it was pure, for my anxiety about his health and welfare continued two years after he left England, though I never saw or heard from him during that time or received a message from him by his sister above twice, though she always wrote about him.

Finally, she came to the conclusion that James had been faithless to her and "used me very ill". She wrote an abusive letter to his sister which ended their friendship. None the less she had a hankering for James for long after.

Meanwhile, the state of affairs between her husband and herself had deteriorated. Strathmore was consumptive and spent much time at Bristol and Bath on his doctor's orders. Mary Eleanor stayed in London with the children and with her old governess, Mrs. Parish, who knew far too much about everything.

She and her husband were extravagant. Strathmore kept up the stud at Streatlam and may have lost a good deal of money on the Turf. He was £30,000 in debt when he died. He objected to some of his wife's friends, in particular Mrs. Montague, whom he described as "a wild, light, silly woman of bad character", and he accused his wife of "folly and extravagance such as the purchase of stuffed animals and other useless and absurd extravagances". This was a dig at her interest in natural history. He also blamed her for being too fond of dogs and cats, of saying clever but malicious things and of giving more affection to her daughters than she did to her sons. Mary Eleanor, in her *Confessions* certainly blames herself for "my unnatural dislike to my eldest son, for faults which, at most, he could only be the innocent cause and not the author of. Of this I have repented many months ago and am most sincerely sorry I did not sooner, in compliance with most sincere and disinterested advice".

Most of these counter-charges between the pair are of no serious nature. The turning-point in her life and the prelude to infinite disaster was her affair with the mysterious Mr. George Grey or Gray. In his sensitive, documented and erudite biography of Mary Eleanor, entitled *The Unhappy Countess* (Constable 1957)

Mr. Ralph Arnold pinpoints this useless fellow in one crystal paragraph:

> We may picture him as a fundamentally dishonest, lazy, amorous, literary, greedy, pussy-cat of a man, attentive, good company, and with plenty of time on his hands, but not too lazy or too stupid to constitute a considerable menace to an unhappily married, lonely young woman . . .

It seems probable that he was the "Mr. Gray" whom Clive sacked from the Council of Bengal for corrupt practices in 1765.

Mary Eleanor met him in London in 1774. Later she wrote of him:

> It was not till after many months of constant attention, and many marks of sincerity and friendship, that just as I was going to St. Paul's Walden for two months [this was early in 1775, Lord Strathmore was taking the waters at Bristol], Mr. Grey ventured to give me some verses which expressed in a delicate though in too tender a manner for mere friendship his regard for me and his great concern at my leaving London. From many circumstances I had conceived so high an opinion of the goodness of his heart and disposition that I was unwilling to lose his friendship; so that, though I made no answer, I expressed no anger, but continued corresponding with him openly and fairly till we both returned to town.

When Lord Strathmore came back from Bristol he went to stay with a friend, a Mr. Palgrave. Mary Eleanor stayed in London with Mrs. Parish. Various circumstances, mainly accidental, then aided the designs of Grey. Lady Strathmore's recollections, as she wrote them, give us a picture of how these circumstances played into the hands of the fortune-hunter:

> The post brought me a letter from Mr. Lyon in which he refused, very uncivilly, to send me a small sum of money I told him I had written for by Lord Strathmore's directions; and another letter from Miss Graham, in which I found she had received a letter from her brother who, as he began to do some time before, never so much as mentioned me but spoke with the highest commendations of a lady at Minorca where he was arrived.

As I was full of resentment at Mr. Lyon, and determined never more to think of Mr. James Graham, a servant brought me a letter from Mr. Grey who, by an Enigma, very ingeniously invented, had pitched upon that very day to see how far he might venture. If I was angry, he might have explained it away; but if I understood it, or pretended not to understand it, then he might speak plain. I chose the latter method and, full of resentment, I thought I had revenged myself on others, whilst I was literally [revenged] on myself, as I felt nothing for Mr. Grey that exceeded friendship or gave me cause to apprehend the consequences of such a connection.

I consented to accept the love of a man whom I could always keep within bounds and whom I had conceived such an esteem for that I reckoned his friendship a comfort I should be very sorry to lose. I saw him three times when I knew Mrs. Parish was at the Museum, and met him for a short time, as if by accident, at the Ring, [the fashionable parade ground for horsemen and carriages] without, I really believe, any suspicion; but as Lord Strathmore was out of town—was expected soon to return—he pressed me to see him oftener at my house and meet him oftener at different places abroad. But this was found impracticable without trusting somebody; and, unfortunately, after taking what we thought all necessary precautions, we agreed to trust George Walker [her footman] whose secrecy and caution we both thought we had reason to be satisfied with. We imprudently allowed him to tell us freely all the reports of the town, on every occasion where either (of us) were in the least concerned.

She went on to make it quite clear how she regarded the affair and on what terms it might continue:

I told Mr. Grey that he had my friendship and esteem; that my heart had long been in the possession of another [James Graham] from whom I had determined to withdraw it, but had done it so short a time that I should think it an injury against the friendship and confidence he was entitled to if I concealed the circumstances from him.

Also, that I had been so unhappy in matrimony that I was determined never to engage myself indissolubly; though I would most faithfully promise, if on these conditions he would be satisfied with my affection, he should have it entire if Lord Strathmore died; that if he recovered he must give me up, and that during my husband's life, he must decline all thoughts of me. To all this, with reluctance, and finding me peremptory, he agreed.

Soon after, Lord Strathmore, now desperately ill, set sail for Lisbon, then the Mecca of rich consumptives. A week or two before he sailed George Grey managed, at last, to seduce Mary Eleanor. "One unfortunate evening", she wrote, "I was off my guard and ever after that I lived occasionally with him as his wife." This happened in mid-February 1776.

Strathmore died aboard ship on 7th March, 1776, and on 6th April the news reached his widow with a letter he had written at sea shortly before he died. A copy of it is in the Bowes Museum.

It is a sad document, much to the point, full of Scots common sense and shows that even in the cold apartness of their latter years he still had her best interests at heart. He may have been insensitive, unsympathetic to her hobbies and her thirst for knowledge, but he was what Grey could never be—a manly man. Here is his letter:

As this is not intended for your perusal till I am dead I hope you will pay a little more attention to it than you ever did to anything I said to you while alive.

I do not mean to study elegance, but truth; and to offer you the best advice my experience will afford.

In the first place I freely forgive you all your liberties and follies (however fatal they have been to me) as being thoroughly persuaded they were not the produce of your own mind, but the suggestions of some vile interested monster.

I next do most solemnly declare (and I wrote this declaration in a full belief that I have a very short time to live) that I am convinced all the prejudices you have conceived against my family are entirely without foundation, and, as such, I would request you would lay them aside, at least until you have fresh matter or cause for complaint.

I must also earnestly desire you would endeavour to give up your foolish partiality for your daughters, and that most unnatural prejudice you have against your eldest innocent son. All children should rank equally in a parent's mind, at least until they have forfeited that regard which was due to them from their birth; favour is commonly more hurtful to the child than the contrary, but either without reason is an infallible mark of the badness of the parent's heart.

I will say nothing of your extreme rage for literary fame. I think your own understanding, when matured, will convince you of the futility of the pursuit.

I recommend you to give a greater complacency to those with whom you converse, and more candour in giving your opinion of those upon [whom] the conversation happens to fall. Above all, I would wish you to avoid all appearance of malice, and entreat you not to be tempted to say an ill-natured thing for the sake of sporting a *bon mot*.

I come now to a point very essential to your ease and comfort, and allow me to say that no one ever studied with more attention to promote the happiness of another than I have constantly done to promote yours. If I have not succeeded it is my misfortune, not my fault.

What I mean to speak of relates to your Estate, the management of which, as you have never known about it, it is impossible you should understand. For which reason I would advise you most earnestly to appoint some person you can confide in, to fix with your sons' trustees for a certain sum payable quarterly or half yearly as you shall approve.

I do not mean that you should receive less than the value of the Estate, that the person you employ will naturally take care of; but that you will know for certain what you have to receive, and be free from the imposition of Steward, the plague of repairs, and many troubles attending to management of a large Estate.

The old Duchess of Portland has at length found this measure necessary, and no one will suspect her of having done it out of favour to her son.

Consult whoever you think proper upon the expediency of what I recommend. If by sensible men you are advised against it, I submit; but yet I assure you upon the word of a dying man it is the well-considered advice of as sincere a friend as ever woman had.

And remember one circumstance, a dead man can have no interest to mislead, a living man may.

This letter must have hit her vanity hard. We do not know how hard. She had little affection for her late husband. Her frustrated capacity to love was centred on the oleaginous Grey.

She was rich. Her income has been estimated at between £16,000 and £20,000 a year. She was now free to make what friends she chose, to follow her intellectual bents and to marry again. She made little pretence of mourning for her husband.

To cap it all she was pregnant by Grey and had to go through the degradation of an induced miscarriage. Mrs. Parish, her old governess, knew all the details—and might, at a pinch, tell everything to the Lyon family or to Mrs. Bowes.

Mary Eleanor Strathmore at this time was deeply involved with a set of bogus-intellectuals of a type one knows only too well today. They were known as "The Bloomsbury Jilts" or "The Male Literati". One or two of them, notably Daniel Carl Solander, a Swedish botanist, and Joseph Planta, brother of Mrs. Parish, who was employed in the Natural History Department of the British Museum had some real claim to botanical or scientific knowledge. Solander, indeed, was a man of some scientific eminence. Another of the set, Mr. Magra, was a serious botanist. Most of them were mere hangers-on and parasites. They flattered Mary Eleanor's ego. Mrs. Parish, the governess, was perhaps the best of the bunch. None the less she was being bombarded by Mrs. Bowes with whom she was most friendly, and by the Lyon relations who were anxious to get at the roots of the scandal with Grey. Either one or both tried to bribe her soon after Lord Strathmore died. Lady Strathmore wrote:

> Mrs. Parish had displeased me so much, and, apt as I am to be imposed on, had shown such proofs of a dirty disinterestedness, that I determined to part with her, but as she had lived with, and partly educated, me so many years, I resolved it should be on good terms. Therefore I resolved to raise £2,000 by any means, the first money I expended. This, I thought, would be sufficient to make her easy in circumstances if she was interested, as I thought her, or, if it was possible I had been mistaken in her character, convince me by her still remaining with me that I had done her injustice. This I concealed from my mother till I put it in execution. . . . My mother,

I believe, did not entertain the most distant thought that she would leave me, except by marrying.

The upshot of it all was that Mrs. Parish finally left her service, and Lady Strathmore carried on her affair with George Grey.

"I saw him only every other night," she wrote. "It was agreed between us, that by the intervention of one night, we might meet the next with more pleasure and have less chance of being tired of each other. Not to mention that it was often four or five in the morning before he went away. . . . I saw him some part of every day, or when I did not, by any accident, he never failed writing. . . . Another crime was plighting myself most solemnly to Mr. Grey, at St. Paul's, to marry none but him."

The reference to St. Paul's means that she had actually met Grey in St. Paul's Cathedral and there formally engaged herself to him, which seems to suggest that she thought, somewhere in her muddled, religious mind, that this gave a semblance of divine approval to her liaison with him.

She had had a second induced miscarriage, but this time she was expecting a third child and nothing she could do would remove it.

Early in 1776 she decided that she would leave England with Grey on about the 8th or 10th April having announced their marriage to the world. The baby was expected in August. They would get married before it arrived and after being abroad for three or four years they could return with the child and no one would ask any awkward questions about it.

2

ENTER STONEY BOWES

UNLUCKILY, a far greater blackguard than George Grey had already entered Mary Eleanor's life. During the previous autumn she met Andrew Robinson Stoney. This man was surely the lowest cad in history. He came of a reasonably good Irish family in Kings County, was utterly penniless and had been bought a commission in the Army by a relative, General Armstrong. He was the type of seedy, gentlemanly bounder, calling himself "Captain", which has flourished in every era of society.

Andrew Stoney, in addition to being a bounder, was cunning, ruthless, sadistic, with rat-like cleverness and a specious Irish charm. He was a fortune-hunter of the worst type.

He had already married a Miss Hannah Newton, daughter of a Durham coal-owner. She had a fortune of between £20,000 and £30,000 and a house and landed property called Cold Pike Hill in Durham. Stoney treated her abominably. Jesse Foot wrote: "In a short time he broke her heart. He knew secret ways of provoking her before company and then, if she looked displeased or said anything tart, he appealed to the company."

Once he pushed her downstairs. He locked her up in a cupboard scarcely larger than a coffin and kept her there for days, feeding her on one egg a day. The neighbours said she was clad only in her chemise. Soon after, the wretched woman, who "bore the character of a very good woman", died. Stoney got her fortune and Cold Pike Hill.

Jesse Foot gives us a good picture of this rat of a man. He was about five feet ten inches high, spoke with a soft Irish brogue, had bright little pig-eyes, light-coloured hair, sandy eyebrows, a quick smile and sharp wits. "He was always the first to laugh at what he said", says Foot, "which forced others to laugh too. There was something uncommon in the connection of his nose with his upper lip; he could never talk without the nose, which was long and curved downwards, being also moved ridiculously with the upper lip. . . . It was seen much more in serious discourse than in light conversation. It was when he meant to be emphatic that it was most discovered. In light conversation he avoided it, by not employing the upper lip beyond a certain extent; and in that case he was necessarily forced to lisp."

This creature was a hanger-on of the third-rate drinking, gambling and cock-fighting clubs of St. James's where, as Foot remarks, "all are much upon a level amongst each other, exchange their horses, their dogs and their mistresses for the capricious accommodation of one another; and keep a sharp look-out for the opportunity of obtaining money and improving their fortunes from heir or heiress, by play or marriage, no matter which." It is a breed which never dies.

Stoney made a dead set at Lady Strathmore. He obviously knew of her affair with Grey, for all London knew it. He probably used his Durham connections to get his foot into her house in Grosvenor Square. It did not matter that she was engaged to Grey, wore his ring and had told her mother that she meant to marry him. Stoney, for sheer cunning, was more than a match for Grey. Foot says, "He was, in the first place, ten years younger; in the second place more cunning; in the third bred up more regularly to the trade; in the fourth had the superior aid, the air, and the necessary art of a man of the St. James's Coffee House. There was no antiquated, dissipated, impudent and profligate nabob a match for him."

Stoney's campaign to win Lady Strathmore and her fortune was devilish in its cunning. He knew that she was credulous, romantic, susceptible to flattery and believed in fortune-tellers. She was also surrounded by flatterers, intriguers and parasites. Stoney pulled all these strings.

She was induced to visit a "conjuror" who presumably told her that she should marry a witty and dashing young Irishman.

Then a mysterious woman in Durham was supposed to have written letters to Stoney reproaching him bitterly for having dropped her in favour of Lady Strathmore. Copies were sent to Lady Strathmore.

When Eliza Planta, sister of Mrs. Parish, who had taken Mrs. Parish's place with Lady Strathmore, eloped to Scotland with a parson and Lady Strathmore retired to St. Pauls Walden, Stoney wrote her a long letter of which this extract is a supreme example of cunning humbug:

> You tell me that your good mother (Heaven bless her) is well employed for an old lady; but by the soul of *Angelica* [a cat] you vow, (and I know she was dear to you,) that her pursuits do not at this time engage your attention. Now by the living sick *Jacintha* [another cat], by everything I have to hope, I swear that I am highly interested in your present thoughts; and were I *Proteus* I would instantly transform myself, to be happy that I was stroked and caressed, like them, by you; and, discovering the secret of your mind, I might experience what I hope Eliza will never be a stranger to, or be placed beyond the reach of further hope.
>
> I am all impatience to see your ladyship; I really cannot wait till Saturday; I must have five minutes chat with you before that time. You will think me whimsical; but upon Thursday next, at one o'clock, I shall be in the garden at Paul's Walden. There is a leaden statue, or there was formerly, and near that spot (for it lives in my remembrance) I shall wait; and can I presume that you will condescend to know the place? Eliza shall be our excuse for this innocent frolic; and the civilities shall never be erased from the the remembrance of your faithful, etc.

He followed this up with more letters from his supposed jilted fiancée in the North. In one of them this woman, if she ever existed—it is more than likely that Stoney wrote the letters himself—accused Lady Strathmore of having stolen her lover "merely because you possess more acres and that you are a Countess".

She suggested also that Mary Eleanor should stick to Mr. Grey since she was not only engaged to him, but he was approved of by her Lyon relations. It seems likely, in fact, that George Grey had more or less got the backing of the Lyon family and of Mrs. Bowes. By this time, however, Mary Eleanor was madly in love with the Irish adventurer.

In the winter of 1776 and January 1777 the *Morning Post*, which had just been founded by that astounding "squarson", the Reverend Henry Bate, brought the whole affair into a blaze of publicity equal to anything that Fleet Street has ever known. Parson Bate, who later became Sir Henry Bate Dudley Bt. has I confess, long been one of my pet heroes. He was an outstanding character. He was not only the first of the great editors, but a sportsman, a man of iron courage and cultivated tastes, a dead shot, an intrepid fox-hunter, a brilliant swordsman and no mean agriculturalist.

He held the living of Bradwell-juxta-Mare in the bright, bleak sea-country at the mouth of the Essex Blackwater where corn-fields step down to the marshes, the saltings run luminous to the sea and the clangour of wild geese is the orchestra of winter dawns. There Bate, or Bate Dudley as he became when he succeeded to the baronetcy, reclaimed hundreds of acres of saltings and hunted a pack of hounds with great dash. He once killed a fox on the thatched roof of the chancel of the little church of Creeksea overlooking the Crouch estuary. He also conducted one of the greatest duck decoys in England, was a bosom friend of the Prince Regent, an elegant when in London, and a man whom you either feared or admired. As a duellist he was deadly. As a boxer he could knock out most professionals.

This formidable figure took a hand in the Strathmore scandal. Letters appeared in the *Morning Post* attacking Lady Strathmore bitterly for her conduct to her husband during his illness and before his death and for her scandalous goings-on thereafter. They spared her nothing. She had, one must confess, asked for it. Other letters defended her. She enjoyed it all and cut out all the letters and pasted them in a press-cutting album.

Whether Stoney himself wrote the letters we shall never know. It is more than possible. It is, however, quite impossible to believe that Parson Bate, a man of strict honour and inflexible courage, was any party to Stoney's designs.

The upshot of the matter was that, whilst London was rocking with the newspaper attacks on Lady Strathmore, Stoney said that if Grey was a man worthy of the name he would challenge Parson Bate to a duel. Any man worth his salt would have done so. Grey knew that, if he did, it would mean his certain death.

Stoney thereupon challenged Bate himself. The "duel" took place in an upper room of the Adelphi Tavern off the Strand. We shall never know the truth of what took place. Stoney had probably invited Bate to discuss plans for the duel to take place elsewhere and at a later date.

Stoney was, at heart, a coward. He was certainly no match for Bate with pistol, sword or fist. Bate was no man to refuse a challenge from any one.

There were various versions of the supposed duel. Some may have been fabricated by Stoney. Jesse Foot's own version clearly states that he personally was called, in great haste, to the Adelphi Tavern on the evening of Monday, 13th January, 1777. There he saw Parson Bate, whom he knew personally, Stoney, whom he had never seen before, a Doctor Scott who had been called hurriedly, and a servant.

Stoney was sitting on a chair looking ready to faint and was wounded twice in the right breast. He had another slight wound also. Bate had suffered one small wound. There were two swords in the room, one of which was bent. The looking-glass had been broken by a pistol bullet.

Another witness said that when he heard the shots in the room he helped to break down the door and found the two duellists in darkness. The candles had been put out.

Sifting the evidence and giving all the benefit of the doubt to Parson Bate it seems more than probable that Stoney induced him to meet him in the room, challenged him and then either shot the candles out or cut them down with his sword, feeling that he would be safer in the dark than in the light. The wound in his breast had apparently gone transversely through his right breast. It could, therefore, have been self-inflicted.

It is more than probable that Bate realized that he had been fooled into a sham duel by a scoundrel. That could be the reason why he refused to throw any further light on the affair. From his point of view it was no duel but a third-rate "scrap" in an upper room of a dubious tavern. The less said about it the better as far as he was concerned.

It was enough, however, to discredit Grey utterly and to throw Eleanor Mary Strathmore finally into the arms of Andrew Robinson Stoney. She had been there already. According to her *Confessions* she had been bedded by Stoney before Christmas, probably at St. Pauls Walden.

She married Stoney at St. James's Church, Piccadilly, on 17th January, 1777. He appeared to be in great pain during the ceremony.

Under the terms of George Bowes' will he took the surname of Bowes and was known henceforth as Stoney Bowes. This opened the door for him to much of her fortune. For her it opened the door to torture, misery, abduction and near-death. Whatever publicity she had reaped in the past was a puff of wind compared to the tornado to come.

George Grey threatened an action for breach of promise. Months later his claim was settled for £12,000.

Then, a few days after the wedding, Stoney Bowes—who nowadays would be known as "Phoney" Bowes—was livid when he discovered that his wife had put all her estate, real and personal, in trust for her life, no matter whether she remained a widow or married again. All monies from these trusts were to be paid to whomsoever she should direct or, in default to be paid to her "for her separate and peculiar use and disposal, exclusive of any husband she should thereafter marry with; and wherewith he should not intermeddle, nor should the same be anyways subject or liable to his debts, control or management".

A clause in the Trust gave her the power to revoke it and to appoint other Trusts if she wished it.

It was a paralysing smack in the face for the fortune hunter. He peremptorily ordered his wife to write to her solicitor Mr. Peele, who was one of the Trustees, demanding that he deliver up the deeds and accusing him of having forced the wishes of Thomas Lyon upon her. It was an insulting letter Peele refused point-blank to deliver the deeds unless Stoney Bowes provided for his wife from his own fortune. Stoney refused.

There seems no doubt that Lady Strathmore had set up the Trust when she intended to marry Grey and that Grey had agreed to the terms in them. Bowes contended, in the long series of Chancery actions which followed, that, since he knew nothing of the deeds when he married her, they "constituted a fraud on him". It should be remembered that, in those days, the husband had complete control of his wife's property, which opened the door wide to fortune-hunters.

Stoney's immediate reaction were those of a bully. He ordered the servants to hand to himself all letters addressed to his wife. He forbade her to use her own carriage without his consent. He refused to allow her to see her daughter alone. When she spoke to a guest in French he sent a servant the length of the room to tell her to speak in English. These calculated insults were nothing compared with what was to come. Bowes was after her money—and he meant to get it.

Scarcely a month after the wedding he stood for Parliament for the borough of Newcastle-upon-Tyne as a Radical under the battle cry of "Bowes and Freedom". There were 2,000 voters and every man had his price. An election campaign in those days needed a bottomless purse. Bowes went straight into the fight and ran up enormous debts. His election address contained this appeal to the voters: "Oh, break the closet-combination of the magistrates and gentry, whose glory it seems to be to treat their inferiors as slaves."

Stoney's opponent was Sir John Trevelyan of Wallington, whose family was justly popular in Northumberland with wide acres and a high sense of duty. Bowes declared that Sir John was "a zealous foxhunter, 'tis true, and loves roast beef and claret as well as any fat-headed Country Squire in Zummerset-zheere—this comprehends the whole of Sir John Trevelyan's merits. . . . You are told by those who canvass for him that your late member on his death bed *recommended* Sir John—is Newcastle, then, to be an *Heir Loom* to Wallington? Or has Sir Walter in his will *bequeathed* You to his nephew?"

Trevelyan's men came back with a straight smack in the eye. If Lady Strathmore should die, they proclaimed, the fortune-hunter "would go back to his original insignificancy. Would it be decent . . . to entrust our rights and properties to a man who, in a few hours, may find himself divested of the very appearance of an estate?" Trevelyan, "was an Englishman of a most ancient and most respectable family, possessed of a large permanent estate."

Lady Strathmore's part in the election, according to a local squire, Mr. Montague of Denton Hall, consisted of sitting at the window of an inn "from whence she sometimes lets fall some jewels or trinkets, which voters pick up, and then she gives them money for returning them—a new kind of offering bribes."

In the end Trevelyan won and Bowes lost by ninety-five votes. He petitioned the House of Commons against the return and lost again.

Then, on 1st May, the Ante-nuptial Trusts were broken and Bowes got full legal control of his wife's estates and income. In the lawsuits which followed she claimed that he had forced her to sign the revocation "by the terrors of personal violence" which is probably exactly what did happen.

Meanwhile, Bowes had to find £24,000 to pay for his futile election and to pay Grey's claims for damages. This money came, in the end, from her estate. In July Stoney Bowes and his wife went up to Gibside. There he made himself thoroughly unpopular as one would expect. A local bard put it thus:

Her Ladyship's tenants first gained his attention,
Whose treatment was cruel—most shocking to mention;
He rais'd all their rents, which if they could not pay,
He crav'd them, and seized them, then turned them away.
The helpless dependants—the labouring poor,
He removed from their work, or horse-whipp'd from his door.

3

THE COUNTESS'S "CONFESSIONS"

In August Mary Eleanor gave birth to George Grey's baby. The explosion of a landmine would have been a puff of wind by comparison. It gave Stoney the final weapon in his armoury of torture and abuse. The only thing that pleased him was the fact that his wife did not die. It would have wrecked his financial plot. The child was a daughter, christened Mary.

Soon after Lady Strathmore wrote her *Confessions*. There seems little doubt that Stoney Bowes made her do so in order that he could use them later as a weapon against her, either in the Courts of Law or as public vilification. Jesse Foot says "They were evidently extorted from her under the tyranny of Bowes", and he added that they contained "many falsehoods and some truths". Whatever the falsehoods poor Mary Eleanor clearly delineated her own faults—a lack of morals, impatience and an unforgiving nature. Whatever her faults, she is none the less a paragon by comparison with Stoney Bowes, who was no Bowes at all.

Next year, in 1779, Stoney actually managed to be elected High Sheriff of Newcastle. He gave great dinners to the Newcastle worthies at Gibside where his table was "enriched by massive plate", says Foot, "but there was always a smack of mean splendour about him, as he did not purchase one single new carriage and his coach horses, originally of high value, were never in good condition".

In February 1780, he actually managed to scrape into the House of Commons at the General Election. His opponents trumpeted: "Can the friends of Mr. Bowes, without blushing, compare a fortune hunter, a Wolf in Sheep's Clothing, an unprincipled Mock Patriot to the Independent, Steady, Consistent Delaval?"

He turned up seldom at the House. He quarrelled with his election agent. He owed money all over the county. Finally, when he found that he could not buy or cajole an Irish peerage from the Government he ceased attending the House altogether.

Mary Eleanor's mother, Mrs. Bowes, died in January 1781 and left St. Pauls Walden and her estate to her daughter. Bowes used the place as a bolt-hole from his creditors. The North was now too hot for him. Streatlam Castle was empty and neglected. Then, on 8th May, 1782, his wretched wife bore him a son, William Johnstone Bowes.

Meanwhile, Bowes was after every woman in sight. No servant girl was safe. Ralph Arnold records that he stood in the garden at St. Pauls Walden one wintry night watching the bedroom window of a serving-maid whom he had tried to seduce. She was secretly married to one of the men-servants. Her husband entered the room as Bowes was watching the window and they put the lights out.

Bowes bounded up the stairs, hammered on the bedroom door and turned the wretched couple out into the wind and rain. They trudged off in the dark down to the lodge at the park gates and were given a bed. Bowes sacked the lodge-keeper in the morning. Then he told the story gleefully to the old family chaplain.

"You did that", exclaimed the chaplain, "and yet you would have ruined her yourself. You shall not turn *me* out. I will be gone directly." He left the house. Bowes refused to let him have his luggage until the parish constable was called.

Jesse Foot records that Bowes used to spy on a tenant farmer's wife and her daughters when they went to bed:

> When the (dinner) company was gone Bowes asked me to walk out with him. He took me to the farm and peeped into the windows where they were all sitting and preparing for bed. Everything, in their innocent custom, was undoing. The dog barked, and I returned and left him there, where he was for a long time.
>
> He told me there was no danger from the dog, as he had made the

farmer tie him up, because, as he said, he had been caught killing some of his own sheep.

He went thus to the window almost every night. In a week after my return to London he sent for me in haste, as he had met with an accident. The farmer, finding that his dog barked thus every night, suspected thieves and determined to let him loose; and the dog, revenging himself against Bowes in one of these excursions, fastened upon his leg, and bit it severely.

Bowes reduced his wife to a dejected, frightened, nervous wreck. All her interests in life, gardening, botany, literature and intelligent conversation were squashed. If ever a woman was ruthlessly brain-washed that woman was Mary Eleanor Strathmore. It says much for her father's early insistence on a healthy, athletic life that her system, both physical and mental, was able to stand up to the strain. Far worse was to come.

When, finally, their marital misery was thrashed out in the High Court, Dorothy Stevenson, the nursery-maid, gave evidence to the effect that not only had Bowes raped her herself, but that he had given Lady Strathmore "many violent blows on her face, head and other parts of the body; he often kicked her and sometimes pinched her ears nearly through".

He threw a dishful of hot potatoes straight into her face one night at dinner. Then he threw a glass of wine in her face "to wash the potatoes off". He made the wretched woman eat potatoes "until she was sick". He refused to let her buy clothes. Her daughters later testified that she lost all interest in dress and became a slovenly drab.

Their baby son, William, had a wet nurse, Mrs. Houghton. Bowes raped her and gave her a child.

When Dorothy Stevenson fled from the houses after Bowes had raped her, a poor little servant girl, young and pathetic, Elizabeth Waite, took her place. Her father was locked up for debt in the King's Bench Prison. Bowes told the wretched child that he would pay her father's debts and see that he was released. She was overcome with gratitude. He forced his way into her bedroom and raped the child. She fled from the house in tears and ended in that house of misery, the Magdalen Hospital in St. George's Fields. It was a charitable institution which cared for the bruised and broken waifs of London.

Jesse Foot records that when he visited Lady Strathmore at St. Pauls Walden for the second time after the birth of her son, he found her

> . . . wonderfully *altered* and *dejected*. She was pale and nervous, and her under-jaw constantly moved from side to side. If she said anything, she looked at Bowes first. If she was asked to drink a glass of wine, she took his intelligence before she answered. She sat but a short time at dinner, and then was out of my sight.
>
> I did get one morning's walk with her . . . into the once beautiful pleasure garden where, in spite of the ruinous state of it, much was left for admiration; because the taste that gave it a creation was not yet totally obliterated. The Countess pointed out to us the concern she had formerly taken in the shrubs, the flower beds, the alcoves and the walks of this most delectable recess. She even pointed out the assistance her own hand had lent to individual articles.
>
> In observing her during her conversation, the agitation of her mind was apparent by its action on her mouth. She would look for some time, hesitate, and then her underjaw would act in that convulsive manner, which absolutely explained her state of melancholy remembrance beyond all other proofs abstracted knowledge could confirm or technical teachers could demonstrate.

Meanwhile, Mary Eleanor's five children by her first marriage to Lord Strathmore were living in the family house in Grosvenor Square in the charge of the family chaplain and his wife. Not one of them was ten years old. The chaplain was a dubious character.

The Lyon family took a strong hand in matters, for the next we know is that young John Strathmore and his brother George were at a private boarding school at Neasden, then well out in the country in Middlesex, whilst the two little sisters Lady Maria Jane and Lady Anna Maria were at a boarding school in Queen's Square, London.

The Lyon family were vigilant on the children's behalf. Thomas Lyon saw to it that they were made Wards in Chancery. This meant that their immediate future was controlled by the Lord Chancellor, who appointed Thomas Lyon and a Scottish lawyer as their legal guardians.

Lady Strathmore was devoted to her daughters but took little or no interest in the two small boys. Mr. Arnold discovered a charming little letter in the Bowes Museum, dated 12th May 1784, written by the small Lady Maria to her mother from the school in Queen's Square in which, pathetically, the child regarded Stoney as her "Papa". She wrote:

> I hope my dear Papa and Mama will not disapprove of my spending the Whitsuntide holidays with them. We break up on the 27th of this month, and as almost all the ladies are to go home I think that Papa and you will not object to my having the same pleasure. We have had two balls which I liked very much. I did not dance, as I have not learned long enough to dare before so much company. . . . I wish much to know that you and Papa are well and that I may have the pleasure of spending the holiday at home. My sister desires her duty.

The guardians stopped this. They objected, perfectly properly, to the influence of Stoney. They took the child from school and put her in her aunt's house in Harley Street. Bowes had already applied to the Lord Chancellor for permission to have the two girls in the house with their mother, but the Lord Chancellor put his foot down.

This latest move precipitated matters. Stoney made his wife write to Lady Anna's schoolmistress, Mrs. Carlisle, saying that she wished to see the child before she left London for Bath. Another letter was sent to Lady Anne Simpson, the aunt in Harley Street, to say that she would like to see her elder daughter. Next day Lady Anna was collected from school and brought to Stoney Bowes' house. Lady Maria, the older girl, was brought by Mrs. John Ord, Lady Anne's sister-in-law. They saw the younger girl looking out of a bedroom window. Lady Maria was sixteen and obviously alive to the situation. She pointed out that her younger sister was already in the house.

Glamis Castle in 1790 (*The Mansell Collection*)

Patrick, first Earl of Strathmore and third Earl of Kinghorne
(*Scottish National Portrait Gallery*)

Mrs. Ord taxed Lady Strathmore with the fact. Mary Eleanor admitted that the other girl was within the house also. She then took Maria into another room. After Mrs. Ord had waited for some time she asked a servant to tell Lady Maria that it was time to go. The servant came back with the message that the girl would be with her shortly. Mrs. Ord waited for a still longer time then she rang the bell and sent the same message. She was told that Lady Strathmore was in her dressing-room. Mrs. Ord, evidently a woman of character, marched upstairs to the dressing-room and tried the door. It was locked. She went back to the drawing-room, thoroughly alarmed, and was presented with this letter from Lady Strathmore:

Madam,

As you have accompanied Lady Maria upon the present as well as a former occasion, on both of which I strenuously requested to see my daughter *by herself*, I conclude that you have some written orders for that purpose from a majority of her guardians; if thus authorized, I should not chuse to interfere in regard to her returning to you today. But if you cannot produce such sanction, you will, I hope, excuse my detaining her till, by representing my case and laying my grievance before my Lord Chancellor, I shall be honoured by his Lordship's command.

However inhuman may be the *behaviour* I have experienced from those who never paid the slightest intentions to my feelings as a mother, and whose professed regard for my children ought to have taught them a very different lesson; yet I hope you will be so obliging as to believe that nothing can be further from my wishes than to treat you with the most distant degree of impoliteness, especially in my own house; but that goodness of heart that I have the pleasure to know you possess will, I doubt not, fully excuse the liberty I now take, and lead you to sympathize in the sufferings of a parent whose children have, for many years, been entirely secluded from her sight, an affliction which, though you have never been so unfortunate as to experience, yet you may easily conceive the severity of; and from your own sensations upon inferior occasions, will form a just idea how impossible it must be ever to exist under such cruel and unnatural controul.

Mrs. Ord took instant action. She sent a footman to her husband asking him to come at once. She then sat down and refused to leave the house. Finally she walked up to Lady Strathmore's dressing-room. The door was open but it was slammed in her face. She heard Maria scream and cried out to her: "Maria! I shall not quit the house till you come to me." She then sat down by the dressing-room door on a chair and refused to budge.

Shortly afterwards Maria was produced and Mrs. Ord walked out of the house with the girl. She discovered that Stoney Bowes had sent her own coachman away. Maria told her that her mother and Bowes had done their upmost to get her to stay with them.

The younger girl, Anna, did not escape. Her schoolmistress was told by letter that her mother intended to keep her with her and she was further led to believe that Lady Strathmore, the child and Bowes had left the house "for an unknown destination".

Four days later the guardians applied to the Lord Chancellor to have the child delivered to them. Stoney Bowes, mother and daughter, were by this time in France. Bowes realized that by kidnapping a Ward in Chancery and taking her out of the country he had really put his foot in it. None the less he tried to bluster his way out of it in a series of letters from the Hotel Luxembourg in Paris.

Lady Strathmore's health was deteriorating rapidly. After they had crossed the Channel Mrs. Morgan, her maid, helped her to undress in an hotel in Calais. She saw a large bruise as big as her own hand on her mistress's upper arm. Next day, in the coach on the way to Paris, Bowes kicked and pinched his wife to stop her from looking out of the window. He was terrified that they would be recognized.

Days went by and his behaviour became worse. One day Mrs. Morgan found Mary Eleanor's sleeve and face covered in blood. She was weeping bitterly. The skin behind one of her ears was badly torn as though she had been scratched deeply by someone's nails. Lady Strathmore admitted, between sobs, that her husband had attacked her because she had tried to look out of the window. He met a Frenchwoman, made advances to her, and ordered his wife to write his own love-letter to her in French. When she refused, he hit her.

Meanwhile, the Lord Chancellor ordered the whole party to return instantly to England. Bowes replied that he would gladly return, but that Lady Strathmore had said she would rather die than be parted from her daughter.

After much legal wrangling the whole party returned to St. Pauls Walden in October. Lady Anna said that her stepfather had pushed a lighted candle into her mother's face and had stuck a quill pen into her tongue. Lady Strathmore, sobbing and broken, said that "she wished God would take either her or Bowes so that her suffering might end". Her maid, Mrs. Morgan, spent £100 of her own savings to buy her mistress decent clothes. Lady Strathmore was in such a state of nerves that she took to laudanum. Bowes egged her on.

None the less Mary Eleanor's spirit was not broken. Bowes sacked Mrs. Morgan but Lady Strathmore got a message to her, through a housemaid, saying that she felt sure Bowes would either murder her or shut her up for life. She begged Mrs. Morgan to help her escape.

That excellent woman immediately got her cousin, a barrister named Shuter who lived in Cursitor Street off Chancery Lane, to agree to give Lady Strathmore sanctuary the instant she could escape from the house in Grosvenor Square.

On 3rd February Lady Strathmore did escape, aided by her housekeeper, housemaid and footman. She got out of the house whilst Bowes was out at dinner, leaving her valuable jewellery behind, and, after a frantic hunt for a hackney carriage, found one in Oxford Street. They were only just in time. A minute or two later Bowes drove past them in another hackney carriage, head out of the window, searching for his wife on the pavement. It was a near squeak. Lady Strathmore had hysterics on the spot.

At Mr. Shuter's house she was joined by Mrs. Morgan and Ann Parks, her housemaid. They took her to lodgings in Dyers Buildings, Holborn. There she was put under the protection of a High Court tipstaff and was registered as Mrs. Jefferies.

In no time Bowes discovered where she was. He took rooms in

the same street but dare not touch her. She dare not put a foot outside the door.

From her lodgings Lady Strathmore took all the legal steps that were open to her, including steps to have the Ante-nuptial Trust re-established, to have the Deed of Revocation set aside and to have a Receiver appointed for her estate. Finally, she started a suit for divorce from Bowes on the grounds of adultery and cruelty.

Legal processes then were cumbersome, long-winded and involved. Matters dragged on. There is no need to go into the tortuous proceedings other than to say that Bowes, after months had passed, saw that matters were going against him. If his wife won her divorce, as seemed inevitable, he would lose his last hope of her fortune. He decided to abduct her. This was the prelude to one of the most dramatic and unbelievable episodes in the social history of England.

The house in Grosvenor Square was besieged by his creditors. He employed more than a dozen secret agents to spy on his wife's affairs. He sat up at night drinking like a fish and eating peppered biscuits. Yet another maidservant was in child by him. He had been bound over for twelve months. The moment that period was up he determined to kidnap his wife, drive her to a remote part of the country, force her at pistol point to sign a document to stop divorce proceedings and also force her to cohabit with him which would, as condonation, end all chances of a divorce.

Meanwhile, Mary Eleanor had moved to a better house in Bloomsbury Square. There she had her own coach and even dared to go for an occasional drive through the streets of London.

Bowes decided to stage a mock suicide so that she would move freely, thinking that he was dead, and so make it easy to kidnap her. This is what actually happened.

He went up to Gibside and bribed a coal-miner named Chapman to go to Lady Strathmore's doctor in Newcastle, Dr. Brown, and tell him that Bowes had shot himself the night before. Soon afterwards, Bowes' groom, Joseph Hill, turned up with the same story and beseeched the doctor to put in a word for him with Lady Strathmore so that he could hold his job. Then came a party of the Gibside coal-miners. They wanted to know who was going to pay their wages. Dr. Brown smelt a rat. He refused to do anything. The "suicide" was a complete flop.

A fortnight later, in mid-October, Bowes came South to London with two tough coal-miners, Chapman and Pigg, and a man called Peacock who was said to be a coal merchant. Bowes called himself Colonel Maddison, proclaimed that he was a Justice of the Peace and wore an enormous bush wig to give colour to it. On the way south at Stone in Staffordshire he took on a post-boy, named Peter Orme, at £20 a year. This youth, eventually, was a powerful witness against him.

Bowes took a house in London at Number 18, Norfolk Street, installed his gang of thugs and kept a sharp watch on his wife. Sometimes he disguised himself as a magistrate in his great long-tailed wig with enormous spectacles perched on his nose. At other times he waddled round "in a sailor's dress with trowsers". Occasionally he drove round Bloomsbury Square in a hackney carriage peering out of the windows. Lady Strathmore soon saw through this and told Mr. Mingay, a barrister who had acted for her, that her husband was dogging her footsteps.

Bowes heard of this, promptly left London with his French valet, named Prevot, and went north to Streatlam Castle where he arrived on 21st October. He left his three thugs behind in the house in Norfolk Street.

At Streatlam Bowes, aided by the estate steward, Henry Bourne, and a local surgeon named Hobson, staged another mock death. All three, Bowes, Prevot and Bourne passed a man named Thomas Collpitts on horse-back, knowing that Collpitts would recognize them. Shortly afterwards Bourne galloped back down the road, waving madly to Collpitts as though an accident had happened. Bourne called Mr. Hobson from his house and told him that Bowes had fallen from his horse and was near death. Hobson found Bowes lying on the roadside and blooded him.

Then Collpitts rode up. To all appearances Bowes was, if not dead, dangerously injured. They told him that Bowes had smashed three ribs and that blood had been coming out of his ear. Bowes was lying with his head on a heap of stones with a handful of hay under him. He looked deathly white. Bourne lifted him into a carriage and, as Collpitts said later, took £1,400 out of his pocket in gold coins.

The local papers were told that Bowes had been seriously injured and would be far too ill to see anyone for months to come.

A week later Bowes was on the road, post-haste for London. He and his gang went to a public house called the "Pyed Bull", in Russell Street behind Bloomsbury Square. The landlord, Edward Crook, smelt a rat. He said later that he took Chapman, Prevot and Pigg "for a gang of thieves and would have nothing to do with them", but when they took him round to see "Justice Maddison", sitting like a judge in a huge armchair, with the formidable long-tailed wig on his head and great spectacles on his nose, the inn-keeper thought their story that they were hunting a gang of robbers must be true. He put them on to a constable named Edward Lucas who had been head-runner to Mr. Justice Walker. He, too, wore large spectacles and was known as "Four Eyes".

They bribed him to go to Lady Strathmore, tell her that he had seen disreputable characters watching her house and offer to act as her bodyguard. Mary Eleanor fell for it. She took Lucas on at twelve shillings a week and he followed her like a watchdog.

The plot was taking real shape. Chapman went to Mr. Justice Walker on 8th November and swore on oath that his life had been threatened by Lady Strathmore's maidservant, coachman and footman. Mr. Justice Walker issued a warrant for their arrest. Lucas persuaded three other constables to join in the plot.

4

THE ABDUCTION

On the afternoon of 10th November Lady Strathmore left her house, entered her carriage and went for a drive with her solicitor's brother, Captain Henry Farrer. Lucas, and the rest of the gang, followed her in two hackney carriages. She stopped at an iron-mongers shop kept by a Mr. Forster in Oxford Street. Lucas and his gang jumped out of their hackney carriages, hauled Lady Strathmore's footman and coachman off the box and announced that they were under arrest. They took them straight to Mr. Justice Walker, Lucas' former employer. Lady Strathmore with her maid, Mrs. Morgan, and Captain Farrer, bolted into the shop, ran upstairs and locked themselves in a room. Lucas knocked on the door a few minutes later.

"Who's that?" Mary Eleanor demanded.

"Your friend, Lucas."

"Oh, Lucas! Come in, by all means."

The door was unbolted. Lucas marched in, pulled out his staff of office, seized Mary Eleanor by the arm and said:

"My God, my Lady, you are my prisoner. I have a warrant for your arrest. I must take you at once to Lord Mansfield at Caen Wood (Ken Wood). It is as much as my life is worth not to execute this warrant."

"But you can't seize a Countess just as you seize a common person," Mrs. Morgan, the maid, protested.

"You keep quiet," Lucas retorted. "I've got a warrant out against you too! You'd better make yourself scarce, quick."

Mrs. Morgan ran out of the shop and went straight to Lady Strathmore's lawyers, Farrer and Lacey.

Meanwhile, Lady Strathmore with Lucas and Captain Farrer came downstairs and got into her own coach, which was driven and guarded by Lucas' gang. She thought she was being driven to Caen Wood, but the coach stopped at Highgate. She was taken to an upstairs room in the Red Lion Inn. There, to her consternation, she found Bowes waiting for her. She rushed to the window, threw it open and yelled "Murder!"

They finally persuaded her that she would have to go to Caen Wood so the whole party got back into the coach, Bowes with them, and drove off. Captain Farrer, who cut no heroic figure, was most reluctant to go. Another coach followed them, containing two of Lucas' constables as well as Chapman and Pigg.

Lady Strathmore noticed they were not going in the direction of Caen Wood at all. Captain Farrer backed her up.

"Hold your tongue, sir, or I will throw you out of the window," Bowes shouted.

"As for you, Madam, damn you, aren't you ashamed of yourself when your daughter lies dying."

Turning to Captain Farrer after the coach had gone a little further, he said:

"You, sir, can get out and leave us. If you don't, I'll knock you down."

"I would have you know, sir, that I am a gentleman and I shall demand satisfaction from you for that expression," Captain Farrer retorted.

In spite of this bold front, when the coach pulled up he got out, as meek as a mouse, and started to walk back to London.

Then started an abduction which set all Britain alight with consternation, rumour and gossip. Everyone, from the Lord Chancellor downwards, could talk of nothing but that mad journey to the North. At Barnet the coach stopped at the "Adam and Eve". There Peter Orme, the postboy, was waiting with a hired chaise. Mary Eleanor smashed the glass window in her coach and screamed "Murder!" at the top of her voice. Ostlers, stablemen and serving-maids gaped in astonishment. "She's mad," Bowes said curtly. "Pay no attention to her. Mad as a march hare! We are taking her to her home."

They set off with a fresh team of horses and drove, lumbering through the night over muddy winter roads in bitter weather, until at one o'clock in the morning on Saturday, 11th November, they pulled up at the "Bell" at Stilton—the famous old coaching inn on the Great North Road in Huntingdonshire where the Stilton cheeses from Leicestershire were loaded on to the London-bound coaches. The moment they got there Bowes hustled Mary Eleanor into a room, made her sit down at a table, thrust a document in front of her and, putting a muzzle-loading pistol to her head, said "Sign it". "I won't sign it for you or for anybody else," she retorted. Bowes threw down his pistol and hit her in the face with his fist.

After a change of horses, Chapman and Peacock forced her back into the coach and Bowes hit her with his fists on the face and on the body. She screamed with agony. He rammed a handkerchief into her mouth. Then he struck her in the face with his watch-chain and a bunch of heavy seals.

Through the dark, in the cold wintry dawn, the coach lurched and jolted through sleeping villages of Northamptonshire, over the bleak fens of Lincolnshire, breasting treeless wolds where the wind blew sharp off the sea. And so into Yorkshire. They pulled up at the "Angel" in Doncaster at midday. The teams were changed like lightning and the coach dashed off for Barnby Moor. For a few moments Mary Eleanor was allowed to go into the inn with the chambermaid. Bowes stood at the bottom of the stairs, shouting to her to hurry up. At Ferry Bridge she again asked to leave the coach as she wanted "to go into the garden". Bowes stood guard outside the door of the inn lavatory, a wooden shack in the hedge.

They reached Streatlam Castle at midnight. They were met by Mary Gowland, a strong, strapping, insolent slut of a maid, one of Bowes' many mistresses. Bourne, the steward, Bowes' confederate, was there also.

As she stepped from the coach Mary Eleanor screamed, "I have been brought here by force." Turning to the postillion, who had been hired to drive the coach from Greta Bridge, she said, "Tell that to the public." Bowes offered the man a handful of guineas to say that the carriage had fallen into the ditch and that was why Lady Strathmore was half off her head.

This nightmare journey from London to Doncaster, through half a dozen or more English counties, took thirty-three hours. A lesser woman than Mary Eleanor Strathmore would have died from fright, fatigue and the hammerings she had received.

Bowes hustled her into the dining-room, put the paper in front of her which he had drawn up at Stilton, making her renounce her suit for divorce, and put a pistol to her head.

"Now say your prayers, woman, because if you don't sign that, I am going to kill you."

"Then shoot me," she retorted.

"By God! You are an astonishing woman," Bowes gasped. He put down the pistol in disgust.

"Take her up to bed," he ordered.

Chapman and Pigg picked her up in their arms and carried her up the stairs.

Meanwhile, things were moving in London. Lord Mansfield, the Lord Chief Justice, issued a write of Habeas Corpus and sent a tipstaff named Ridgeway to Streatlam Castle with the writ and a "Rule for Information against the persons concerned in seizing and carrying off by force the Right Honourable the Countess Dowager of Strathmore" and urging that "all Persons would give their Assistance in having her Ladyship produced to the Court of King's Bench".

An astounding scene developed at Streatlam. John Langstaff, one of Lady Strathmore's colliery managers, heard that Bowes was holding her a prisoner in the castle. He roused the pitmen. They marched in a great body into the park carrying torches and lit a ring of bonfires round the castle, roaring out that they would rescue Lady Strathmore, dead or alive.

Meanwhile, Thomas Bowes, the Darlington solicitor who acted for Stoney Bowes, turned up on Sunday night, 12th November. He found the doors bolted, all the windows shuttered and the place in darkness. When he announced who he was the front door was cautiously opened and he was let in.

Next day, Ridgeway, the tipstaff, arrived from London. He

hammered on the front door and tried to serve the writ of Habeas Corpus on Thomas Bowes who answered the door. Thomas Bowes refused to accept the writ and banged the door. Ridgeway pushed the writ under the door and shouted, "Take notice, I have served Andrew Robinson Bowes by putting a copy of the Habeas Corpus under the door, and I deem it good service."

James Farrer, the lawyer, came hot-foot from London. He arrived at the castle on Wednesday and demanded to see his client, Lady Strathmore. They banged the door in his face. He came back next morning and Thomas Bowes insolently said that he might come in "on parole, to converse with me and no one else".

The moment he got into the castle, Farrer, who had far more courage than his brother, searched the place from top to bottom. The bird had flown. Bowes had taken his wife away just before midnight on Monday night.

"I wouldn't be in your skin for all the land in the county of Durham," James Farrer said to Thomas Bowes.

Had Farrer only known, his client, Lady Strathmore, was shut up at that moment in a little dark room in a nearby cottage, in which lived Mary Gowland's father. Bowes, realizing that his enemies were closing in on him, had taken her there on the Monday night. She was dressed in a man's greatcoat and a servant's bonnet and was put up on a horse behind Chapman. Bowes told her that if there was any more nonsense she would be certified by "a madman's doctor" and put into a strait-jacket.

This was the beginning of the final fantastic flight of that nightmare abduction in the depths of winter. Snow lay on the moors. Rivers and pools were frozen. The wind, shrewd as a questing witch, cut to the bone when, at midnight on Thursday, 16th November, Bowes drove Mary Eleanor over Bowes Moor to a gamekeeper's cottage at Argill. Mary Gowland, Chapman, Pigg and Matthew Shields, the gamekeeper, were all in the plot. When they got to Shields' cottage Mary Eleanor was made to go to bed in a room with two beds. Two of the men-servants slept in the other bed. They got there at six in the morning and after a few hours tortured rest Lady Strathmore was forced to get into the coach and take the rough, moorland road again. It blew a gale. Sheets of rain, alternating with frozen sleet, hammered on the coach window. At six that evening it pulled up at the turnpike keeper's house at Brough Corner. Bowes carried his wife into the house and told the gatekeeper, David Kirk, that she was on her way to see her daughter who was lying-in.

Kirk, who was suspicious, noticed that she had lost a shoe and a stocking, was shivering with cold, apparently terrified out of her wits, and mumbling to herself. Bowes let her warm herself in front of the fire for a quarter of an hour. Then she was bundled into the coach and they drove off into the night towards Appleby in Westmorland.

They stayed that night in an inn at Appleby kept by James Aungier. They took the road early in the morning for Penrith. This seems to argue that Bowes intended to take Mary Eleanor by ship to Ireland and hold her prisoner with some of his relatives.

When they were three miles on the road to Penrith Bowes heard that a post-chaise, full of men, was chasing them.

He stopped his carriage, mounted Lady Strathmore on a pillion behind Chapman on another horse, and told the post-boy to drive on to Penrith in order to fool his pursuers.

Later that afternoon Bowes turned up at Brampton in Cumberland, saying that he was Dr. Hopper, in charge of a lunatic woman, and that as his carriage had had an accident he wanted a horse to take him to Coupland Beck where he would be met by another carriage.

The party rode on in bitter, snowy weather by moorland tracks to Esplan Moor and then across the hills to Burton, where they stopped at a cottage. The cottager noticed that the woman of the party was weeping and wringing her hands and blue with cold. "Dr. Hopper" said that she was mad and when Mary Gowland shook Lady Strathmore he said that she had to be controlled.

Snow lay on the moor more than a yard deep. The wind was freshening and more snow was on the way. At one point the horses stuck in snowdrifts and Lady Strathmore had to be carried. A moor man called Lamb, who was acting as a guide, heard her say, "Tell them I'm here, tell them I'm here." He, one imagines, did not know whom to believe.

Across the moors, through the dark night, in snow and sleet, the party struggled on until, at 4 a.m. on Sunday, 19th November, there came a knock on the door of Thomas Bowes' house in Darlington. The party stayed the rest of the night there. Lady Strathmore was put in a shuttered bedroom.

That afternoon she was hustled downstairs, pushed into a chaise and driven all the way to Newcastle where they changed horses and set off in a storm of wind and rain for Chollerford. At Harlow Hill, with the horses steaming and sweating, the carriage windows broken, rain and sleet driving in, the chaise was taken into a stackyard where a herd of pigs rushed grunting out of the straw. There Lady Strathmore stayed a prisoner, with Mary Gowland as her jailor, from 10.30 p.m. until three o'clock the next morning.

At that unearthly hour Bowes ordered the hired post-boys, whom they had taken on at Newcastle, to drive to Morpeth by back roads. The post-boys refused. They said it was madness in such weather and in the dark. Bowes, who had evidently expected reinforcements to reach him, told them to drive the party back to Newcastle. He seemed, at last, to have lost his nerve.

When they got to Newcastle he gave the post-boys a guinea each and told them to keep their mouths shut.

Meanwhile, the whole countryside was on the alert. Next day, 20th November, James Farrer, Lady Strathmore's lawyer, broadcast the following notice with a reward of £50:

> The Court of King's Bench has granted an Attachment against Andrew Robinson Bowes Esq., for forcibly taking away the *Countess of Strathmore*, and Mr. Ridgeway, his Lordship's tipstaff, and others, are in pursuit of him to execute such Attachment. Any Person concealing or secreting the said Countess of Strathmore, or aiding, abetting, or assisting the said Andrew Robinson Bowes in taking the said Countess of Strathmore from place to place to elude Justice, shall be Prosecuted with the utmost Rigor and Severity of the Law.
>
> Whoever shall bring the said Countess of Strathmore to James Farrer, Esq., now at Carlisle, shall receive a Reward of *fifty pounds*

from that gentleman. The like Reward will be paid by Mr. Farrer on bringing the said Andrew Robinson Bowes Esq., and his armed ruffians, to him at the City of Carlisle aforesaid.

N.B. An Express is arrived from Newcastle mentioning that Bowes and his Ruffians, with Lady Strathmore, set off from that Town yesterday, and are supposed to be going to Port Patrick, and from there to Ireland.

On 21st November James Farrer issued this description of "Lady Strathmore, Mr. Bowes and his Ruffians":

Mr. Bowes is above the middle size, sallow complexion, large Nose which stands rather one side, and lisps in his speech.

Lady Strathmore is a little woman, a longish Face, with fine dark brown Hair, rather Bulky over the Chest—Mr. Bowes gives out that she is Dumb, and sometimes Disordered in her Mind—Her Ladyship does not speak.

Edward Lucas, one of Mr. Bowes' Ruffians, is a Middle Aged Man, looks quick, an acquiline Nose, a striped second Mourning Coat, and a light coloured Great Coat, a light two or three Curled Wig, in general wears spectacles.

Francis Peacock, a very tall and stout Man, above six feet four inches high, dark Complexion, a little pitted with Smallpox. Lucas and Peacock were yesterday at Carlisle, lurking about and looking for Intelligence.

The news travelled like wild-fire. Moor shepherds who covered miles of sheep tracks in a day; game-keepers on their long and lonely rounds; farmers in the dales and, above all, ostlers, coachmen and inn-keepers spread the news by the "bush telegraph" of that wild and lonely countryside.

Bowes took instant fright. He set off from Newcastle with Mary Eleanor and Mary Gowland in a chaise, driving like the devil for Durham. Prevot, the French valet, followed on a horse.

Half a mile or so behind galloped one Abraham Dunn. He had been hired by Mrs. Liddell, Lady Strathmore's aunt, to warn all inn-keepers not to provide Bowes with fresh horses.

Dunn shadowed the party. He saw Bowes prime a pair of

pistols. At Aycliff near Darlington a man called Robert Thornton recognized Bowes and the hunt was up. He joined Dunn. In a few moments Bourne, the steward, came thundering up on a mud-bespattered horse and shouted out to Bowes that the whole countryside was up in arms and after him.

Bowes leapt out of the chaise, took one of the horses out of the shafts, strapped a blanket on the horse's back behind the saddle, mounted the animal and with Lady Strathmore sitting behind him on the blanket, galloped off across snow-covered fields, bounded by stone walls, swampy and desolate. Dunn and Thornton followed.

When they got to the village of Neasham they called out the parish constable, Christopher Smith, and told him to arrest Bowes. Smith jumped on to a horse and, with half the village of Neasham following like a lot of moorland fox-hunters, they galloped across soggy, wintry moorland and hill pasture hunting Bowes like a pack of hounds.

Constable Smith told the story afterwards in a remarkable affidavit:

> An alarm was given by a man on horseback that Bowes had killed his wife and the country was in arms to take him. I had seen a man ride past with a woman behind him, without a pillion, attended by another man on horseback, wanting a hat or any covering on his head, and a bare sword by his side, and took them for pickpockets.
>
> Upon this, I ran to the door and said to my brother, "Let us each get a stick, and we will go and take him." We went after them, as did several of the village, about a mile into Sockburn Lane. Upon our coming up, Mr. Bowes said, "What do you want?" I said, "The country is alarmed with a bad report, we are come to take you." Mr. Bowes presented a pistol and said he would blow out the first man's brains that dared touch him. I said, if he would surrender, we would not hurt him. He again said he would shoot anyone that came nigh him, and that he would pay anyone who would take him to Northallerton. John Gunston said the Tees was too deep at Sockburn, he must go back to Neasham. I said he should not stir from the place till he was taken, and if he would not submit we would set upon him, and take him at all events; for he was a suspicious

person, and had surely done something bad, or he need not ride through the country in the manner he did.

Mr. Bowes turned about his horse, seeming to go away, when the woman slipped off from behind him and, clasping her hands together, said, "I am Lady Strathmore, for God's sake assist me." I said, "Are you indeed Lady Strathmore?" She said, "I am, and am forced away contrary to every inclination by that man (pointing to Bowes)." I said, "If you are Lady Strathmore, we will secure your person, and take him"; and bade the men get sticks and we would set upon him, and take him at all events.

Anthony Claxton put off his hat, and went near Bowes, which, I perceiving, told him to put on his hat and be upon his guard; and seeing Bowes rest the pistol upon the other I rushed upon him and seized them both, and called for assistance, when John Wainton came and took hold of the horse and led him past me. While Bowes struggled with me, one of the pistol handles broke in my hand, and by pulling them away, the guard of the trigger cut a piece out of the foremost finger of my right hand. I threw that pistol away, and with the other gave Bowes a blow upon the right side of his head which knocked him from his horse.

Fearing he had more pistols about him, and that he might shoot some of us, I gave him another blow upon the back part of his head, and cut it about two inches. Lady Strathmore asked if he was killed, and desired we would not strike him again, and several times bade us search his pockets for pistols and take care he did not shoot some of us. Her Ladyship, being then upon horse before Gabriel Thornton, bade us farewell.

I sent John Gunston away for the surgeon to dress the wound, and took him to Eliza Shutt's till Thomas Bowes, Mr. Turner, and Mr. Rudd's man came and dressed the wound, and then carried Bowes away to Thomas Bowes' house in Darlington. And on the Wednesday he was conducted to London by three men.

The cool courage of this moorland village constable deserves to live for all time.

Lady Strathmore went straight to London and was put to bed in Mr. James Farrer's house in Bread Street Hill. She was in such a frightful state that the surgeon who examined her doubted if she would live. She could neither stand nor walk by herself for a

Bowes Museum, Barnard Castle

Mr. and Mrs. John Bowes, creators of the Bowes Museum (*The Bowes Museum*)

whole month. None the less through her lawyer, Farrer, she again swore Articles of Peace against Bowes citing numerous acts of cruelty.

Bowes reached London on 27th November, 1786, guarded by law officers and asked Jesse Foot, the surgeon, to come and see him at Atkinson's Hotel in Dean Street, Soho. Foot found him looking as white as death, his head swathed in a blood-stained cloth, his shirt bloody and a week-old beard on his chin. When he was given a glass of wine he was sick.

The Court officers said that he must go at once to Westminster Hall. Bowes said he was too sick to go. A second doctor was called in. Both he and Foot said that their patient was well enough to attend. He promptly vomited twice again. When he entered Westminster Hall, hanging on to Foot's arm, he was booed and hissed by the public who packed the place to the doors.

His counsel pleaded that he was too sick to be sent to prison. Thereupon the Marshal of the King's Bench Prison said loudly, "I can accommodate the gentleman in my quarters." This caused a roar of laughter.

Bowes was taken straight to the Marshal's house in St. George's Fields where he was given a suite of "state rooms" for which he paid the Marshal rent. He remained in the prison, or, at least, subject to its rules, for the next twenty-two years of his life.

Foot found out, a day or two later, that his patient's vomiting and deathly white face were due to the fact that he had bought some ipecacuanha on the way to London and had swallowed it as soon as he reached the hotel "in order that his appearance might excite commiseration and avoid if possible being committed to prison".

Thereafter there ensued a long-drawn series of law-suits between Bowes and Mary Eleanor. It was a lawyers' harvest. Bowes was bound over to keep the peace for fourteen years in securities of £20,000. He still had control of his wife's income and estates.

Unbelievable though it may sound, he bought the controlling share in the newspaper *The Universal Register* and virtually ran it from his rooms in the prison Marshal's house. Under various *nommes de plume* he attacked and defended himself in a series of letters—as Mr. Ralph Arnold says, "a hero fighting with his own shadow". He also attacked James Farrer in his newspaper and accused him of having designs on Lady Strathmore.

He and his gang of conspirators came up for trial on 30th May, 1787, in the Court of King's Bench on various charges including the abduction of Lady Strathmore and an attempt to make her drop her divorce proceedings. They were also accused of conspiring to imprison her, assaulting her, and "imprisoning her without stating a conspiracy". The Special Jury found Bowes and his gang guilty on all charges. The judge, Mr. Justice Buller, said that he would announce sentence later. He took twenty-seven days to do so. During that time Bowes had the effrontery to publish this advertisement:

> Preparing for the Press and shortly will be published, *an account* of the life of M. E. Bowes, including a Narrative of her Conduct from the age of thirteen till a short time previous to her elopement from her present husband. Written by herself.

This so-called narrative was in fact the wretched woman's *Confessions* which, in all probability, Bowes had forced her to write. It was perhaps the lowest act of his despicable life.

Finally, on 26th June, Bowes and his confederates came up for sentence. He was fined £300 with three years' imprisonment "at the expiration of the said term to find securities for fourteen years, himself in £10,000 and two securities of £5,000 each". Lucas was fined £50 and sent to jail for three years. Peacock got two years and was fined £100. Prevot was given one year in jail whilst Bourne got off lightly with a fine of £50 and six months' imprisonment. For some strange reason Thomas Bowes was not prosecuted.

Bowes was promptly moved into "inferior state rooms", in the Marshal's house and not in the actual prison. There he lived in comfort with a staff of servants, including Mary Gowland, Mr. and Mrs. Peacock and their daughter and his little son, William Johnstone Bowes. His life for the next year or so consisted of endless legal wrangles, consultations with his lawyers and preparation to fight suits pending against him in the Ecclesiastical Courts and in the Chancery Court. He hoped to retain enough of his wife's estates and come out of prison an immensely wealthy man. To bolster his claims he broadcast this letter from prison:

> No person has any right to receive the Streatlam Estate rents except the receiver or receivers appointed by the Court of Chancery under the claims of a mortgage for the sum of £6,500 raised by the late Earl of Strathmore and that when the transfer of the mortgage is made (as it will be soon) then *the rents of the estate will revert to me* or Mr. H. Bourne. Lady Strathmore *never can or will* possess any power over, or any right to receive the rents of the said estate during *the term of my life.* I will only give her an allowance or alimony unless she quits the society of artful, interested attornies and menial servants . . . or unless some respectable persons among her relations or former friends will take her under their charge and protection.
>
> No debts incurred by Lady Strathmore or Mrs. Morgan, since Lady Strathmore's elopement, will be paid by me or, according to my firm belief, by any other person whatever.

In another letter he blackguarded her lawyer, James Farrer, in the *Newcastle Chronicle.* Lady Strathmore was then confined to bed in Farrer's house, very weak, still desperately ill, but apparently with her spirit unbroken. Farrer lent her a good deal of money to tide her over until she was able to claim the income from her estate. Three days after Christmas Day in 1786 she published the following in the *London Packet*:

> Lady Strathmore returns her sincere and hearty thanks to her friends . . . for their humane and spirited exertions towards the restoration of her liberty, and the preservation of her life. . . . She is able to inform her friends that she is at length in a fair way to recovery from the painful and alarming effects of her late sufferings, and gains strength daily.

She was then just able to get about on her feet with a stick although she recorded that she had feared "a mortification of my limbs". On the last day of the year she managed to walk downstairs and in January the Farrers took a house for her in Holles Street. There she lived with the devoted Mrs. Morgan in constant attendance.

After more than a year of legal wrangles the Lord Chancellor restored Lady Strathmore's estates and income to her, dismissed Bowes' cross-petition and the latter was ordered to repay £10,295 11s. 1d. plus Lady Strathmore's taxed costs. The Lord Chancellor, in his judgement, was more than caustic. He said he would say nothing of the morality of the transaction between the two parties. Man and wife "seemed to have been pretty well matched . . . Marriage in general seemed to have been Lady Strathmore's object; she was disposed to marry anybody but not to part with her fortune".

Finally, her divorce suit was heard. In the course of his address Lady Strathmore's counsel, Dr. Bever, said:

> My Lords, this kind of conduct is capable of very great exaggeration and will alter its complexion and will on many occasions become much blacker and will also on many occasions become more and more atrocious, it will become more and more so in accordance to the Education, the Fortune, the Rank and the Condition of the Person both of him who inflicts and of her who suffers it. My Lords, the case now before your Lordships is not upon the common wranglings and disputes between John and Betty, that kind of beating can do no worse, perhaps, than break a head without wounding a heart, and does not consist in anything more than broken heads and bloody noses which are the common consequences of the marriage state and which are very easily and very happily made up by a little matrimonial consolation at night—that is not the cruelty we complain of.

The whole shabby story of Bowes' appalling cruelty was brought out. In defence his counsel said that Lady Strathmore committed misconduct with her footman, George Walker. There was not a shred of evidence to prove it. Bowes said that she had been "extravagant, lustful, wicked and abandoned in temper and religion". He said that she had run deeply into debt before he married her owing to "the indulgence and gratification of her lusts and other profligate means". An odd way to describe an extravagant gardener and a botanist who bought rare shrubs.

One of his witnesses, Eliza Stephens, said that Lady Strathmore was irreligious, immoral—both charges had more than a little truth in them—that she drank heavily and had set her clothes on fire when drunk. Eliza Stephens said that Mary Eleanor had told her that she "loved cats better than her children". In short, Bowes' witnesses, including the contemptible parson, Henry Stephens, lied their heads off in order to paint Mary Eleanor in the most lurid colour and to picture Bowes as "invariably kind and indulgent".

Bowes attempted to submit her *Confessions* but they were not allowed as evidence.

Finally, on 2nd March, 1789, the Lords Commissioners having heard the arguments of both sides, solemnly pronounced that:

> Andrew Robinson Bowes, being unmindful of his conjugal vows, and not having the fear of God before his eyes, did, on the several days and times mentioned in the pleadings of this case, commit the several acts of cruelty therein mentioned, and did also on the days therein set forth commit the heinous crime of adultery. The Court therefore order and decree, that the said Andrew Robinson Bowes and Lady Strathmore be divorced, and live separately from each other; but that neither of the parties marry during the natural life of the other of them.

The *Gentleman's Magazine* commented:

> Lady Strathmore was at length restored to the large possessions of her family, and divorced from a marriage contracted in an evil hour.

5

STONEY BOWES' PRISON ORGIES

BOWES' life in prison was an incredible orgy of riotous living, drunkenness, lechery, gambling, fighting and public mischief-making. The diseased mind of a certain type of Hollywood script-writer could produce nothing more flamboyant.

He had two mistresses almost from the moment he entered prison, Mary Gowland and a pathetically charming little girl called Jenny Sutton. Jenny's father was imprisoned for debt. When she visited him Bowes determined to have her. He sent Jesse Foot to bring her to him. Foot says that she was "a girl of perfect symmetry, fair, lively and innocent. She was feeding a pigeon with split peas out of her mouth". Bowes said he would pay her father's debts. He installed her in a room on his own staircase. Foot says she had "a native cheerful disposition and [she] found a channel for her affections in her children. She had ever been a child of misfortune; all which particulars marked, adapted and qualified her for being a true and rare representation of *a female of fortitude*". This poor child bore Bowes one illegitimate infant after another.

His behaviour in prison was astounding. In October 1790 another debtor, Dr. Hodson, ran a gaming table in the King's Bench. Another prisoner named Vardy sat down to play with £80 in bank bills in his pocket. Bowes stole them. When Vardy told Bowes they were missing he seized Vardy by the throat, slung him to and fro in the air and threatened to throw him out of the window. He told Vardy he had the bills and would stick to them. Vardy sued him. The judge reproved them for gambling in prison and fined Bowes 6s. 8d.

Later another prisoner, du Buisson, was standing in front of the fire warming himself. "Get out of my way or I'll break your head with this pewter pot," roared Bowes. He hit du Buisson in the mouth and broke his teeth. Next year the prisoners rioted because a Parliamentary Bill which would have helped insolvent debtors was thrown out. Bowes sided with the prison officials and was made chairman of the Prisoners Association. Later, it was said that the prison marshal would "testify to the strict propriety of his conduct"!

Meanwhile, his old enemy, the Reverend Sir Henry Bate Dudley, editor of the *Morning Post*, was hot on his trail. That eminent newspaper came out in October 1788 with this sly dig:

> To some people—but we do not allude to *debtors*—to some people a commitment to Banco Regis is no great punishment. A certain delinquent daily eats, drinks and gets merry, and though surrounded by as many wives and children as *Macheath*, keeps them all in good order. . . . Among the evils that arise from imprisonment for debt may be reckoned the increase in female incontinence—the young women who attend on their unfortunate confined relatives being generally seduced. A recent instance of this kind has taken place wherein, poverty having expelled every generous feeling from the parent, he permitted the prostitution of his child to supply his wants, and she now lives openly with a prisoner of a different description. . . .

Bowes did not only attack his wife from prison. He went for the wretched Captain Henry Farrer whom he had turned out of Lady Strathmore's carriage on the day that he abducted her. Bowes discovered that Henry Farrer had married beneath him, had kept the marriage secret from his family and, Bowes alleged, had never given his wife a home or income. She had had to work "as a cleaner of silk stockings and a clear-starcher of muslin and gauze".

Bowes said that her husband had committed adultery with a Mrs. Parks and that "he carried on an intrigue of a still more nefarious and degrading nature—that he was connected with a married woman and for purposes the most wicked. The personage I refer to is the Right Honourable the Countess of Strathmore. . . . The Captain now had two ladies to attend, and one of them a Countess—in such a situation he could not but consider that household-plague, a wife, except as an impediment to his pleasure and a drawback to his interest".

This tarradiddle was printed in a book entitled *The Appeal of an Injured Wife against a Cruel Husband, written by Mrs. Farrer and dedicated to the Countess of Strathmore.* There is no doubt that Bowes wrote it. It bears his trademark of vicious slander and specious humbug. He went on to say, writing as Mrs. Farrer, that Farrer had attempted to seduce his own wife's sister and that Lady Strathmore had often been to his chambers in the Temple, which the modern barrister will be enchanted to know was described as "a place where few modest women venture to visit".

Bowes actually had Mrs. Farrer to stay in his rooms in the King's Bench Prison and arranged for her to take the star role in a play at the Haymarket Theatre. He advertised it thus:

> The Lord Chamberlain has granted a licence for the performance of *Tamerlaine* at the Haymarket Theatre this present evening, in which Mrs. Farrer, who a short time ago published a pamphlet dedicated to Lady Strathmore, will perform the part of Arpasia, and there are flattering expectations that from her person, voice and expressive countenance she may prove a successful candidate for the winter theatres. . . . The Public are respectfully informed that the utmost care and attention will be taken to render the performance respectable and to merit their appreciation and support.

Lady Strathmore's successful divorce and her recovery of the estates knocked most of Bowes' nonsense on the head. Foot records:

> Thus mauled, stripped, disgraced and blasted, the prison bolts flew open, all of a sudden he bade adieu to the outer state rooms, and entered into the walls, in a pickle not unmerited, and in a state which, to some, death would have been comparatively an *Elysium*. . . . Like a tree struck by lightning, he had still a few green branches

left. He had the best rooms within the walls and, as birds do when they are reconciled to the cage, he began to plume himself, to pick and meditate upon the possible smiles the place could afford him. He took an analysis of the inhabitants; and particularly all those he could make useful to his purpose he tempted by his dinners.

In 1800 Bowes actually managed to gain permission to live outside the prison in a house in London Road, St. George's Field, but he was bound to abide by the prison rules.

Jenny Sutton went with him with her crew of illegitimate children and a mob of half-starved cats and dogs. There he took on a second mistress "a very neat and modest young woman, a sempstress who had visited her sister in the King's Bench Prison who was associated with a gentleman there, a clergyman". That is Foot's picture of the girl.

Bowes tried to bring his new mistress into his own house when Jenny Sutton was away, but her children ran her out of the place. Bowes set her up in a second house in the same road. There she had a child by him. Bowes bribed her to say that the father was one of the prisoners in the King's Bench.

So the sordid, evil life of this monstrous cad dragged on. Even poor little Jenny Sutton who was devoted to him, was traduced. Bowes told one of his own sisters that Jenny was a vicious, abandoned, heartless strumpet and that he was going to leave all his money to his sister. On the strength of this he tried to borrow money from his sister's husband. The husband would not play.

Creditors beseiged the house daily. It became a squalid slum. Foot says, "His two daughters went down upon their knees and gathered up the dust with their hands". Poor Jenny Sutton got only one meal a day.

The end came in January 1810. Jenny Sutton sent for Foot and told him, in a storm of tears, that Bowes was near death and had left her completely out of his will. Foot went to see Bowes' lawyer, Mr. Robbins.

The pair of them set off to see Bowes on his death-bed. There they found Bowes' sister and a Mr. Sampson Perry, who had been doctoring Bowes.

This is the deathbed scene as Foot described it:

> All being now assembled, as if from sympathy, all were devoted to see if Bowes could be prevailed upon to give anything to Miss Sutton. It ought not to be omitted that Bowes' sister, from the goodness of her heart, had at her own expense called in the clergyman of the parish. With these powerful engines; with the particular address of Mr. Sampson Perry, with the intercession of all around him, with the begging of the children advancing to the bedside one after the other, Bowes at length gave way, opened his mouth, and consented to Miss Sutton having one hundred pounds per annum. This being avowed to Mr. Perry by Bowes, and legally put down by Mr. Robbins, witnessed by him, his friend and myself, we took our leave. I ought to observe there was not a shilling in the house, till Mr. Robbins left a sum . . . a ready display of direct humanity upon this necessitous occasion.

Six days later the Devil claimed his own. Bowes died in squalor and filth on 23rd January, 1810. His bones lie in the vault of St. George's church in the Borough in South London.

Foot, that diligent chronicler, the Boswell of this blackguard, said:

> He was a villain to the backbone! In every turn of his affairs, his passion indicated all the sufferings of a coward, without the smallest show of fortitude. . . . To sum up his character in a few words, he was cowardly, insidious, hypocritical, tyrannic, mean, violent, selfish, jealous, revengeful, inhuman and savage, without a single countervailing quality. Let us hope when he departed, that never before nor since there never was, nor ever will be, taking him for all in all, his parallel.

Thus died the greatest cad of all time.

Meanwhile, Mary Eleanor Strathmore had lived a retired life. She kept a scrap album in which she pasted every cutting she could collect concerning herself, Bowes and their lawsuits. She was, like many a London hostess of today, a glutton for publicity. She had never been a good mother, but she did, in her latter years, pay far more attention to her children, including her eldest son, John Strathmore. One entry in her album says: "My son did come over for ten days just to see me". When the dust of battle and the stink of scandal had blown away even the Lyon family unbent towards her.

One extraordinary incident stands out. Lady Strathmore had had such a sickening of marriage that she virtually shut up her young daughter, Lady Anna, in the house and refused to let her meet any young men. The result was that Anna fell violently in love with a young law student named Jessup, who lived on the other side of the street. She had only seen him once looking out of his window. That was enough.

When Lady Strathmore and the servants had gone to bed, Anna slowly pushed a long ladder out of her bedroom window across the narrow street to her lover's window opposite. He caught the other end and held it on his windowsill. A plank was then pushed the length of the ladder. Anna, who must have had nerves of steel and the balance of a tight-rope walker, crawled across the swaying, bending ladder. Had it snapped she would have broken her neck.

She and Jessup ran away, married and had two daughters. He died while still a young man. She lived to a good old age in Bird Hill House in the park at Gibside where her brother gave her a pension.

There is no doubt that John Strathmore brought a great deal of happiness, peace and common-sense management into the last years of his mother's life. He was kind-hearted, generous, immensely good-looking and had a strong sense of family. He came of age in 1790 as the tenth Earl of Strathmore. His mother made over the estates and their revenues to him with due allowances for her two youngest children, Mary and William Johnstone Bowes. She had just regained custody of them both. Mr. Ralph Arnold unearthed, in the Bowes Museum, a touching little letter from Mary Bowes:

Newington,
Surrey.

... I cannot express the joy it was to me to be informed by my Lady

Wright of my turn of Fortune in being now, I hope, under your Protection. When I parted from you, I was much too young to know the loss of a mother. I am sensible of the duty and affection I owe to you and my Brother. . . . I long very much to see you and hope there is nothing more now wanting to complete my happiness. I am sure you will be very glad to see my dear little brother William, indeed he is a very fine Boy. Although I have been almost five years absent from you I have not forgot any place where I spent my infancy and believe I could find my way over one half of Paul's Walden and Gibside houses etc.

Pray assure the Earl of Strathmore of my grateful love, my dear Mama,

Your dutiful and affectionate daughter,

Mary

Her second son, George Bowes, came of age in 1792 and she made over to him St. Pauls Walden with its estate of some 1,800 acres. She moved to Purbrook Park near Cosham, not far from Portsmouth. Mr. Ralph Arnold unearthed the interesting fact that a very old farmer, living in the neighbourhood in 1877, remembered Mary Eleanor Strathmore in her old age. Two of her daughters lived with her and the ever-faithful Mrs. Morgan was her maid-companion. She had a full staff of servants and the farmer related:

She kept little company, and was much occupied with pets, especially dogs, of which she had many. Each one had its own bed in a basket, with everything to make it comfortable. Meat was regularly provided in the room which they occupied. Every day a hot dinner was cooked on purpose for them and each dog had its own place set apart for him, with a plate and a dish.

When that devoted woman, Mrs. Morgan, died in 1796 Lady Strathmore had her buried at Christchurch. There, today, one may see her monument. It bears this dedication composed by Mary Eleanor:

Dedicated to the most rare of all connections, a perfect and dis-

> interested friend, by the Countess of Strathmore, who, conscious of the treasure, valued its possession and mourned its loss. . . . To her heroic qualities, her cool deliberate courage, and her matchless, persevering friendship, the tears of blood shed by one who despises weakness, the records of law and justice, and perhaps even the historic page, will bear witness to an astonished and admiring posterity.

Lady Strathmore died on the 28th day of April in 1800. Thirteen days later, clad in her wedding dress, she was buried in the South Cross of Westminster Abbey.

Thus, in the odour of solemn sanctity, ended the life of a woman who was perhaps the most controversial and dramatic woman of the eighteenth century. Her story is unique. It has never been paralleled.

William Johnstone Bowes, Stoney Bowes' son, joined the Navy and made his little niche in history by walking eight miles over pack-ice to the shore when his ship, the frigate *Proserpine*, was jammed in ice at the mouth of the Elbe in 1799. A few days later he walked back to the ship without telling the captain. That night a gale broke up the ice and the frigate was driven ashore on the Island of Baltrum. William Bowes lived to tell the tale. He was drowned in the *Blenheim* in 1817. Mary Bowes died a spinster in Bath. Thus ended the last living link with Stoney Bowes.

6

THE WILD AND LOVELY LADY TYRCONNEL

WHEN the wretched Mary Eleanor, ninth Countess of Strathmore, died in 1800 her eldest son, John, by her first husband, was twenty-nine, handsome, kind, quick-witted. He adored lovely women and good horses.

First he fell in love with a married woman, Lady Tyrconnel. She was slim, wild, lovely and rackety. She was the daughter of Sir John Hussey Delaval of Seaton Delaval, later Lord Delaval, and was married at sixteen to Lord Tyrconnel, her father's friend, which explains a lot. When she rode a horse "her hair floated on the saddle". Frederick, Duke of York, adored her and there is no doubt she was his mistress for a time. He let her down badly. John Strathmore fell head over heels in love with her when he was only twenty-two.

Tyrconnel did not bother his head much about his wife's lover. She and Strathmore rode together, raced together, danced and made love. He worshipped the turf on which her thoroughbred hunter trod.

Then, in 1800, the year of Mary Eleanor's death, the lovely "Hussey" Tyrconnel died of consumption in her lover's mansion at Gibside. Today Gibside is a roofless ruin. Owls and jackdaws possess the stately rooms where "Hussey" Tyrconnel, her golden hair a cloud about her waist, lay in young Strathmore's arms. Her ghost, they say, haunts the place to this day. One could have worse ghosts.

Strathmore gave her a funeral which almost ruined the estate. For, says the chronicle: "Her face was painted like the most brilliant life. He dressed her head himself! And then, having decked her out in all her jewels and covered her with ruffled lace from head to foot, he sent her up to London, causing her to lie in state at every town upon the road and finally to be buried in Westminster Abbey."

John Strathmore was so utterly heart-broken that he did a thing few men have ever done—which only a wild, desperate, broken heart could excuse—he fell in love with "Hussey" Tyrconnel's own daughter, the child of his mistress, by, one hopes, Lord Tyrconnel.

He proposed to her. She was Lady Susan Carpenter. That proposal is described in a letter (still in existence) to the then Lord Delaval: "The fascinated Lord Strathmore stared at her intently, seemed to be on the point of making some declaration, only to withdraw so abruptly that she was quite put out of countenance by his apparent rudeness".

The heartbroken Strathmore saw in the young girl the living image of his adored mistress. He was in love, not with a ghost, but with the living replica of an imperishable memory. They did not marry.

Strathmore turned to thoroughbred horses for consolation. He rebuilt Gibside. He planted woods. He laid out gardens. He threw his heart and his wealth into the creation of beauty amid the stark contours of the Durham moorlands. He created at Gibside "one of the most exquisite works of English classical architecture . . . a fragment of the majestic landscape conception of which it formed the culmination". You can still see at Gibside in the layout of the woods and the planning of the landscape the genius for beauty of that heartbroken young man.

Then happened a strange, wild freak of passion. Apart from Gibside, he owned, also in Durham, Streatlam Castle. Near it lived a gardener named Milner. He had a beautiful daughter, Mary Milner. She became a housemaid at Wemmergill Hall, Strathmore's shooting box on the Yorkshire Moors. She was tall, with natural dignity, great charm. She was also intelligent. These things do not always go together.

Strathmore fell in love with her. They lived together at Wemmergill and in Paradise Row, Chelsea. On 29th June, 1811, she gave birth to a son who was baptized as "John Bowes, son of John and Mary Milner". A year later the three of them moved to Streatlam Castle. Then they lived in London. Strathmore made a will, leaving all his English estates, worth £21,000 a year, "to my son, or reputed son . . . called or known by the name of John Bowes". That was in 1817.

Three years later, Strathmore fell desperately ill. At 4 a.m. on Saturday, 1st July, 1820, he sent for Mr. John Dean Paul, the banker, and said that he wished to marry Mary Milner, and asked him to get a special licence. The Archbishop of Canterbury refused it. Mr. Dean Paul got it through Doctor's Commons the same day. Twenty-four hours of hullabaloo and heartbreak.

Next morning, at 8 a.m., Lord Strathmore was carried from his bedroom by four men-servants. They put him in a sedan chair. They lifted it on their shoulders and took the dying man to St. George's Church, Hanover Square. There the Dean of Carlisle and four witnesses were waiting.

The Dean told Lord Strathmore, dying though he was, that he must get out of the sedan chair and stand and kneel at the altar rails at the precise moments when the service demanded it.

Lord Strathmore was supported, deadly pale, by his friends. But he gave the responses in a clear, ringing voice. He signed the register. Death was waiting round the corner. But with death beckoning he determined to make Mary Milner an honest woman, her son his legitimate heir.

Immediately the service was over a letter was sent by a man galloping on horseback at headlong speed to a school-master, the Reverend William Goodenough at Ealing, to tell him that his pupil, John Bowes, was now Lord Glamis. The school-boy held that title for one day only.

His father, Lord Strathmore, died at two o'clock the next morning. The boy's legitimacy was challenged immediately. The case went before the House of Lords. Mary Eleanor's third but only surviving son, the eleventh Earl, assumed the title of Earl of Strathmore and Kinghorne and challenged the right of young John Bowes to that title.

The case hinged partly on the fact that, under Scottish law, children born out of wedlock are legitimatized by the subsequent marriage of their parents. The law of England does not allow that relief. A shining example of our national humbug. John Bowes lost his claim on the grounds that he could not be a lawful son in one country and a bastard in another, and that, since his parents had married in England, their marriage was covered by the law of England. He failed to win the Earldom of Strathmore.

On the other hand, Mary Milner, the gardener's daughter, became Countess Dowager of Strathmore. She carried her new dignity with poise, charm, intelligence and beauty. Many a blue-blood has looked less the part than Mary Milner, the gardener's daughter, born at Stainton, in County Durham. Later she married William Hutt, who became M.P. for Hull, Paymaster General, Vice-President of the Board of Trade in Gladstone's Government, Privy Councillor and Knight Commander of the Bath. Hutt had been the tutor of her son. Old men remember him.

Meanwhile, John Bowes, the son who failed to win the Earldom, went to Eton and Cambridge. He had not won a coronet, but he had the Durham estates—43,000 acres, worth £20,000 a year, plus coal mines, iron-works, and a thoroughbred stud. When he came of age 300 tenants were entertained with roast beef and plum pudding. He lived at Streatlam Castle in splendour. He became M.P. for South Durham. The course was set for him to be a county squire of vast wealth, an English "Milord" without a coronet.

He founded the great business of John Bowes and Partners, which flourishes today. He operated twelve collieries. He started a ship-building company at Jarrow. More than that, he won the Derby four times. Many a rich Englishman would rather have that honour than be Prime Minister.

Then came the anti-climax. John Bowes, tall, bearded, pale-faced, well-built, with large, intelligent eyes, loved the theatre. He also loved Paris. He was perhaps more at home on the Left Bank than on Newmarket Heath. He loved his race-horses, but he also loved fine furniture, old books, delicate porcelain, medieval tapestries and Old Masters. He bought works of art as other men buy stamps. He also bought the Théâtre de Variétés in

Paris and married a French actress. Her name was Josephine Benoite Coffin-Chevallier, Contessa di Montalbo. Her grandfather had been a clockmaker at Lyons. Her parents, who made money, bought the title from the tiny state of San Marino.

The new Mrs. Bowes supported her husband loyally. She ran true to the Mary Milner form. She never let him down. She was small, black-haired, with piercing, hawk-like eyes, a tight, rather sharp mouth, altogether a little forbidding. She made up her eyes rather too heavily and her fingernails were invariably black due to her habit of taking a very odd bath of "coal black acid".

She must have cut a foreign figure among the gentry of the North Country, but there is no question that she was devoted to her husband, highly artistic, a good painter on a bold and rather splendid scale and a connoisseur of pictures, china, furniture and other works of art. An oddly assorted couple who, none the less, suited each other down to the ground.

They were married at St. Marylebone Church in London in 1854 and it seems that Bowes kept the marriage quiet for a few years. He had a house in Paris, Number 7 Rue de Berlin, and two years after his marriage he bought the splendid house which Louis XV had built for Madam Du Barri, the Château de Louveciennes. They spent much of their early married years between the two houses in France, but John Bowes sold the château in 1862 and sent the contents over to Streatlam Castle. During that year, and for two years afterwards, he bought most of his pictures. Sixty-four of them, including three Goyas, a Zurbaran, Antonio More and the El Greco of St. Peter, came from the collection of a Spanish connoisseur, the Conde de Quinto, who, fortunately, had the pick of some of the best pictures in Spain.

Meanwhile Streatlam Castle, which had been building for some years, was finished by 1860. The architect was John Dobson who, incidentally, built Newcastle railway station.

That incorrigible country-house guest, Augustus Hare, who stayed in half the big houses in England and noted in his diary what he saw and what he thought of them, gives one an interesting little cameo of life at Streatlam when John Bowes and

"Madame" Bowes, as she was called, were in residence there in 1861. He says in his biography, *The Story of My Life*, which is full of fascinating country house gossip and ghost stories:

> September 25th—I came with Cousin Susan to this curious place, to which my cousin, Mr. Bowes, has welcomed us so very cordially. The house is in a hollow—an enormous building of the last century, enclosing a mediaeval castle. I sleep in the ghost-room, looking most grim and weird from its black oak with red hangings, and containing a tall bed with a red canopy. "Here", the only existing Handbook says, "the unfortunate Mary Queen of Scots expired in captivity." I am afraid that the next Handbook will have to confess that she was beheaded at Fotheringay.
>
> The long galleries are full of family portraits—Hyltons, Blakistons, and Bowes'—one of whom, Miss Bowes of Streatlam, was Mrs. John Knox! More interesting to me is the great picture of Mary Eleanor, the unhappy Countess of Strathmore, walking in the grounds of St. Paul's Walden.
>
> September 27th—This is the oddest house I ever was in! Everything is arranged for you, from the moment you get up till the moment you go to bed, and you are never allowed to deviate from the rules laid down: I even write this in time stolen from the half-hour for dressing. We are called at eight, and at ten march into breakfast with the same procession as at dinner, only at this meal "Madame Bowes" does not appear, for she is then reclining in a bath of coal-black acid, which "refreshes her system" but leaves her nails black.
>
> After breakfast we are all set down to employments appointed for the morning. At twelve Madame appears, having painted the under-lids of her jet-black eyes with belladonna. At two the bell rings for luncheon, and we are fetched if not punctual to an instant. At three we are all sent out driving (the coachman having exact orders where to take us) immense drives (twenty-four miles today) in an open barouche and pair. At seven we dine in great splendour and afterwards we sit in the oak drawing-room and talk about our ancestors!

Rather different a picture of life at Streatlam was given by Thackeray who visited the place in the summer of 1841 before

John Bowes had married and when he was fighting a parliamentary election. He had known John Bowes as an undergraduate at Cambridge and they had been friends, on and off, for years. One entry in Thackeray's letters says: "I went to see Bowes [in Paris]. He has £40,000 a year and palaces in the country, and here he is manager of the Théâtre de Variétés—and his talk was about actors and coulisses all the time of our interview—I wish it could be the last, but he has made me promise to dine with him and go I must, to be killed by his melancholy *gentlemanlikeness.*"

Thackeray is supposed to have based his novel, *Barry Lyndon*, on the life of Andrew Robinson Stoney Bowes, and it was during one of his stays at Streatlam in June and July 1841 that he read Jesse Foot's *Lives* which could have given him just the material he needed for *Barry Lyndon.*

Thackeray wrote a description of his visit to Streatlam in *Frazer's Magazine* in the autumn of 1841 in the form of a skit on an American journalist's version of an English country gentleman's Parliamentary election campaign.

He describes how he drove from Darlington Station to Streatlam in a gig and how a very precise old lady, the lodge-keeper, opened the park gates. He was greeted at the castle by a St. Bernard dog, a black Newfoundland retriever and various other dogs. Bowes was away, so Thackeray found himself, for the moment, the temporary "lord of a grand house and park, of a stable full of horses, a garden full of good things and a hall full of servants".

The housekeeper showed him into a dining-room where he was to dine alone at "a great stiff shining damask table cloth, opposite which is placed a tall red chair. On the left hand side imagine a fire, such as they usually light here in the summer months, and containing at least three degenerated scuttlefuls of London coal. Opposite is an array of gold plate, polished up to a pitch of supernatural brightness, flanked on each side by a decanter in a filigree stand. In the midst of this array is a jug of the commonest earthenware—a 3d. yellow jug, inscribed "Britton for ever".

His pseudonym for Bowes was "Britton". After dinner the

butler took him up a stately staircase "to a tall tester bed covered with four blankets and a counterpane". He was woken by "a gentleman in black" at 8 a.m. who brought up his hot water and he breakfasted at 9 a.m. He even went to the length of describing his table thus:

> A clean table cloth and napkin, on it arranged: Dry toast, Eggs, Hot cakes, Bread brown, Butter, Bread white, Cup, Tea, Coffee, Cup, Cream, Milk.
>
> On the right of the plate, letters and newspapers. On the side table grilled ham, a silver mustard pot, a cold chicken, and a sort of pig's head jelly—very good indeed.

In 1873 John Bowes' income from coal alone was more than £1,000 a day. That, in the debased values of today, means rather more than £4,000 a day in our paper money.

Between them they created, on the edge of the desolate Bowes Moor in Durham, a temple of beauty, which today is one of the little-known treasures of England, the Bowes Museum, near Barnard Castle. It stands like a vast château, dominating, with cold grandeur, the bleak moorlands where Dickens laid the scene for Dotheboy's Hall. It is packed with good pictures, furniture, tapestries and other works of art. It is unique in England—enormous, dominating, utterly out of place, terrifically imposing. The late Sir Albert Richardson, Past President of the Royal Academy, rightly said that it "looks like a château that has been transported by a magician from France".

It even has Madam Du Barri's bedroom! The pictures include the El Greco, worth a fortune, some Goyas which would convulse Christies, Reynolds' portrait of Mrs. Thrale, Dr. Johnson's friend, and works by Corot, Fantin-Latour, Fragonard, and others, cheek by jowl with stuffed birds, an enormous canvas of a Durham ox and a perfect example of an eighteenth-century gentleman's library. Their fantastic house framed in cold moorland, instinct with beauty, was born of a great passion and an enduring sense of public service. It is typical of the way in which the Bowes-Lyon blood runs. Whatever their tragedies of light and darknesses, service for others is the key-note.

7

THE GYPSY AND THE QUEEN MOTHER

Two small girls played in the sunshine, under the embattled gateway to the park of Glamis Castle. Two life-size savage warriors in stone gazed down on them impassively. Behind them, at the end of the mile-long drive, sword straight, soared the pink-grey mass of the most romantic castle in Scotland. A fairy-tale pile of pepperpot turrets, battlements, towers, cupolas and a forest of chimneys. From the ninety-feet-high keep above the great black clock with its gilt hands floated the house-flag of Lyon of Glamis—a family whose royal roots are 600 years deep in history.

On that sunny morning in 1907, or thereabouts, when kings and emperors ruled the world of Europe, there was no thought of an impending throne in the mind of anyone at Glamis. All that sort of thing had been buried in 1372, when the White Lyon married Princess Joanna, daughter of King Robert II of Scotland and was given this great castle and all the wide lands which went with the thanage of Glamis.

The two little girls playing in the gateway certainly had no thought of such vaunting splendours. Their life was lived with pet dogs, ponies, their mother and father the Earl and Countess of Strathmore, the castle housekeeper, the dairymaids, their nannie, and, as special village friends, the people who kept the post office and sold two pennyworth of "black balls" to eager little fingers, or with Mrs. Crabbe, the head forester's wife. They often tapped at her door after a run down the village street and asked to be allowed in for "a wee rest".

Suddenly, on that sunny morning, round the bend of the park

wall, on the Kirriemuir Road, came the clip-clop of horses' hooves, the jingle of harness, the rumble of caravan wheels. Motor-cars were rare in those days.

"Oh, look, Elizabeth! The Tinkies! Here come the tinkies!' Let's have our fortunes told!"

The caravan clattered slowly by. A swarthy woman with beady eyes, like onyx, sat on the shafts, smoking a pipe. Gold ear-rings glittered in her ears. She saw the two little girls holding up their pennies. She jerked at the reins. The scrawny horse stopped, thankfully. After all, a little fortune-telling for the young and credulous is part of the stock-in-trade of that wild-eyed, frowsty-haired race of travelling tinkers, half-gypsy, half God-knows-what, who, for centuries, have been part of Highland life.

"Well, my wee girlies, what do you lack?" she asked. "Wull the auld gypsy wuman tell the young leddies fortunes?"

The woman with the witch-hair and onyx eyes took the tiny hand of the smaller girl in her own grimy paw. She looked piercingly into the eager little face. The blue eyes, framed in soft brown hair, were entrancingly shy. The gypsy woman spoke with sudden, intense fierceness. A touch of awe.

"You will live to be a queen—and the mother of a queen," she gasped, half to herself. She dropped the tiny hand and gazed at the child with compelling intensity.

"Ah canna tell thee ony muir," she added. She flicked the reins. The scrawny horse jerked into his collar. The caravan rumbled on.

That is the story told to me on the Glamis estate. It may be no more than a local legend. True or not, is is by no means the only uncannily prophetic happening in childhood life of the Lady Elizabeth Angela Marguerite Bowes-Lyon, Queen Mother of this realm and daughter of the fourteenth Earl of Strathmore and Kinghorne.

As a very small child she had great poise and unaffected charm. An uncanny, instinctive tact. She was utterly unselfconscious. Those grey-blue eyes, which every Lyon seems to have, the flower-like face and the soft voice belied one's first impression of shyness. She was never shy. She was far too pleased to meet people, to entertain them and welcome them. Sargent, that prince of portrait painters, said of her: "She is the only completely unselfconscious sitter I have ever had."

She was not more than three or four when a party of neighbours turned up one afternoon at Glamis for tea. They arrived early. They were shown into the drawing-room. Lady Strathmore had not yet come down from her room. When she entered the drawing-room a few minutes later, she was astounded to see the grown-up guests sitting dutifully in a ring round her small daughter, who was solemnly pouring out tea, holding the large silver teapot unsteadily in two tiny hands and engaging the visitors in small talk.

When her mother took over the teapot Elizabeth retired into a corner. Before doing so she gripped a distinguished gentleman, at least fifty years of age, firmly by the hand, and said: "Come along! Shall us sit and talk?"

The housewife instincts were always strong. Aged about six, she opened the stillroom door one day and said to the dairy-maid: "If you could make the pats of butter small, I think it would help mummy. Persons do leave some of the big pats on their plates—and that is very waste."

Another day she knocked on the stillroom door, popped in with a guilty look and said with an excited gasp: "May I come in and eat more—*lots more*—of that lovely chocolate cake. I didn't like to eat it all while it was upstairs."

She entered the drawing-room one day whilst guests were having tea, wearing a ring on one finger.

"Ah, so I see you're engaged, Elizabeth?" said one lady.

"No, not quite yet. It was only mummy what gave me this ring."

The Strathmore children were never overloaded with pocket money. Scots thrift was instilled into them. When therefore her supply of pennies ran out, she took toll from the stillroom maids, who adored her. One day, feeling particularly broke, at the age of five, she asked shyly: "Do you think I might have silver pennies this time?"

Then there was a fearful crime, committed at the age of six, and confessed to a neighbour whom she adored. Wriggling into her arms the little Elizabeth breathed confidentially: "Do you know I've been so naughty this afternoon. I'll tell you 'cos I like you, but you mustn't tell mummy before I do."

"What have you done, Elizabeth?" the visitor asked.

"Mummy gave me a pair of scissors, so I've just been and cut up all my new sheets into long ribbons."

"Heavens, child, what on earth will your mother say when you tell her?"

"Oh, she'll just say: 'Oh! Elizabeth!' "

This is precisely what Lady Strathmore did say!

Once she was stung by a bee. This flattered her ego. She rushed into the castle shouting: "Clever me! I've been stung by a bee. There's a whole sting in my chin. Would anyone like to pull it out?"

Those are some of the local memories of her early childhood. Miss Clara Cooper Knight, who was her nurse from the time she was a month old until her eleventh year remembers the Queen Mother as "an exceptionally happy, easy baby, crawling early, running at thirteen months and speaking very young".

Her brother David, later prominent in big business and President of the Royal Horticultural Society, undoubtedly had the gift of second-sight as a boy, and indeed well into later years. This was oddly demonstrated whilst he was at school in the third year of the First World War. His eldest brother, Fergus, had been killed. Then his next brother, Michael, was reported killed. The Strathmores were heartbroken. David was sent home from school. He went to lunch with a friend of the family, a middle-aged man. The latter looked at him gravely and said: "David, I see you are not wearing a dark suit and a black tie. You know you really shouldn't wear coloured clothes so soon after Michael has been killed."

"But he's not dead," David protested. "I've seen Michael twice. He's in a big house, with fir trees all round it. He's not dead. But I think he must be very ill, because his head is tied up in a cloth. I won't wear mourning for him, because I've seen him twice and I know he's alive."

Three months later, Michael Bowes-Lyon, who had been shot

through the head, let his amazed family know that he was still alive and in a prison hospital in Germany.

In those early years David used to see "grey people" in various rooms at Glamis. I know at least two other senior members of the family who have assured me solemnly that they have seen the same ghostly inhabitants of the old castle, particularly the Grey Lady, who is a regular visitor to the family chapel.

It may have been a mere quirk of coincidence, or, as I like to think, a touch of the same Scottish second-sight, which suddenly prompted the small Lady Elizabeth on a sunny afternoon in 1910, solemnly to foretell her own rise to royal dignity. It happened in the magnificent drawing-room at Glamis. She and her brother David danced a minuet in historical dress before the Reverend John Stirton, Minister of Glamis, and other local friends. At the end of it she bowed gravely to the parson.

"And who are you?" he asked, referring to her costume.

"I call myself the Princess Elizabeth," she replied with impressive gravity.

Five years before that happened she was invited by Lady Leicester to a children's party in London. She went with her brother David. She wore a long blue and white frock. Her dark curls were tied with a big floppy bow. She took off her velvet wrap in a spare bedroom and then, gripping brother David possessively by the hand, led him forward to meet their hostess. Even at five years old she was always completely at ease, with perfect poise. The Countess of Leicester came forward leading three other children, two boys and a girl. "Here is another David," she said. "And this is his brother Bertie and his sister Mary."

Little did the five-year-old Elizabeth know as she shook hands with the three children that the other David was to become Edward VIII of England, now the Duke of Windsor. Still less did she guess that "Bertie" would woo her less than twenty years later, and take her to the throne which the gypsy had prophesied. Mary was to become the Princess Royal and her own sister-in-law. Now the odd thing is that little Bertie never forgot the small girl in the blue and white dress with the big blue bow. She made an impression on him which never left him. Such is the stuff of romance.

In those enchanted childhood days, spring and summer were spent at the Hertfordshire house, St. Paul's Waldenbury. At the bottom of the garden was a wood. The Queen Mother describes it as "my childhood haunt of fairies". Under the big oak she read her first books with two pet doves, whom she christened Caroline-Curly-Love and Rhoda-Wriggley-Worm, cooing to her from their wicker cage. Little did she realize that years later, H.R.H. The Duke of York would propose to her in that very spot on Sunday, 14th January, 1923. His proposal was witnessed by "The Running Footman" and "The Bounding Butler"—family nicknames for two statues of a running Greek god and a Greek discus-thrower.

She spent only two terms at school, which she disliked intensely. The rest of her education she had from her mother and from governesses. From the very first she was able to entertain visitors and to receive them as though she was the chatelaine of Glamis.

One afternoon the front door bell rang at Glamis Castle. Little Lady Elizabeth rushed to answer it. It was always a smart race between the butler and herself. Usually she ended by peeping at the visitors from behind the butler's trousers. This time she showed the callers, two ladies, into the drawing-room. They sat down to tea with her mother. Little Elizabeth went off to play in the corner. The visitors started to discuss a well-known local bachelor.

"How sad that no one will marry the poor man except for his money," said one. A second's pause whilst this fact was digested. Then a little voice piped up from the corner:

"P'raps someone will marry him 'cos she loves him. She ought to, you know." That closed the discussion.

Her habit of rushing downstairs to greet guests reminds me of a story told of her when she was only four years old. Mr. Ralston, the estate factor, called to discuss business with Lord Strathmore. Lady Elizabeth met him in the drawing-room. She held out her hand with grave dignity and shook hands with him. "How do you do, Mr. Ralston," she said. "I haven't seen you look so well for years and years. I am sure you will be sorry to learn that Lord Strathmore has the toothache."

Ralston blinked for an instant. Then with true Scots gravity he answered: "I am truly sorry to hear that, Your Ladyship. Toothache can be most painful as we know. I hope that His Lordship will soon recover from it."

She was never bored. She read every book she could lay her hands on. She kept budgerigars, rabbits, chickens, dogs, frogs, goats, tortoises and pigs. She had a Shetland pony called Bobs, on which she used to gallop about the park at Glamis in a little red riding habit. When her pet bullfinch, Bobby, who used to eat off her plate at meals, was murdered by a cat she rescued the body, put it in a cedar-wood pencil box and dug a deep grave. She then lowered the tiny coffin reverently and stood, head bowed, hands clasped, tears streaming down her cheeks, solemnly intoning an interminable funeral oration, of her own devising.

Once, and once only she embarrassed her mother. Lady Cynthia Asquith tells the story. It happened when Lady Nina Balfour, who was a great friend of the Strathmores, arrived one afternoon.

"We haven't had no presents lately, Elizabuff," brother David remarked.

"No," she said brightly. "But p'raps we'll have some big ones now Nina has come."

Almost her earliest literary composition turned up not so long ago, in an old school copy book. It was short and to the point: "Some governesses are nice and some *are not*."

She was a good tennis player, but loved climbing trees and running races rather than playing the usual games. Dressing up in historical costume fascinated her. There is an enormous dower chest at the far end of the Crypt at Glamis, full of historical costumes. The Queen Mother tried most of them on as a child. When the castle, in the First World War, became a hospital for wounded, she dressed her brother David up in a skirt, blouse and bonnet, and took him round the wards, introducing him as a distinguished lady visitor. He hoaxed the lot.

In 1916, when she was only sixteen, she woke up one night to find the ninety-feet-high keep of Glamis on fire. The oak beams and floors of the top floors were crackling fiercely. Flames burst from the towering keep and lit the wild park with unearthly light. Cattle stampeded. Servant girls screamed. Down in Glamis village the flicking tongues of flames from the highest tower of the castle caused something like panic. Ghillies, foresters, farmers, gardeners and cottagers ran across the park to the Castle. They found "our Lady Elizabeth" calmly directing everything. Whilst others flapped she telephoned the Forfar Fire Brigade. Then she organized a chain of forty servants to pass pictures, furniture, silver and china out of the castle on to the lawn.

Suddenly there came a roar of flames, a torrent of sparks from the top of the keep, and a vast hissing cloud of steam which blotted out the moon. The great lead water tank had melted. Waves of water poured down the stone stairs and threatened to flood the State Rooms. "Get every broom in the house and *sweep* the water out of the passages down the stairs," she ordered. That quick thinking saved thousands of pounds' worth of damage to carpets and antiques.

Then she rang the Dundee Fire Brigade. They covered the fifteen miles to the Castle in record time. Finally, with all pumps going, the fire was put out. Blackened walls, burned-out rooms, a roofless keep and pools of slimy, steaming water were left. Scotland's most famous castle had been saved by a hairsbreadth. That night, as the Minister of Glamis said afterwards: "Our Lady Elizabeth was cheered and toasted in every house in Glamis and far beyond".

8

THE DUKE OF YORK PROPOSES

As she grew up Lady Elizabeth Bowes-Lyon began to show the qualities which have since won her the love of millions. Her quiet courage when fire threatened to destroy Glamis Castle is something the villagers will never forget. In her later teens she was gracious and good mannered, with an enormous sense of fun.

This was the young woman, with the will and mind of her own, who completely captivated the heart of H.R.H. Prince Albert Frederick Arthur George, Duke of York, Earl of Inverness and Baron Killarney, second son of King George V.

The Duke of York was born at York Cottage, Sandringham, on 14th December, 1895, which made him about four years older than the little girl with the blue bow whom he had first met at Lady Leicester's party, when she was five.

As I remarked earlier, he never forgot her from that first childhood meeting. As they grew up, they met from time to time with fair regularity. The Duke was shy because, in those early days, he had a bad impediment in his speech. He stuttered, paused and sometimes took seconds to find the next word. I remember him speaking in the Cambridge Union when he was in his early twenties. It was painful to listen to him and even more painful for the Duke. But he did it; his will was unconquerable. The shy man had, in reality, an iron courage.

There is no truth whatever in the story, often quoted, that he sent a friend to propose to Lady Elizabeth Bowes-Lyon on his behalf, because he feared that his voice might fail him at the critical moment. The truth is that he asked his father, George V, and his mother, Queen Mary, beforehand, if they would approve of the match. They did so gladly.

This was no light matter because, although in Tudor days the kings of England had not hesitated to marry the daughters of noblemen or commoners, when the House of Hanover came to the throne it was laid down, with Teutonic thoroughness, that a Royal Prince must marry a woman of Royal rank. If he should marry a subject, the marriage would not be recognized officially, and his wife and children would have no Royal or official position or rank.

Queen Victoria, a womanly woman if ever there was one, broke this stiff-necked rule. First, she agreed that her daughter, Princess Louise, should marry the then Marquess of Lorne, who later became Duke of Argyll. Later she agreed to her granddaughter marrying the Earl of Fife. As a wedding present she made him a Duke at the breakfast table.

George V wisely swept away all these German ideas. First, he changed the Royal Family name from Guelph to Windsor. Secondly, he decided that if the younger children wished to marry out of Royalty they could choose their spouses from the first three ranks of the nobility—dukes, marquesses and earls.

So it was that, on Saturday, 13th January, 1923, the Duke of York motored down to stay the weekend with Lord and Lady Strathmore at their house in St. Paul's Waldenbury, in the green and pleasant countryside near Hitchin. On the Sunday morning the rest of the party went to church. He and Lady Elizabeth went for a walk.

They walked to the wood of her childhood "where the sun always seemed to be shining". The wood which she had written of in those childhood days as "the haunt of fairies". When they walked out of the wood on that Sunday morning on 14th January, 1923, Lady Elizabeth Bowes-Lyon, descendant of the ancient kings of Scotland, had agreed to marry the second son of the King of England and Emperor of India.

The Duke went back to London the next day and straight on to Sandringham to tell his parents. And a few days later Lady Elizabeth wrote to a girl friend: "I feel very happy, but quite dazed. We hoped we were going to have a few days' peace first, but the cat is now completely out of the bag and there is no possibility of stuffing him back."

That cat was out with quite a vengeance. The Strathmores' town house in Bruton Street was besieged, day and night, by reporters and photographers. Her name blazed from every newspaper placard in the kingdom.

The following Sunday she went down to Sandringham to meet her future parents-in-law. One can imagine the feelings of any girl, newly engaged, who goes "on approval" to meet her parents-in-law-to-be. In this case they were the King and Queen. She received a welcome whose warmth and affection never diminished from that day.

Soon after the engagement, the Duke went up to Glamis, the old castle that had seen 600 years of Scottish history pass down the ages in stately procession. There, for a few days of blessed family quiet, he enjoyed the atmosphere of feudal benevolence, unaffected simplicity, and open-hearted neighbourliness in which his bride had grown up. They were married in Westminster Abbey on April 26th. Ministers of State; soldiers in scarlet; admirals glittering in gold braid; Indian Princes, splendid with jewels; ambassadors; Members of Parliament and Men-at-Arms in scarlet, carrying pikes, made a dramatic background of colour.

In the splendour of the Abbey long shafts of light, through stained windows, lit the gilded reredos of the altar, where golden vessels glowed and candles flickered. In that dim place of ancient peace the blaze of uniforms, of blue and gold, scarlet and silver, with jewelled turbans and shining swords, gave a splendour and dignity which the drab trappings of a Republic could never match. A man and woman of old and Royal blood were being united in marriage. And Elizabeth Bowes-Lyon, now Her Royal Highness, the Duchess of York, took her place on the splendid stage of British history.

They spent the first few days of the honeymoon at Polesden Lacey, that lovely house in Surrey which belonged then to the late Mrs. Ronnie Greville and is now a National Trust showplace. Then they went up to Glamis. The Duchess's own troop of Girl

The village of Glamis and the Castle in 1876 (*Radio Times Hulton Picture Library*)

Lady Elizabeth Bowes-Lyon with her parents, the Earl and Countess of Strathmore and Kinghorne, and her

Guides were on the station to meet their District Commissioner's train. So was Fairweather, the keeper, and his old enemy, the stationmaster. And Alfred Crabbe, the head forester, and Alec Craig, the piper. And Mr. Ralston, the factor, and every other man, woman, child and dog in the thanage of Glamis.

It was a great homecoming.

They moved into the suite of rooms in the Castle which are still kept for the Queen Mother to this day. There is a sitting-room, not too large, low-ceilinged, lit by deep latticed windows with an open tiled fireplace, holding a lovely Adam grate and a carved oak chimneypiece above it. The furniture is good, plain and comfortable. A long, deep settee. Two comfortable, modern armchairs. One or two round, mahogany wine-tables. Another little table with a lacquered tray top on wrought-iron scroll feet. There is a magnificently carved dark oak cupboard, rather like a Flemish armoire. Tapestries and family portraits on the walls.

The Queen Mother's bedroom has cream coloured walls, antique furniture, and a most elegant gilt Chippendale four-poster bed, with an ornate foliated gilt headboard on glass. The bed is covered with a superb, patchwork, silk counterpane, worked by the Queen Mother's mother, Lady Strathmore, who was an outstanding needlewoman. She made all the chair covers in the Queen Mother's sitting-room, and framed tapestry in the small dining-room. I wince to record that trippers, not so long ago, snipped out pieces of that wonderful silk counterpane.

The rest of the suite consists of another bedroom, a plainly furnished room, still known as the King's Bedroom, in which George VI used to sleep, and a bathroom.

After their honeymoon at Glamis, the Duke and Duchess eventually set up house at White Lodge, in Richmond Park—a gracious Georgian house, built by Queen Caroline, added to by Princess Amelia, her daughter, and finished by Lord Bute.

After they had settled into their home there followed visits to Serbia, Northern Ireland, East Africa, the industrial North of England and endless public engagements.

One close friend tells of a luncheon party which they both attended soon after Lady Elizabeth Bowes-Lyon had become

Duchess of York. Attended by stiff and pompous individuals, the luncheon promised to be unbearably dull.

"Can you laugh?" the Duchess said suddenly, turning to her friend. "I mean laugh as though you mean it. Laugh to order, in fact."

"Yes, I think so," her friend replied.

"Will you laugh with me at luncheon then, whenever I raise my left eyebrow?" the Duchess replied.

"Let's practise now."

For the next few moments their left eyebrows shot up and down with such rapidity that both dissolved into laughter.

The luncheon began with conscious pomposity. Then came that infectious laughter which had distinguished "Elizabuff" from childhood. Within minutes the atmosphere became human.

This was the girl who set to work to help her husband by every means in her power. He was shy. He stammered. Her gaiety conquered his shyness. Her moral support was tremendous. She taught him music, she helped him to forget his stammer, she gave him confidence in his own speech. "When he rose to speak she flashed a quick smile. It was their mutual 'telegram'. It gave him just that spur which he needed." That is how a friend at Buckingham Palace summed it up to me.

Within a year or two the Duke, thanks to his wife and the speech-training methods of Mr. Lionel Logue, an Australian, spoke splendidly. A deep voice gave dignity and authority to his words.

Then, on 21st April, 1926, their first baby, the little Princess Elizabeth, was born in the Strathmores' house in Bruton Street. She was only eight months old when the Duke had to open the first Australian Parliament, in the new capital of Canberra. The Duchess went with him. It meant leaving their baby behind, so they missed the first words, the first staggering steps, the change from a helpless plaything to a tiny mite beginning to lurch to its feet. That is part of the price that Royalty pays.

They came back at the end of June in *Renown*, and never did any ship carry so many toys, from so many people, for one small girl; there were literally, and actually, nearly three tons of presents. Her father and mother came back to a baby who had already learned to hold out her arms to a crowd, and smile them into utter devotion. Her brilliant blue eyes and mop of golden curls had already captured London to such a degree that her nurse had to stop taking her for outings in the Park. The perambulator was mobbed. Her governess summed her up in a phrase: "Always lively, but always good..'

Princess Margaret Rose was born four years after her sister, at Glamis. That is a bald statement of fact which gives little idea of the intense excitement which pulsated throughout that otherwise level-headed little Scottish village all through the night of Wednesday, 20th August, 1930.

"Not a man, wumman or bairn slept that night," a forester said to me. "We were a' awake and waitin'. The Earl o' Airlie at Cortachy Castle, eight miles awa', was waitin' for the summons.

" 'Twas early in the morn on Thursday the 21st, wi' a rare storm blowin', when we saw his motor-car come up the road, swing in under the great stone gates and away up the long drive to the Castle. There we all stood in the pourin' rain—and a grand cheer went up! For we knew that our own lassie's bairn was born.

"When the Home Secretary got to the Castle, he found the wee lassie kickin' in her cradle in the Tapestry Room, holding her first levee, as you might say! Kirk bells rang out doon in the village.

"Up on the top o' Hunter's Hill where they used to hang the evil men in the auld days, we foresters had built a grand bonfire. It went up in a rare blaze, roarin' and cracklin' in the rain—great logs of spruce and larch, beech, holly and oak. We had four wee lassies to light it wi' the same torches that had lit a bonfire on the same spot when our own bonnie Lady Elizabeth had been marrit to the Duke, seven years before."

Ever since that day, more than thirty years ago, the Queen Mother and Princess Margaret—before her marriage—had made it a rule to visit Glamis at least once a year, and sometimes oftener. "The Princesses always regarded St. Paul's Waldenbury as home, and Glamis as their holiday home," I was told by one who has known them all their lives. He added: "But I think Glamis is still home to Princess Margaret. She loves the place."

As it happens, Princess Margaret came over to Glamis for a flying visit from her cousin, Lady Elphinstone, on the morning of the Sunday on which I arrived at the Castle, late in the afternoon. "She dashed up the great stone staircase, like a two-year-old, with a party of friends," I was told. "Within an hour she had shown them almost every room in the Castle. She was as excited as could be. She loves every stone of this place." Here, perhaps, I may tell my own little story.

In 1937 I was asked by a friend the late Lady Annaly, then Lady-in-Waiting to the Duke and Duchess of York, to be an "uncle" at a children's party at Viscountess Lymington's house in Dean's Yard, Westminster.

"Princess Elizabeth is coming. She has a bird book of yours in her nursery," Lavinia Annaly said, "so be prepared to answer a lot of questions about birds."

The party day came. The children, twenty or thirty of them, arrived. Lady Annaly advanced on me with two small girls in hand. "This is Uncle Wentworth," she announced. "This is the Princess Elizabeth and Princess Margaret. Now you must ask him all the questions you wanted to ask about birds!"

We sat down in a corner. Princess Margaret, with a confidential smile, hitched herself on my right knee. Princess Elizabeth did not sit. She stood, quite regally, against my left knee, and regarded me with a solemn penetration which gave clear warning that no fairy-tale nonsense would be tolerated.

"Tell, me, Uncle Wentworth, all about the tiny little birds that snuggle into the feathers on the back of big white owls and then fly all the way across the sea from Norway," the seven-year-old Princess Margaret invited. Her smile would have warmed a dead university don to exhilarated eloquence.

"Well", I began cautiously, "the story is that the golden-crested wren, who isn't much bigger than a shilling, and quite as bright as a jewel, snuggles into the feathers on the back of the big snowy owls, who sometimes fly to Scotland from Norway and," —rather lamely—"well, that's how they get here. Airborne and nice and warm."

Princess Elizabeth regarded me with the cold stare which Queen

Victoria undoubtedly gave to those who did not amuse her. "They couldn't," she announced firmly. " 'Cos if they did, the owls would eat them as soon as they got off their backs." And that seemed to be that.

"Now, tell me," she went on firmly, obviously determined to give the criminal a last chance. "How is it that herons catch fish, just by standing still in the water?"

"Well," I remarked, with rather more certainty, "herons have oil in their legs which floats off into the water when they stand in it. This oil attracts the fish. So they swim towards the heron. And the heron darts his beak down and catches them. You see, the oil is his natural fish bait."

"That sounds more like true," Princess Elizabeth remarked firmly.

"I still like that bit about the little birds who arrive on the big bird's back," Princess Margaret said. "And I don't believe they eat them. If they wanted to, why don't they catch them when they're getting on their backs?"

Shortly after, I was invited to dine privately with the Duke and Duchess of York at Mary Lymington's tiny little panelled house in Gayfere Street, off Smith Square in Westminster. I sat on the Duchess's right and fell under the spell which has captivated so many. She talked of birds and children, of elephants and angling, with knowledge and gaiety.

At the end, the ladies rose. She touched me on the shoulder and whispered: "Now, we are only three women and you are only three men, so don't stay too long over the brandy and leave us to gossip among ourselves. We've lots to talk about." Surely it is this touch of intuition and unaffected friendliness which has made the present Royal Family the most beloved in the world.

Do you wonder that, today, at Glamis, the attitude of the local people towards the Royal Family is one of possessive pride. They adore the Queen Mother. She is still "our little Lady Elizabeth". The Queen is "their ain lassie". Princess Margaret commands positively possessive affection.

"I mind me sitting in the Brush Room one day, trying over a few notes on my chanter," Fairweather, the former head keeper, said to me. "Suddenly Princess Elizabeth and Princess Margaret popped in like sprites. I asked them what air it was I was playing. 'That was "The Road to the Isles",' Princess Margaret piped up straight away. She knew them all! Aye, Glamis is their home," he added thoughtfully, "away from the wide world." That is the local touch—Glamis, the ultimate sanctuary of peace.

One day Fairweather went up to the Castle and saw the lawns covered with people. The family, servants and children were all creeping about, bent double, peering anxiously at the grass.

"What's toward?" he asked.

"I've lost my necklace," Princess Margaret told him. She was then a child.

"Ooh! I'll get rid o' ma dogs an' come down and find it for ye," Fairweather replied.

"You won't," said Princess Margaret. "No one else can find it."

"Well," said Fairweather, telling me the story, "that kind o' put me on ma mettle, y'know. So when I'd kennelled ma dogs I went down and said to the wee Princess:

" 'Did ye go to feed your ponies, the morn?'

" 'Yes,' she said. 'Lillibet and I both went to feed them.'

" 'Did ye go through the gate?'

" 'No—we didn't—we climbed through the wire fence.'

"So", said Fairweather, "that gave me ma clue. Away down to the wire fence I goes, an' sure enough, there in the grass on the other side lay the wee girlie's necklace under an auld tree. There it lay—in two pieces. The half of it was trampit into the ground by the ponies. So I picks up the two pieces an' away to the Castle wi' them.

"The Queen sends for me to go round to the front door, and when I gets there she thanks me hersel'—and down comes the wee Princess Elizabeth in her dressing-gown and says: 'Oh! Fairweather, thank you so much for finding ma sister's necklace. Have a piece o' cake.'

"An' she hands me a slice o' the cake she was eatin' for her supper!

"The next morn the two children was out wi' their wee jacket pockets stuffed wi' lumps o' sugar for the ponies—and Princess Margaret wi' a big box o' chocolates.

" 'Are those chocolates for the ponies, too?' says her sister.

" 'No, they're not—they're for Fairweather. He found my necklace.' "

When Princess Elizabeth was about to be married to Prince Philip, the Queen Mother said to Fairweather: "Are you coming to the wedding?"

"I hope so. If I'm not invited, Your Majesty, I'll be there," he answered. "If the train's full up, I'll walk."

He breakfasted and lunched at Buckingham Palace that day, and said dryly to me: "There I sat in state, being waited on hand and foot, as though I'd a right to be there." He added: "The greatest assets of the Royal Family today came from Glamis."

Glamis and its hills and silences. St. Paul's Waldenbury with its green vistas of peace. The tall house in Piccadilly next door to Apsley House, at Hyde Park Corner, their London home. Between the three the two Princesses lived a typically British upper-class life. Simple, unaffected, reasonably disciplined, governed always by a sense of duty towards others.

Their father was a splendid shot. He was a cunning fly fisher, good at tennis and cricket and, above all, extremely fond of sailing boats. Princess Elizabeth learned from him how to shoot. Today she is a first-class rifle shot with many a good stag to her credit. She is a good fly-fisher too—her fishing book carries a long toll of salmon and trout. If she were not a Queen she would hunt and be in the first flight across country. These were the good and simple outdoor values which the children learned.

When old King George V, bearded, paternal, gruff-voiced, but always smiling, died, it seemed like the end of an era. Then came the brief, unhappy, uncrowned reign of Edward VIII. It ended on 11th December, 1936. On that day, the Duke of York, who wanted nothing better than the cheerful company of his own family and the lesser duties of a Royal Prince, was summoned to the Throne.

That shy, diffident man with the none-too-robust constitution was crowned with all the splendour of the ages on 12th May, 1937. There sat beside him, at that supreme moment, she who, not so many years before, had played under the park gatehouse of Glamis when the gypsy's caravan crawled to a jingling stop. The prophecy had come true.

Westminster Abbey, on that spring day of bright sun, was a mystic world of ancient truths and old splendours. The solemn words were spoken. To the new King "our little leddie from Glamis" gave at that moment, as she had always given, that inner strength, that uplifting confidence, that sense of utter loyalty which, in the harsh, bitter years of war, so soon to come, sustained him. She tempered the steel within the King. She gave him strength. What woman could do more?

The strain of war tragically shortened his life. Today his widow, the Queen Mother, carries on the Bowes-Lyon tradition. Glamis, "the Castle of Queens", may take some credit.

Much of her childhood and young womanhood was spent, as I have said, at St. Paul's Waldenbury, the Hertfordshire house, because it was so much nearer London than Glamis. The house stands, rose-red, on a green rise in a park, with black Angus cattle fly-flicking under great oaks. Like almost everything English, it has been added to over the centuries. The result is a mixture of Georgian elegance and Elizabethan mellowness—a house of warmth and loveliness.

The front glows with roses, crimson, yellow and red. A great magnolia sentinels the door. A green mantle of forsythia climbs half-way up a tower. There is the scent of honeysuckle and roses . . . and the cooing of doves . . . and the peace of a wood whose green alleys recall the formal grace of a French château. Above all, this house of flowers and trees has the atmosphere of a lived-in, much-loved family home.

That is one's instant impression of St. Paul's Waldenbury, in recent years the home of the late Sir David Bowes-Lyon. He was a great gardener and President of the Royal Horticultural Society.

The house stands in its park in rolling country, great woods marching on the skyline, four miles from Hitchin, in the green of Hertfordshire. It is not a lordly mansion of Whig magnificence, but the sort of old, warm, red and rambling house in which you would expect an English squire to live. That, precisely, is this house, which takes its name from the Dean of St. Paul's, who owned the manor in 1544.

Early in the eighteenth century Edward Gilbert, a Georgian squire, owned the estate. He built the quite lovely and beautifully proportioned Georgian house with rococo wings, to which the fourteenth Earl of Strathmore added the Elizabethan-style front in 1887.

Edward Gilbert laid out the gardens on magnificent lines but to a modest scale, in about 1725–30. Today they are the enduring background of the Queen Mother's childhood memories. "My quite unexceptional garden," David Bowes-Lyon once described it to me, and added, "It has had more than its share of publicity."

I thought, as I walked round lawns and rock gardens, the pools and roses—hundreds of roses of an incredible variety of species—and down the avenue of pleached limes and honeysuckle to the wood that not one of the 4,000 or 5,000 people who pass that way each year will ever forget it. For it is a garden of spells, of old enchantments, of green and lucent peace. There are three acres of flowers, perhaps seven of lawns, about two and a half miles of beech hedges, and forty acres or so of wood. The wood of oaks and beech, of dark firs and silver birch, through which Le Notre or one of his many pupils cut those star-shaped green alleys of smooth grass which lead the eye to a statue against the sky or the village church tower, alight with chuckling jackdaws. The secret of the garden is its utter informality and individuality.

"All gardens are individuals," David Bowes-Lyon remarked gently. "Except great formal places like Versailles. They should look natural. That's why I dislike square beds and dead-straight herbaceous borders. One must get away from regimentation. Break the lines and break the height. Plant all sorts of things in clumps.

"I am my own head gardener for the flowers. Each morning before I leave for the City I tell my two chaps what to do. The whole family do a lot in the garden at weekends.

"The other four gardeners work in the kitchen gardens, which are run commercially. We sell fruit and vegetables locally.

"I loved gardening when I was a boy. When I came into this

place I had a flying start. One just decided to do all the things in a garden that one had always wanted to do."

Now, in the wood where the Duke of York proposed to the Queen Mother when she was Lady Elizabeth Bowes-Lyon, on a January Sunday in 1923, they have opened up new vistas of rhododendrons and azaleas, crimson, pink, mauve, and white, against the green of oaks and the silver slenderness of birches.

9

THE CINDERELLA OF GLAMIS

THE tall, fair-haired girl with cornflower eyes stood behind the counter of the little shop in Powis Terrace, Kittybrewster, which is the charming name for a rather dull working-class district in Aberdeen. The shop sign outside told one there dwelt J. Smith, "Newsagent, Hairdresser, and Shaving Saloon". He also sold fruit, sweets, cigarettes and matches, and ran a little circulating library. The girl behind the counter had just sold two pennyworth of butterscotch to a grimy, bow-legged little urchin, who hurtled out of the shop yelling to the rest of his gang on the other side of the street. The fact that the girl had a low, musical voice and a complexion like a tea-rose made no impression on that little barbarian.

Smiling quietly to herself the girl slipped the two pennies into the till, picked up a newspaper and read it. It was dated 26th April, 1923. It headlined the marriage of the Lady Elizabeth Angela Marguerite Bowes-Lyon to His Royal Highness Prince Albert Frederick Arthur George, Duke of York, second son of King George V of Great Britain and her Dominions beyond the seas. The papers had been full of it for days. Every girl in Britain envied the young Scottish noblewoman from the haunted castle of Glamis, in the ancient land of Angus, who had been courted among the bright fields and tapestried woods of St. Paul's, Waldenbury, in the far southern county of Hertfordshire, by a Prince of the Blood Royal. A great day for Scotland. A gallant day for England. A poignant day for the girl behind the sweet counter.

"Gi'e us an ounce o' shag an' a box o' matches, Connie Bain, please, ma dear," said a blue-jerseyed trawlerman, who darkened the door. His face was graven with the fine lines of wind and sea. He slapped down a florin and smiled shyly at the girl. "Yon's a leddy," the seaman thought to himself. Connie Bain wrapped up his twist of tobacco, gave him his change, and a slow, shy smile. He went out.

"Bain!" she thought to herself. "I'm no Bain. I'm a Lyon—a Lyon of Glamis Castle. A cousin of the girl who is marrying the Royal Duke of York today. I know it in my bones." She had known it for a long time.

When the little shop shut on that bright April afternoon Constance Mary Bain—or Lyon—fair-haired, nineteen years young, with the step of a fallow doe in spring, went home to the little, back-street, semi-detached house, number fifty-five, Elmfield Avenue, Aberdeen, where she lived with her guardian, one Bain, a bookmaker. She had been transferred to their care a few years previously. Mr. and Mrs. Bain, a douce, decent couple, had registered the girl in their own name at Sunnybank School, in Aberdeen. It was just the ordinary sort of secondary school to which decent working people sent their children to learn reading, writing, arithmetic, and no nonsense.

There was a long talk round the tea-table that afternoon, in the clean little living-room of Mr. and Mrs. Bain.

"Connie, my girl, ye're no' a Bain. You're a Lyon—a cousin to the bonny leddy that's become a Royal Duchess today," said Mr. Bain. His voice was flatly definite. "Ye may work in Smith's shop, but your right place is in a castle. We'll see the lawyers aboot it." They did.

Fourteen months later the girl with the cornflower-blue eyes, the sun-kissed hair, the indefinable air of blood and breeding, stood in the witness-box in the majestic Court of Session in the Ancient and Royal See of Edinburgh. There the Lord Lyon King of Arms rules in all matters of blood and precedence, heraldry and pedigree. Formally she applied to the court for a declaration that she was "the legitimate, eldest, lawful child of Hubert Ernest Bowes-Lyon, Esquire, grandson of the thirteenth Earl of Strathmore and Kinghorne, and the late Miss Mary Agnes Hay Smeaton".

Connie Bain, the girl who sold sweets and cigarettes, submitted to the learned Court of Session that although her parents were unmarried when she was born on 24th December, 1904, she was, none the less, legitimized under Scots law by their subsequent marriage on 14th January, 1905, a bare three weeks after her birth. Her mother had died on 5th March, 1914. She had never seen either her mother or her father since babyhood.

Those were the bare bones of the buried love story which shook all Britain and sent a gale of whispers through the crimson corridors of Buckingham Palace and Windsor Castle. The action was undefended. Less than a month later, in June 1924, the Court of Session declared that Constance Mary Bowes-Lyon was the legitimate eldest child of Hubert Ernest Bowes-Lyon and therefore second cousin to Her Royal Highness the Duchess of York, later Queen of England, today Queen Mother of this Realm.

Mr. Herbert Mellor, of Edinburgh, examined by Mr. A. M. Mackay, K.C., said that he had obtained a birth certificate of Miss Lyon's mother, who had been born on 16th October, 1885. He had found it difficult to get a photograph of Mr. Lyon, the girl's father, but he produced a cutting from a Sunday pictorial paper which was described as a portrait of Mr. Lyon.

Then Miss Elizabeth Mackie of Lyon Street, Glasgow, a middle-aged, self-composed woman of forty-seven, gave evidence. She held the court in fascinated attention. She had lived in 1904, she said, in lodgings in Edinburgh, with Miss Mary Agnes Hay Smeaton. Miss Smeaton did not get on very well with her parents so she had shared lodgings with Miss Mackie. One night in March 1904 Mary Smeaton went to a dance in the Egyptian Rooms in Edinburgh. There she met a well-set-up, handsome young officer in the Black Watch, with a sweeping moustache. His name was Hubert Lyon. After the dance he brought Mary Smeaton home to her lodgings. It was love at first sight.

Within a few weeks Mary Smeaton and Hubert Lyon began to live together. Mary was only eighteen. They were infatuated. Soon after, Hubert Lyon took a house in Blackford Avenue, Edinburgh, and he and Mary Smeaton lived there. She, Miss

Mackie, visited the couple almost every day. She saw Mr. Lyon there on many occasions during that summer.

Counsel: Did you know he stayed there every night with her?

Miss Mackie: Yes.

Counsel: I think you often left that house late at night, when they were just preparing for bed?

Miss Mackie: Yes.

For a time, added Miss Mackie, the couple had a maid, but afterwards they did without one. After they had lived together for a little time, Mr. Lyon resigned his Army commission.

Later on Mr. Lyon left Miss Smeaton in the house at Blackford Avenue and went to London. Miss Mackie remembered Mary Smeaton showing her a letter which contained £15 and a request that she should go to London. At that time Mr. Lyon had taken a furnished flat at Tavistock Chambers, Hart Street, London. Mary Smeaton joined him at that address, the furniture also being sent there.

Counsel: Did you know before Mary Smeaton left for London that she was going to have a child?

Miss Mackie: Yes.

Counsel: Did she say who was the father?

Miss Mackie: Mr. Hubert Lyon.

Miss Mackie said that in December 1904 she was invited to Tavistock Chambers, where she found Mr. Lyon and Miss Smeaton living together as man and wife.

Mary Smeaton asked her to find a doctor and nurse for the confinement. After returning to Edinburgh Mary Smeaton wrote to her. She said that a baby girl had been born. She did not want her parents to know about it, and she certainly did not want "the Bowes-Lyon people" to hear a whisper of it. She asked Elizabeth Mackie how the child could be tactfully brought up without anyone knowing about it.

She, Miss Mackie, said she knew of a Mrs. Collie in Aberdeen who might look after it. So, in January 1905, Mary Smeaton arrived in Scotland with the baby. Miss Mackie met them in Edinburgh and took mother and child to Aberdeen. The baby's leg was in plaster. Mary Smeaton mentioned that she had been married to Hubert Lyon only the day before. The baby was called Connie.

Counsel produced a photograph of Mrs. Collie and Connie, taken when little Connie was about six months old. Miss Mackie identified them both. She added that, although Mr. and Mrs. Lyon had lived later at Maidenhead and at Dorney, near Windsor, they visited the baby when they were both staying at the Calendonian Hotel at Edinburgh. She seemed to remember that Mr. Lyon gave her some money. Mrs. Collie was receiving 6s. per week for the upkeep of the child at that time.

Then about the middle of 1907 the parents asked Miss Mackie to take little Connie to Dorney for a fortnight. Mr. Lyon saw his little daughter daily. Later on she visited Dorney again, but she added that her correspondence with Mrs. Lyon ceased about 1912. After that she knew nothing of the parents until she saw an advertisement relating to the case then before the Court of Session. She added that she last saw Constance when the child was about five years old. Miss Lyon was then asked to stand up in court. Miss Mackie looked straight at her. "I am sure that is the girl," she said. "She isn't as tall as her mother, but otherwise the likeness is very noticeable."

In reply to Lord Morrison, the judge, Miss Mackie said that when Mr. Lyon visited her house she said: "This is Connie's father, this is Mr. Lyon." Mrs. Lyon was then present.

Mrs. Margaret Ingram, of Aberdeen, formerly a neighbour of Mrs. Collie, said she remembered Mrs. Collie telling her that she had charge of a child from London and that the father was a friend of the Strathmores. Mrs. Ingram added that she knew the child for six years. At the present time Constance Lyon was "not so tall as her mother", but took more after the Bowes-Lyon side.

Miss Constance Lyon then gave evidence. She said she remembered Mrs. Collie from the time when she was about five years old until Mrs. Collie died in 1912. She added: "I have always had trouble with my left leg. I felt pain in it if I walked a lot."

Lord Morrison gave judgement in her favour.

Afterwards Connie Lyon, the shop girl whose name had been thus dramatically cleared, said in that low, rather shy, musical voice: "I was always called 'Miss Bain' because Mr. Bain had been my guardian for seven years, but I always had the instinctive feeling, from the time I was old enough to entertain such thoughts, that I belonged to a different kind of life from that I am now in. It is only a year ago that my guardian, Mr. Bain, took the steps that led to the present legal proceedings. I am quite happy now that my name is cleared. That was all I wanted."

A neighbour, who had known her since childhood, said: "She was very quiet, self-possessed, and lady-like. She always impressed one, in a vague way, as being superior to her surroundings."

Why did the parents of this utterly delightful girl cause her to be brought up in obscurity? Why did they never see her after her early childhood days? Why did they not keep her in their own home after their marriage, when she was a mere three weeks old? We shall never know the answers. Illegitimacy, like bankruptcy, and suicide were unmentionable in early Edwardian days. Unmentionable in England. Unthinkable in Scotland. There is no doubt that the parents were deeply in love. There is equally no doubt that Hubert Lyon never denied the paternity.

It seems likely that Mary Smeaton, coming from a strict middle-class Scots family, terrified of her parents or at any rate on unfriendly terms with them, had made up her mind that whatever happened the love-child should not ruin her romance with the scion of one of the oldest and noblest families in Scotland. Snobbery, if you like.

As for Constance Lyon, the girl who might so easily have swum into the limelight as the newly-discovered Royal cousin in the star-dust trail of the Royal wedding—she chose obscurity. She had won her little battle.

This is not quite the end of the modern Cinderella story of Glamis. The quiet girl with the cornflower eyes married her prince in June 1933. He was George Dow, of Kilmarnock. He owned great tobacco plantations in the Blantyre Hills of East Africa. He offered her not only love, but a white, large and lovely bungalow, a little palace on the African hillside, with a troop of servants and a great estate which stretched into the blue of the bush. You may be quite sure that she married for love.

Lady Elizabeth Bowes-Lyon and her brother,
the Hon. David Bowes-Lyon, at Glamis Castle in 1909

The crypt of Glamis Castle

A dark corner in the passages of the Castle (*The Mansell Collection*)

"I am going out there for ever," she said. And that finality slammed the door of the glass coach of the Cinderella of Glamis. Somewhere in the African hills, a story lingers.

Ten years before the wedding in Westminster Abbey and the dramatic appearance of Connie Bain to claim her rightful name, a tragedy which shook London struck the Bowes-Lyon family.

A summer thunderstorm had blown itself out in the dawn sky over Surrey on 10th July, 1923. The last spear of lightning had flickered on the skyline. Rain pattered on the leaves. The peace of night had fallen after the torture of the skies. The artillery of the clouds was muted. The stars shone coldly on a motor-car, silent under dripping trees. Its lights were still on in the pale dawn. A man, picking his way through puddles, glanced casually inside the car as he passed. He recoiled with a gasp of horror. Drooping over the front seat was the body of a young man. Half his head was shot away. His white dress-shirt and dinner jacket glistened with blood. The stars winked dispassionately on the silk hat beside him—and on the blue steel of a double-barrelled gun.

When the police came, they found that the body was that of Angus Patrick Bowes-Lyon, cousin of the Lady Elizabeth Bowes-Lyon. That dreadful vision in a leafy lane, near Ripley, Surrey, was the first stunning news of a tragedy, epic in its pathos, which cast the Strathmore family into gloom for many months.

Angus Patrick Bowes-Lyon was only twenty-three years old. He was the younger son of the Hon. Patrick Bowes-Lyon, who in turn was a younger brother of the Earl of Strathmore. Angus had an elder brother. He was killed in action in 1917 in the First World War. More than one Bowes-Lyon died in that welter of slaughter which decimated the old families of the realm and brought ruin to so many ancient estates.

Angus went out to fight when only nineteen. Soon after he landed in France the Armistice was signed. The gunfire died. The night skies were no longer lit by the ghastly flare of star shells and the dead lay alone in sudden silence. Every mother in Britain who had a son in that grey land of quick death heaved a sigh of unbelievable relief. It seemed too good to be true. Britain lost her young men at the appalling rate of up to 60,000 killed, missing and wounded in one day. The Second World War was chicken-feed by comparison.

Mrs. Patrick Bowes-Lyon was one of thousands of mothers who welcomed Armistice Day, 11th November, 1918, as the farewell to tragedy, the open door to her son's future life. Tragedy lay less than five years ahead for her.

Angus Bowes-Lyon resigned his commission in the Grenadier Guards soon after the war ended. He went into the family firm of Lyon and Company, stock jobbers of Austin Friars. He worked in his father's office. He lived in the dignified family house in Cadogan Square. His mother and father adored him. One son had already gone. Angus, by the luck of war, had been snatched from almost certain death. Life now seemed set fair.

London in those immediate post-war days was a riot of gaiety. Balls, dances, receptions, first-nights, cocktail parties and weekend house parties in the country were the rule. Those who had been through the valley of the shadow of death were only too eager to forget it. So the first few London Seasons after the war shone with a brilliance which almost matched the magnificence of the Edwardian period and certainly eclipsed that period in daring and high spirits.

A year or so before his death Angus met an enchanting girl named Alfreda Mary Parsons. She was the daughter of Major-General Sir Charles Parsons of Onslow Square, Kensington. She had a charming personality, lustrous eyes and a wave of dark hair, swept back from a parting on the right side of her head. She was a good dancer, one of the most popular girls among the Younger Set in Society.

Angus fell in love with her. They were inseparable. For nine months or more they were semi-officially engaged. Then, in about May 1923, he gave her an engagement ring. They were officially engaged, but the announcement was not made public because Major-General Parsons was away at the time.

Some time early in July the first breath of the tragedy hit young Bowes-Lyon like a blow in the face. Lady Parsons had a few words with her daughter. We shall never know precisely what was said. Freda Parsons sat down and wrote Angus Bowes-Lyon a letter. In it were these words: "Mother does not think I ought to marry you, if I am not really in love with you. She does not think I could make you really happy. I am not sure that she is not right."

How many mothers have whispered those words of caution to their daughters? How many daughters have not written in much the same strain to young men, whose whole world dwelt on their smiles?

The full story, so far as we shall ever know it, came out at the inquest, in the drab surroundings of Woking police court, on 11th July, 1923, the day after the tragedy.

First, Superintendent Boshier of the Surrey police told Mr. Hubert White, the coroner, that after the finding of the body had been reported to him by a workman named Henry Best of Ripley, he, the superintendent, went to the fern-bordered road in which Bowes-Lyons' car stood. The body was slumped in the driving seat. Half the head was blown away. A garage proprietor who went with the police superintendent had to get into the car and drive it six miles to the police station, with the dead man's body on the blood-soaked seat beside him.

In the police court sat a pale, white-faced girl, with unseeing eyes. She was dressed from head to foot in black. A girl friend sat beside her, quietly holding her hand. The girl in black was Freda Parsons. Mr. W. A. Wardley, a solicitor, represented her. She was not called to give evidence.

When the police superintendent had finished his macabre evidence the dead man's father, the Hon. Patrick Bowes-Lyon. rose to give his evidence. Sixty years of age, grey-haired, distinguished-looking, he was the picture of tragedy. He said in a quiet voice: "I was having dinner alone the night before, at half past eight, when he [Angus] came in and sat and talked to me. I asked him to join me at dinner, but he refused. He was very agitated. Previously I had seen him in his bedroom alone three times, and urged him to have dinner with me. He said, "I cannot, I must go into the country.' "

Mr. Bowes-Lyon added: "Later, he [Angus] spoke to his

mother and asked her to see me as I was dining alone. Angus was at the office during the day. I was there too. He received a letter which upset him. He was in love for nearly a year with Miss Freda Parsons. He had been going about with her as semi-officially engaged for about a year. About three months ago they became officially engaged. Miss Parsons accepted that engagement ring and Lady Parsons assented to the marriage."

Coroner: Was he greatly in love with the girl?

Mr. Bowes-Lyon: Yes, it became the whole of his life.

Coroner: With the exception of this love affair there was nothing else?

Mr. Bowes-Lyon: Absolutely nothing.

Then the father added the one simple, shattering phrase: "His heart was broken—that was all."

There was a moment's silence in the police court. Then Mr. Bowes-Lyon added: "Last Friday Lady Parsons sent for him [Angus] and said the engagement must be broken off. I knew that he wrote to Miss Parsons and got a reply in which there was the phrase: 'I don't love you'. This really broke his heart.

"On the day on which I last saw him he made a final effort, a last stroke. Miss Parsons would not see him. Her married sister saw him instead. It was no good. He was in despair. This was the end."

At this point the grey-haired father broke down. His voice faltered. With tears running down his cheeks he repeated the words: "The boy's heart was broken. He was in despair and drove off. That was the end." He added that his son had gone out to the Front at the age of nineteen, just before the Armistice was signed. In that final phrase one sensed the whole tragedy of the family who, having lost their eldest son, Gavin Patrick Bowes-Lyon, in action, had seen this son snatched, as it were, from almost certain death in Flanders, only to die by his own hand in a country lane at midnight.

The next witness was Mr. Ralph Leslie Tritton, an officer in the Brigade of Guards. He said that Angus Bowes-Lyon had been "his dearest friend". He had seen Angus on the Sunday night before the tragedy. He knew that Angus had had an interview with Miss Parsons on the Friday. They played tennis together on the Sunday and Angus talked a great deal about Miss Parsons. He seemed moderately cheerful.

Then, on the night of the tragedy, Angus rang him [Tritton] up at the Guards Club. He said that he was fed up. He was going to kill himself and was going off to the country instantly.

Tritton said: "I talked to him for some time, but while doing so I ordered a taxi. As soon as he rang off I jumped into it. I went to the most likely place I knew of to find him. That was the Hyde Park Hotel. When I arrived he had gone. I think I missed him by about twenty seconds. I went after him in the taxi, but failed to find him."

The coroner asked: "Did he give you any suggestion on the Saturday that he would take his life?"

"No. Not exactly," Tritton replied. "I thought that period was over. On Friday at his house he had his gun ready. But he seemed quite cheerful on the Sunday."

Having said this, which ended his evidence, Tritton turned sharply round and threw a verbal bombshell into the silence of the court room.

"I wish to say this," he said loudly to the coroner. "Having seen this affair for the past ten months, and having been introduced to Miss Parsons, I say she was in no way to blame."

Mr. Patrick Bowes-Lyon, father of the dead man, sprang to his feet and cried passionately: "Coward! It is the most dastardly thing to say. If Miss Parsons is not to blame then my poor boy was. It is cowardly!"

Tritton, facing the distraught father, said lamely: "Your son was my greatest friend. I apologize. I do not reflect on him in any way."

The coroner interposed: "Had I known what you were going to say I would not have allowed it."

Tritton answered: "There appears to be a good deal of feeling in this affair. I did not wish to reflect on him."

Mr. Patrick Bowes-Lyon, his face drawn with grief, said shortly: "It was very badly expressed then. I am now sorry that I spoke. I accept your apology."

Superintendent Boshier then said he had found a letter signed "Freda" on the dead man's body. The coroner thereupon produced it and said in a low voice: "This is an eight page letter, such as a woman who has been engaged to a man for a little while might write. She writes on Saturday: 'Mother does not think I ought to marry if I am not really in love with you . . . she does not think I could make you happy . . . I am not sure she is not right.' "

The coroner was proceeding to read more of the letter when the Hon. Patrick Bowes-Lyon interposed: "I do not wish any of the references to selfishness or anything of that kind put in."

"I do not propose to put it in," the coroner replied.

"I think really the whole point," said Mr. Bowes-Lyon, "is where she says 'I do not love you'."

The Coroner looked up and, glancing at Mr. Wardley, the solicitor representing Miss Parsons, said: "There is nothing in this letter which could be said to be to the prejudice of your client, Mr. Wardley."

Mr. Wardley replied: "There is nothing in the letter which reflects on anybody."

"No," the coroner replied. "The only possible verdict is that Mr. Bowes-Lyon took his own life while of unsound mind. I have not the slightest doubt that his mind was unbalanced through terrible agony over the breaking of his engagement."

That ended the bleak tale of official evidence.

10

"QUEEN OF THE SLUMS"

WHEN the maid opened her mistress's bedroom door in the pleasant old house in Brompton Square, Kensington to take in her early tea, on a bright July morning in 1949, she found her dead in bed. Both her legs had been cut off. Her hands, which had written some of the outstanding poetry of the present day, were crooked and crippled.

This was not murder. It was the price paid for nine years of heroic war work among the bombs, mine craters, stinking deep shelters and shattered slum tenements of Bow and Stepney. The dead woman in the bed was Miss Lilian Bowes-Lyon, cousin of the Queen Mother.

She need not have died so soon, since she was only a little over fifty. Sick and frail, she had no need to give the last heroic days of her life to the care, day and night, of slum children and their mothers. She was rich. She left a fortune of more than sixty-five thousand pounds. It could have taken her anywhere, beyond the reach of bombs and the disease which killed her. That, however, is not the Bowes-Lyon way. They have a tradition of unselfish service for others.

Lilian Bowes-Lyon was one of the most remarkable women of this century. She was an outstanding modern poetess, with a classic style. She wrote vibrantly. She interpreted the dark abysses of suffering in poignant words. Equally, she put the stark beauty of her beloved Northern fields and hills into words as clear as spring water. She had her feet firmly on the ladder of literary greatness.

She was an odd paradox, this frail woman with the burning

heart. Born in 1895, daughter of Francis Bowes-Lyon, brother of the fourteenth Earl of Strathmore, she was brought up at her father's seat, Ridley Hall, in Northumberland. They were rich. They had great estates. She, herself, had money.

She loved the bold Northumbrian hills, the tapestry of woods lordly on the skyline. The best music to her ears was the chatter of moorland becks and the slow thunder of long seas on that whinstone coast; the whistle of curlew in the dawn; the bleating of sheep on empty moorlands; above all, the white silence of a snow-bound countryside. These were the sights and sounds she loved. They influence her poetry, shine in her written words.

Yet when the 1914 war broke out she was nursing the wounded, with their boils and sores and festering cuts, amid all the stinks and horrors, at an age when other girls of her background were thinking of dances and "deb" parties.

Suffering and poverty took early hold on the great heart in that small body. Above all, though she never married, she adored children.

When the Second World War, after a phoney start, broke suddenly in a maniac fury of fire and bombs and choking smoke upon the defenceless dwellers of the East End, Lilian Bowes-Lyon left her comfortable home in the West End with its pictures, glass, damasks and flowers—and her beloved books. She took a flat in a tall, grey-brick Victorian house at 141 Bow Road, Poplar. There she lived and worked in two bedrooms, a sitting-room, a kitchen and a bathroom.

To this house came the Queen Mother, the Duchess of Kent, Mr. Anthony Eden and many others, great and famous, during the bitter days of the war. Lilian Bowes-Lyon had them all down to visit her in her tiny East End flat, so that they could see for themselves the misery and heroism of her neighbours.

She worked day and night. She nursed the wounded. She pulled dead bodies from smoking ruins. She dressed the wounds of the injured. She made tea by the bucketful. She lived and worked night after night in stinking tenements and foetid shelters, packed with unwashed humans. It is an austerely heroic story. She was already becoming crippled by arthritis. She moved with pain. Yet through nights of fire and bombing, when gas mains blew up and tube stations were full of the dead and dying, when police stations had their corridors packed with collapsible coffins, ready to cart away corpses by the hundred, this woman of royal blood and great riches took scores of children, mainly under five years old, from the East End to the green peace of the country. Duncote Hall, a country mansion in Northamptonshire, was one of the rest homes for the tiny mites from Bethnal Green and Stepney.

She became a bosom friend of the mothers of Bow and Stepney —"the Queen of the Slums". When she walked down the shell-torn streets in the grey light of dawn, after the last bombers had droned seaward down the Thames and the smoke of fire blinded the rising sun, she was cheered by Cockneys who had very little strength left to do more than croak.

Yet she could still write poetry. Arthritis was slowly, cruelly, crippling her own legs. Every step she took was a step of pain. She knew that she was one of the incurables. Yet, down there, on the grey cobbles of Bow Road, with the smell of death in the air and ashes on the wind, she wrote these undying lines:

Down here a commoner jewel glows
  The all-undaunted foot of patient men
I might have passed that bravery by for ever. Now
    I've lost
  My soaring heights. I borrow things from those
Who plod, yet sing. Who walk in dust.

Were the "soaring heights" her memories of the bold Northumbrian hills, the towers and battlements of Glamis? If those were her memories, she saw a greater majesty in "the all-undaunted feet" of those "patient men" of the East End, who each bitter dawn and agonized night trod the grey and slimy pavements in bomb-flash and gun-fire, who in their Cockney bravery "plod yet sing"—"Who walk in dust".

Do you wonder that Cecil Day Lewis, that prince among modern poets wrote: "She was an incredibly brave woman, but she was not the ordinary kind of heroine. The appalling pain she suffered . . . could be felt in her writing. That writing was influenced by another great war poet, Edward Thomas. Lilian Bowes-Lyon, as Edward Shanks once said, "was the sole living inheritor of that lonely magic".

Let Mrs. Ellen Beckwith, of 7 Mostyn Grove, Bow, tell the story. I went to see Mrs. Beckwith. She was Lilian Bowes-Lyon's housekeeper, companion and close friend during the six years of war, and the pain and final tragedy of death.

Mrs. Beckwith is small, bright-eyed, with pink cheeks and grey-gold hair, a neat figure, a mind as clear as well-water, and a rare gift for putting humanity into plain words. She is an East Ender with a proper pride in the fact. A Cockney who adds dignity to that old and humorous race of the English.

"Lilian! She was the Florence Nightingale of the East End. That's what you ought to call her when you write about her. No monument would be too big to put up for her. I always called her Lilian because she told me to. When she took that little flat at 141 Bow Road, in 1942, she went to the Town Hall to organize help for all the women and children round here.

"She was head of the Women's Voluntary Services, you know. Everything else, too. She was nurse, doctor's assistant, ambulance helper, welfare worker, tea-maker—anything that came along.

"She wanted a housekeeper and the Town Hall found me. When I first met her I thought: 'What a sweet, lovely lady—a real aristocrat.' She was tall and slim, you know, with lovely brown hair and big brown eyes, with a dimple in her chin and a very soft, musical voice. Always humming Scottish tunes. A real comic, too. She never lost her sense of humour.

" 'We're going to be chummy,' she said, straight away. 'You must call me Lilian. Bowes-Lyon is too much of a mouthful.' So Lilian and Ellen it was from the start.

"She had a very simple bedroom and a plain little sitting-room. There were photos of the Queen Mother, the Duchess of Kent and her children, and of Captain Ronnie Bowes-Lyon and her sisters on the mantelpiece. And a lovely one of a handsome sailor. 'Who's the pin-up boy, Lilian?' I said one day. She gave me a long look out of those big brown eyes of hers: 'Oh! That's a sad story, Ellen. He was drowned. I was going to marry him.' I reckon that sailor boy was the love of her life. He must have been lost in the First World War.

"After that she gave up her life to doing good for other people —and writing poetry. Beautiful stuff, too. All the big poets praised her work. She knew them all.

"Some of the big people that came down here to see how we were getting on in Bow, just because Lilian asked them to, would surprise you. The Queen Mother came one day. No fuss. She had a cup of tea with Lilian in the flat, and Lilian told her just what we needed down here.

"And then Lilian had the Duke of Kent down, and Mr. Anthony Eden. He was Foreign Secretary then, and Leader of the House of Commons. So she said: 'I'm going to get him down here and give him a good talking-to and just show him what Bow needs.' So down he came and she took him round.

"Whenever the siren went she was out of that front door like a flash with her tin hat on, and her first-aid box under her arm. Wherever the bomb fell she was there with the ambulance. Many a night she spent in the deep shelters making tea, handing round food, seeing that the women and children all had blankets, and cheering everybody up.

"Often I have known her come back home late at night or early in the morning, black with smoke and dust, perhaps smothered in blood, her hands all cut with flying glass. She'd just pop into the bath, give herself a good clean-up and then say: 'Come on, Ellen. Let's sing "Come Ye Back to Bonnie Scotland".' When she'd had a meal she'd sit up late, writing poetry. Then, perhaps two or three hours in bed, and up again at five or six o'clock in the morning.

"She thought of everyone. Dustman, postman, tradesman, whoever came to the door was asked in for a cup of coffee. Then she'd find out how they were getting on at home, if they had any bomb damage and if their wives and children were all right. Whatever they wanted—clothes, blankets, food, medicine—she saw that they had it.

"Then came the terrible day when she was coming back from

the docks, where she had been serving out hundreds of cups of tea. I think she had been down to Tilbury. Anyway, she came back in a bus. A bomb suddenly came down and went up with a roar. It blew all the glass out of the bus windows and nearly turned the bus over. There was a terrible panic. People fighting and scrambling to get out of the bus. Poor Lilian was kicked cruelly in the leg. It was black and blue. She could hardly hobble on it. It was a terrible shame, because when she first came here she used to stride along with a real vigorous walk. You could tell she was a country woman just by seeing her walk. As though she was going over the moors.

"She got back to the flat that day, cut, bleeding and bruised. 'Oh! my poor leg, Ellen,' she said. 'What am I to do about it? I can't walk. But we must get on with the work. We can't let this hold us up. I shall have to think of something.'

"Next morning she went out and hired a Cockney greengrocer's van, with a little, rough pony. 'I'll be the driver and you'll be the van-boy,' she said. 'We can get about with this.' Well, d'you know, she groomed that pony, fed him, cleaned out the stable, made his bed for him, harnessed him in the van and took him out again at night. She knew how to handle horses all right. The moment a bomb fell, off we'd go, trotting away in the van loaded up with blankets, medicines, bandages, brandy flask, food and hot drinks. She was always on the spot within a few minutes of the bomb dropping. And that pony seemed to know that he was doing a good job, too.

"Then she adopted two Polish boys. One was about sixteen and the other seventeen. A ship came into the docks one day, packed with refugees. Lilian went down and watched them coming down the gangway. She picked these two out, because, as she said: 'Their lovely sad eyes looked at me. They touched my heart. So I asked them if they'd like to call me Auntie.'

"She had them both sent to a hostel where she paid for their food and clothes, and then sent them to a good school. She gave them a thorough education. One of them got a very good job after the war as a window-dresser at Simpsons in Piccadilly, and the other one went to Canada. That was typical of Lilian.

"Finally her leg got so bad that the doctor said: 'You must be operated on. You must go into a West End hospital.'

" 'What! Leave Bow? Not me,' she said. 'I want to go into St. Andrew's Hospital here.'

" 'You can't possibly go into a poor hospital like that with your name and your Royal connections,' the doctor answered.

" 'Of course I can,' Lilian said. 'I can go in as plain Mrs. Brown. What does it matter, anyway? Please, Doctor, do let me go into hospital here in Bow.'

"They sent her to St. George's Hospital, and to University College Hospital for massage and all sorts of treatment. It was no good. One leg had gone all black and turned to gangrene. They had to cut it off above the knee. That was at the end of the war.

"Then came the big victory celebrations. I went to see her in the flat which she had taken in Pont Street. All the flags were flying in the West End. The bands were out. Troops were lining the streets. The King and Queen were making a state drive and the crowds were singing and dancing. London was truly gay that day.

"Poor Lilian was hobbling about on a crutch. 'How's my Bow?' she asked, the moment I entered the room. 'Are they having a gay time? Have they got the flags out? Are they celebrating?'

" 'They haven't much time to celebrate,' I said. 'All the evacuees are coming back in swarms. People are hunting high and low for somewhere to sleep. They are queueing up for bread and potatoes all over the place. Blankets, too. Their trouble is to get hold of enough food to feed the families that are pouring back every day.'

" 'Heavens!' she said. 'We must do something about this. I'll speak to the Queen, at once. Now, you listen to this, Ellen, and we'll see what we can arrange.'

"She reached for the telephone, called Buckingham Palace, and asked to be put through to the Queen. She was told that Her Majesty was getting ready to go out on the State drive round London with the King. So she spoke to one of the Queen's

Ladies-in-Waiting who was a friend of hers, instead. She said: 'I've just heard that my poor people in Bow are without enough food to give them a square meal. They're even queueing up for bread and potatoes. What a state of affairs on a day of celebration like this! Will you tell the Queen that I'd like all those mobile canteens, especially the big new American ones that are hanging about in Hyde Park at this minute, doing nothing, to be loaded up with food and hot drinks right away, and sent down to the East End for free distribution. Then the East End can join with the West End and share their happiness on this special day. If you'll send somebody round I'll give them a list of places to send the canteens to.'

"She sat down there and then and wrote out a list of distribution centres in Bow, Stepney, Whitechapel, Poplar, the docks and other places, and within an hour all those big canteens were off in one tremendous fleet, loaded with free food for Lilian's people in the East End. That was the way Lilian got things done.

"Yet all the time poor Lilian was getting frailer and frailer. For years she had suffered from sugar diabetes, and one day as I was bathing her I suddenly noticed that the toes on her remaining leg were going black. Gangrene again! Not long after she had to have the second leg cut off, yet she never once complained.

"Years before I had admired a little black glass vase in which she used to put roses. She offered it to me then because she knew I liked it. I refused it. The day before Lilian died a friend of hers arrived at my house with the little black glass vase, and a message to say that she would write to me if she could. She must have had a premonition that she was going to die, for that very night she died."

Mrs. Beckwith looked at me with those clear eyes of hers. "That was Lilian Bowes-Lyon. The greatest friend, and the greatest lady, that the East End ever knew. Never snobby, always kind and straight, and she treated you so well. No monument could ever do justice to Lilian."

That is the first-hand testimony of a woman, proud to be a Cockney, to the woman whom she rightly describes as "The Florence Nightingale of the East End".

Through all this pain, death and suffering, the little woman with the blue blood, the cousin of the Queen of England, had a little friend who shared her heart. He was a lonely, unknown, little man from the slums called Jimmy Leach. He had been paralysed from the age of seventeen. He was crippled by Parkinson's Disease. He could scarcely speak or move. Yet, as Dr. Maurice Marcus of Turner Street, Stepney has said: "She made this poor little man happy. There was a great affinity between them."

Until a few weeks before her death Lilian Bowes-Lyon went in her wheel-chair to the Royal Hospital for Incurables at Putney to give the blessing of her smile, her warm heart and her ready hand—a hand that was already crippled—to Jimmy and others like him. Then, when she could no longer leave her house at Brompton Square, little Jimmy Leach turned up, trundling along in his wheel-chair, to say the last goodbye to the woman who had brought great friendship and surpassing understanding into his own bleak life.

The wording of her will was typical. She left £65,000. Dr. Williams Dunham of Hampstead was left £1,500 "as a gesture of affection and gratitude on behalf of incurable patients like Jimmy and on my own behalf with true affection". She added the typical rider—"hoping he will spend the bequest in some personally agreeable and recreational way, so as to give him more 'breathing space'." There was £3,000 for Dr. Maurice Marcus "in token of friendship which never failed". And £250 "with special love" to Ellen. Ellen was Mrs. C. Beckwith of Mostyn Grove, Bow. One of her West End friends Mrs. Sylvia Bradbrooke of Carlisle Square, Westminster, was left "any souvenir, ornament, picture, clothing or furniture she likes, in token of my grateful friendship and go ahead!" This was the friendly jest of a dying woman. The rest of her estate went to her brother, Captain Ronald Bowes-Lyon, at Ridley Hall, Northumberland, with the final, charming direction that he should "choose as charming a present as he can find as a small token from me to his wife Cecilia".

Having written these words and left another sum of money to

provide play centres for slum children she turned her face to the wall and went to her God. It was all in the Bowes-Lyon tradition. Warriors in war—service to others in peace.

Regard another side of that family picture. When 3rd September, 1944, dawned over the battlefields of France Hitler's armies were on the run. Mussolini's Fascists were scuttling like rabbits.

Three months before we stormed ashore on the beaches of Isigny. All Normandy had gone up in gun-smoke. The Allied armies overran France. On 1st September they entered Arras. On the same day Verdun, the "Gibraltar of the North" fell. The Gothic Line was smashed.

On that third day of September a British tank unit rumbled forward to Pont à Maroq in Northern France. Its guns were blazing. Suddenly an anti-tank shell hit the gun-turret with a smack like a thunder-bolt. The officer was wounded. He continued to fire his guns. A second anti-tank shell smacked into his tank. Seconds later a third shell hit it again. It burst into flames.

Yet in those few minutes between being hit by the first and third shell, the major operating that tank knocked out two German 88 mm. guns. Then his tank caught fire. He jumped out. Under a hail of machine-gun bullets he leapt into a ditch and ran to a troop in action on his left flank. He took command. Within minutes they knocked out two more German anti-tank guns.

Another tank troop lumbered into action. The young British major leapt on to the leading tank. He swooped round to the right flank of the British attack in support of another company of the Grenadier Guards. They "cleared the area".

The bald words of the official citation say this: "Throughout the action this officer showed a complete disregard for his personal safety and by his cool leadership and example was largely responsible for the many successful actions fought by his squadron".

Men have been awarded the V.C. for less. Instead, Major Francis James Cecil Bowes-Lyon, second cousin of the Queen Mother, was awarded a bar to his Military Cross, for "great gallantry in Northern France". Today he commands the second battalion of the Grenadier Guards.

This is the Grenadier Colonel who was burnt in effigy by Windsor school-boys in October 1957 because they believed that some of his men had set fire to their bonfire on Bachelor's Acre, Windsor. "Old Bowes and Arrows Lyon", as they called him, retaliated by inviting all the school-boys to a bigger and better bonfire at the barracks.

There are plenty of other Bowes-Lyons who do their job of service without fuss. They are workers. Mayfair parasites have never flourished in that family. Anne Bowes-Lyon, who worked in the Advice Bureau as a secretary at Chelsea Town Hall, has written good poetry. The love of fine English runs in the family. Davina Bowes-Lyon, daughter of David Bowes-Lyon, the Queen Mother's brother, who was a big gun in the City, first of all worked in Sotheby's, and then became librarian to Sir Malcolm Sargeant, with 2,000 musical scores in her charge. Diana, another of the Queen Mother's nieces, was a secretary in the British Embassy in Madrid and then became secretary to Lady Jebb at the British Embassy in Paris. This is blue blood which works—and is proud of it.

11

THE "MONSTER" OF GLAMIS

THE Earl of Strathmore, in gumboots and shooting jacket, bounded up the dark stone staircase of Glamis Castle. I stumbled after him, striking matches. He flung open a door, high up in an uninhabited tower of the hundred-room building. "This is where the ghost of Earl Beardie gambles with the Devil," he announced. "There's the trap-door in the floor through which the Devil vanished—so they say!"

We were in a long, bare, white-walled room with two doors. Dusk was falling. Outside, snow whitened the far tops of the Grampian mountains. "Earl Beardie was a far-off Lord Crawford," Lord Strathmore went on. "A master of all the vices. He was gambling here one Sunday with one of my ancestors, Lord Glamis. They quarrelled. Lord Glamis threw Beardie—a huge man—down the stone staircase."

Thereupon, says the legend, old Beardie, in a rage, stamped up to this room in which we stood. He roared out for a servant to come and gamble with him. Not one dared. The chaplain forbade it.

"The Devil take you!" Beardie stormed. "If no man will gamble with me I'll play with the Devil himself." The door was flung open instantly. A tall, dark man in a cloak strode in. He nodded, sat down. They started to play for high stakes. "If I can't pay I'll give you a bond," old Beardie grunted. The stakes mounted like mercury. Curses and shouts flew like buckshot. They stamped and swore.

Outside, the butler, true to form, put his eye to the keyhole. He fell back with a piercing shriek. His eye was burnt, ringed with ghastly yellow. The door flew open, Earl Beardie stormed out. "Kill any man who leaves that room," he shouted. Then he said: "That man—or Devil—playing with me suddenly looked at the door and said, 'Smite that eye!' A sheet of flame darted to the keyhole. Serves you damn well right," he added to the butler. He stamped back into the room. The Devil had gone. So had Earl Beardie's bond. Five years later he died.

Ever since, they say, the ghost of Beardie has gambled, stamped and sworn with the Devil in that narrow, white, empty room with the two doors and the trap door in which I stood in the winter dusk.

Florence Foster, the apple-cheeked Australian-born cook at the Castle, told me her tale. "I've heard them rattle the dice, stamp and swear," she said. "I've heard three knocks on my bedroom door and no one there. And I've lain in bed and shaken with fright."

The Hon. Mrs. Wingfield, daughter of the late Lord Castletown, woke up one night when she was staying at Glamis. In the words of Lord Halifax, she saw "seated in front of the fire, a huge old man with a long, flowing beard. He turned his head and gazed fixedly at her, and then she saw that, although his beard rose and fell as he breathed, the face was that of a dead man."

Now for my own discovery. Lord Strathmore gave me the freedom of the Charter Room, a secret cell in the fifteen-foot-thick walls, guarded by a low, immensely strong steel door. I spent days going through family papers ranging over the last 500 years, secrets seen by few.

There I found a hand-written sheet of paper signed by Mrs. Augusta Maclagan, wife of a former Archbishop of York. This is what she wrote:

The Dean of Brechin, Dr. Nicholson, was once sleeping in the room on the central staircase called, in my sister Charlotte Strathmore's time, "Earl Patrick's room". He locked the door before going to bed. Suddenly he became aware of a tall figure in a cloak, fastened with a clasp, standing by his bed. Neither spoke. Presently the figure disappeared in the wall, where there was no door. The door on the staircase was still locked. The Dean told the Bishop of Brechin, Dr. Forbes, who teased him by saying "Mr. Dean, you are the best beggar in Scotland. I am sure you laid the ghost by asking him for a subscription."

The following year the two met at Glamis for the Chapel Festival, with the Provost of Perth. Passing Earl Patrick's room, the Provost told the Dean he had once seen a ghost there. They compared notes. Both had seen the same ghost. Bishop Forbes offered to exorcise it. The thirteenth Lord Strathmore was afraid to agree to it.

"How true is all this?" I asked Lady Granville, elder sister of the Queen Mother, next day.

"When I lived at Glamis," she said, "children often woke up at night in those upper rooms screaming for their mamas because a huge, bearded man had leant over their beds and looked at them. All the furniture was cleared out a dozen years ago. No one sleeps there today—nor in the Hangman's Chamber.

"You see, centuries ago, we held the rights of High, Low and Middle Justice. We kept a private hangman. Criminals were hanged on Hangman's Hill. The Hangman's Chamber was said to be haunted. In fact a butler once hanged himself in it.

"Some years ago, Arthur Lowther, son of Mr. Speaker Lowther, later Lord Ullswater, asked my father if he could sleep in the Hangman's Room. He got up in the night and walked about. The floor gave way. His legs went through the ceiling of the room below. Colum Stuart was sleeping there. He woke up with a shower of plaster on his face and saw two legs waving through the ceiling at him—far worse than a ghost!"

What of the ghastly Glamis secret? About a century or more ago, the legend says, a monster was born into the family. Shaped like an egg, he was immensely strong. He was the heir—a creature fearful to behold. It was impossible to allow this deformed caricature of humanity to be seen—even by their friends. In Scotland—country of clan feuds—there were always enemies and their scorn would have been unbearable. But, however warped and twisted his body, the child had to be reared to manhood—in secret. But where? Glamis, with its sixteen-feet-thick walls had many answers.

I found one of them in the *Book of Records* of Earl Patrick, a man with a passion for secret hiding-places. On 24th June, 1684, he recorded this transaction in his archaic English:

> Agried with the four masones in Glammis for digging down from the floor of the littil pantry off the lobbis a closet designed within the charter-house there, for which I am to give them fifty lib. scotts and four bolls meall. [£50 and some porridge meal.]

A later entry reads:

> I did add, to the work before mentioned of a closet in my charter-house, severall things of a considerable trouble, as the digging thorrow that closet againe, so that as now I have the access off on flour (one floor) from the East quarter of the house of Glammis to the West side of the house thorrow the low hall, and am to pay the masons, because of the uncertainty four days wages, and just so the wright and plasterer.

So, in 1684, the first Earl of Strathmore had a secret room built, with an entrance from the present Charter Room. The Monster was probably imprisoned there, though there are other secret rooms in those monumental walls. One assumes that he ate and slept in a smallish room, ten feet wide by fifteen long, lit dimly by small windows high in the walls. Here he lived while generations of his family came and went. One wall of his evil-smelling cell was guarded by a great iron "yett" or grille. A similar "yett" still clangs shut behind the nail-studded, oaken entrance door of Glamis.

The Monster, we assume, was immense. His chest an enormous barrel, hairy as a doormat, but it is said that his head ran straight into his shoulders and his arms and legs were toy-like.

To keep the shocking secret, only four men at a time knew of his existence and whereabouts. They were the Earl, his eldest son, the family lawyer, and the factor, or agent to the estate. Each eldest son was told the secret when he attained his majority and was shown the Monster, who was the rightful Earl. The factor, the man who ran the estates, collected the rents and paid the bills, knew all the family secrets. That is probably the reason why, though the office is not hereditary, it always passed from father to son. Only two families served as factors between 1765 and the 1940s. No Countess of Strathmore was ever let into the fearful secret.

The initiation of the son and heir into the family secret must have been a spine-chilling ceremony. The solemn procession of three would be led by the Earl from the dining-room, through vaulted, echoing stone passages to a far, uninhabited part of the castle . . . the unlocking of a creaking door . . . the worn steps . . . a solid iron-handled door let into the wall. And, after that, the "yett", massive, unyielding, locked.

In the sudden lamplight a creature, half-man, half-ape, stands, grips the iron bars and stares blindly at them.

"This, my boy," you can hear the Earl of Strathmore say with bitterness and grief; "This is your great-great-great-uncle. The rightful Earl." Silence, a horror-filled silence, as the young Lord Glamis recoils from the dull-eyed, uncomprehending creature behind the bars. The oaken door shuts behind them and the Monster—a century or more old—goes back to his animal sleep. Before their twenty-first birthdays several heirs lightheartedly promised their friends that they would reveal the secret as soon as they knew it. None of them did.

The Monster is believed to have lived to an incredible age—anything up to 150 years, or more. An Admiral, who knows the story, and is an outstanding hero of the last war, believes he lived until about 1921.

Peter Proctor, who served the family from 1765 until 1815, was almost certainly the first factor to see the Monster, and be sworn to secrecy. He was succeeded by his son, David, who was factor for forty years and died in 1860. Mr. Andrew Ralston followed him and reigned for fifty-two years. He was succeeded by his son, Mr. Gavin Ralston, M.V.O., who died only a few years ago.

The late Lady Strathmore, the Queen Mother's mother, once asked Mr. Ralston to tell her the full, true story. He looked at her gravely and slowly shook his head. He said: "Lady Strathmore, it is fortunate you do not know it and will never know it, for if you did you would never be happy."

Ralston was a hard-headed, dour man, greatly respected and no person to be easily scared. Yet he would never sleep under the roof of Glamis. Once he was dining with the late Lord and Lady Strathmore on a winter's night when the ground was already snowbound. It snowed again, heavily. Soon, the park was four feet deep in snow and Ralston lived about a mile away.

"You can't possibly get home in this," said Lord Strathmore as they sat after dinner in front of a great fire. "Stay the night. There's a bed ready for you."

Ralston refused point-blank. Nothing would induce him to spend a night in the Castle. Instead, he got every gardener and stableman on the place out of bed to dig a path through the snow to his house.

Another odd fact is that no Lord Strathmore, for the past century or so, has been a very happy man. Augustus Hare, who stayed at Glamis, wrote of a house party in 1877:

> Only Lord Strathmore himself has an ever-sad look. The Bishop of Brechin, who was a great friend of the house, felt this strange sadness so deeply that he went to Lord Strathmore and, after imploring him in the most touching fashion to forgive the intrusion into his private affairs, said how, having heard of the strange secret which oppressed him, he could not help entreating him to make the most use of his services as an ecclesiastic, if he could in any way, by any means be of use to him.
>
> Lord Strathmore was deeply moved. He said that he thanked him, but that in his most unfortunate position, no one could ever help him.

I asked the Dowager Lady Granville, sister of the Queen Mother, what she knew of the story. She looked serious, was silent for a moment, then said: "We were never allowed to talk about it when we were children. Our parents forbade us ever to discuss the matter or ask any questions about it. My father and grandfather refused absolutely to discuss it."

I asked Lord Strathmore what he knew. His answer: "Not a thing. It may have died with my father, or with my brother who was killed in the last war. I feel sure there is a corpse or a coffin bricked up somewhere in the walls. They are immensely thick. You could search for a week and find nothing."

Now consider the evidence of that assiduous ghost hunter, Charles, Viscount Halifax, father of the first (and later) Earl of Halifax, and author of *Ghost Book*. Lord Halifax had Lyon blood in him and knew Glamis well. He relates that, in 1870, he met a Miss Virginia Gabriel who had just returned from a long stay at Glamis and was "full of the mysteries which had assumed such prominence since the death of our poor brother-in-law in 1865. . . . The gossip was that the ghosts were endeavouring to terrify Claude [Lord Strathmore] and his family from making the Castle their home". Miss Gabriel told Lord Halifax "that after [his] brother-in-law's funeral the lawyer and the agent initiated Claude into the family secret. He went from them to his wife and said: 'My dearest, you know how often we have joked over the secret room and the family mystery. I have been into the room; I have heard the secret; and if you wish to please me you will *never* mention the subject to me again.' "

During that time Lord Strathmore was making a good many alterations to the Castle. Lord Halifax records that, whilst the family were in London "a man working in, I think, the Chapel, came upon a door opening up a long passage". He explored the passage, "became alarmed", told the Clerk of the Works who immediately stopped all work and sent a wire to Lord Strathmore in London and one to his Edinburgh lawyer, Mr. Dundas. Both of them caught the next trains and immediately cross-examined the workman as to what he had seen. The upshot was that the man and his family "were subsidised and induced to emigrate".

Lord Halifax says that "after the revelation of the secret, Claude was quite a changed man, silent and moody, with an anxious, scared look on his face." He says that the knowledge of the secret had such an effect on the father that when his son Glamis reached his twenty-first birthday in 1876 he "absolutely refused to be enlightened".

Lord Halifax was firmly convinced that Glamis had ghosts other than the Monster. He records that Mrs. Munro of Lindertis was sleeping with her husband in the Red Room, with their small boy sleeping in the dressing-room, when she was woken in the middle of the night by feeling a beard brush her face. She asked her husband to find the matches. Winter moonlight shone palely into the room. In the half-light she saw a figure pass into the dressing-room. Then she found the matches and struck a light, calling to her husband, "Cam, I've found the matches."

There came a sleepy grumble, "What are you bothering about." He was still lying by her side in the bed. The next instant the small boy in the dressing-room screamed in terror. He said he had seen a giant. A moment later there came a fearful crash as though a wardrobe had fallen over and the big clock in the turret struck four.

At breakfast another guest, Lady Fanny Trevanion, who was Lord Strathmore's sister, said that she had had a bad night. Her lap-dog had woken her by howling. Her nightlight had gone out. She and her husband were hunting for matches when they heard a frightful crash—and the clock struck four. The next night the two couples, with the Streatfeilds who were also staying there, waited in their respective rooms to see what would happen at four o'clock in the morning. None of them saw anything, but they all heard the same loud crash again—and the clock struck four. This performance was not repeated the following night.

Lord Halifax was convinced that the Blue Room at Glamis was haunted by the ghost of Old Beardie and he had a nightmare in which the ghost spoke to him and said that he had been weighed down by "irons ever since 1486". He also dreamt that on the day previously a maid, whilst cleaning the grate in the Blue Room, had lifted a stone in the fireplace which had a ring in it and had removed pieces of iron from beneath it. Years later he told the story of this dream to Lady Strathmore who said: "Oh, that is too odd. It *was* in 1486 nearly four hundred years ago."

One year when he and his wife arrived at Glamis they "found the whole house in great excitement as the White Lady had been seen by Lady Strathmore, her nieces and Lady Glasgow, from different windows at the same moment. Their descriptions were exceedingly vague and incoherent."

Lord Halifax ended his fascinating chapter on Glamis by

recording that when he used to visit the place during the early years of this century, that is just before the First World War, two of the children "Rose, the second girl [now Dowager Countess of Granville] and David, the youngest boy, often [saw] shadowy figures flitting about the Castle. They [were] not alarmed by them, but Rose said she would not like to sleep in the Blue Room."

To return to the Monster, a Mr. Paul Bloomfield carried out a great deal of patient research within the last year or two and came to the conclusion that the "Monster" was the son of Thomas, Lord Glamis, (heir to Thomas, the eleventh Earl) who married a girl called Charlotte Grimstead on 21st December, 1820. Charlotte gave birth, according to Burke's Peerage, to an heir Thomas George on 22nd September, 1822. In due course he became the twelfth Earl. Mr. Bloomfield points out that the period between the marriage and his birth was no less than *twenty-two months*. "Room for the arrival of a first-born child unnoticed by Burke, perhaps?" he observes drily.

Then, turning to Douglas' *Scots Peerage* he finds that Lord Glamis and his bride, Charlotte Grimstead, who were married on 21st December, 1820, had "a son born and died, October 21st, 1821". Cockayne's *Complete Peerage* also records the birth and death of this first son, but gives the date as 18th October and not 21st October.

Mr. Bloomfield assumes from this that the son and heir born in October 1821 was so hideously deformed at birth that his parents decided to record him as dead since he could not possibly inherit the title and estates. They hoped perhaps that the poor, deformed little creature could not live for more than a few days. "While he lived he would be well cared for", Mr. Bloomfield reflected, "and, if God willed, by the time he died another heir would have been born. But he lived and he lived."

Twenty-one months later a second son, quite normal, was born on 22nd September, 1822. That was Thomas George who became the twelfth Earl. He, presumably, was in due course "initiated" into the secret of his physically and mentally deformed elder brother when he became of age. Thomas George was succeeded by his brother, Claude, the thirteenth Earl, born in 1824, and he, in 1904, was succeeded by his son, Claude George, the fourteenth Earl, the father of Queen Elizabeth the Queen Mother.

We assume, therefore, that Thomas the twelfth Earl, and Claude the thirteenth Earl both knew of and *saw* the pathetic "monster" but that Claude George, the fourteenth Earl, who was born in 1855, was not "initiated", in other words not shown the Monster when he attained his twenty-first birthday on 14th March, 1876. Some time just before or after that date the wretched "Monster" probably died, having lived far longer than anyone ever expected him to do. The precise date of his death will never be known. One thing seems highly probable—the workman who was "subsidised and induced to emigrate" saw *something* alive in a secret room in 1865. It seems likely that the "Monster" died shortly afterwards, possibly (in spite of Lord Halifax's observation) before Claude George came of age in 1876.

It is obvious that the "Monster" was well cared for during his lifetime. He probably occupied a fair-sized room and, never having known liberty, did not miss it. Equally probably, he was exercised on the leads of the roof at night hence the name of "The Mad Earl's Walk" still given to a part of the roof. He may, once, have escaped and been recaptured. That would account for the legend told me by Sir David Bowes-Lyon of "Jack-the-Runner" racing across the Angles Park in the moonlight. It all fits in.

That is the story as I have pieced it together from scraps of evidence in the old papers and from other writings. I believe it to be true. There is enough testimony—apart from the legends and the whispered rumours—to show that the Monster of Glamis must be accepted as a fact and not merely as a legend.

He lived. He is dead. His story will endure whilst Glamis stands.

Finally, to cap this extraordinary tale, I may quote a letter written to me on 6th March, 1965, by an old friend, Sir Shane Leslie, Bt., the distinguished poet, author, teller of ghost stories, and a cousin of Sir Winston Churchill:

Dear Day,

I am glad of a break of day from you after so long! You should do a thrilling history of Glamis. Alas, I never reached there though I could have when I was at Ludgrove with Pat Lyon (the last to know the secret). Abbot Hunter Blair was very interesting about the haunt, but referred to two "traditions" (not quite theories) as to what the monster was—I did not use what he said in my ghost book and now memory is not to be depended upon. I wonder he did not record them in one of his books. My idea, taken from him, was that a monster was born through some curse and would have been destroyed at birth but unluckily was baptised by someone so it was kept alive as a human Christian—which it hardly resembled. Of course it was kept secret and he did die but the secret was handed on—and this was officially brought to a close in 1921.

The walking ghost was old Beardie who was seen by my Aunt Mary as a guest.

Yours ever,
Shane Leslie.

Glamis has literally a host of other ghosts or, to be precise, legends of other ghosts. One, at least, is genuine. That is the Grey Lady. Lord Strathmore and the Dowager Countess Granville have both seen her within the last few years and are quite decided about it.

"I was sitting in the chapel one sunny afternoon playing some music," Lady Granville told me, "when I suddenly had an odd feeling that someone, or some thing, was just behind me. I turned round and looked.

"There, kneeling in one of the pews, was our little Grey Lady. She was praying. I distinctly saw the detail of her dress and the outline of her figure—but the sun, shining through the windows, *shone through her* and made a pattern on the floor. No one knows who she was, but several people have seen her. She is a sweet little person and harms no one. I haven't the faintest idea why she comes here. When I had finished playing my music she vanished."

Lord Strathmore told me his own version:

"Oh, I can agree to that," he said. "You know there are a lot of pictures in the chapel painted by the Dutch artist, de Wint. He painted Our Lord with the face of Charles I and put a sort of Cavalier hat on His head.

"I wanted to check the detail of the picture for some reason or other and walked into the chapel one afternoon to have a look at it on the wall. When I turned round there was the Grey Lady kneeling, praying, more or less as my aunt saw her. I forget what my reaction was. I think I didn't want to disturb her devotions, so I tip-toed quietly away.

"Others say they have seen her at different times but we have no idea who she was."

One night I was working late in the Charter Room when, suddenly, the lights went out. The Castle was plunged into utter darkness. Lord Strathmore and the butler were both away. The housekeeper and cook were in the housekeeper's room, far away down echoing passages. I was alone, in sudden darkness, in that vast, battlemented fortress with its grim legacy of secrets.

I struck a match and groped my way to Duncan's Hall, the vaulted, stone-floored chamber where Duncan was murdered by Macbeth. The half-open iron grille or "yett" of a prison cell in the wall gaped in the flickering match light. A stuffed grizzly bear six feet high, fangs bared and claws extended, leered at me. It was, the moment, of all time, to decide for oneself whether Glamis was haunted or not. I let the match go out. The blackness was so oppressive that one could almost cut it. The silence was, as Mark Twain would have said, deafening. I stood there, immobile, ears strained for the slightest sound. Not even a mouse scuttled in that oppressive black silence. Suddenly came ghastly laughter, the demoniac baying of hounds, high in the night sky. Wild geese on flight!

Next morning I told Lady Granville of that fruitless vigil when a sudden snowstorm fused the electric lights. She laughed. "When my sister, the Queen Mother and I were children," she said, "we would sometimes be sent downstairs to fetch something. We always raced through Duncan's Hall and the Banqueting Room. As for King Malcolm's Room, where Malcolm was murdered, there was a bloodstain on the floor which would *never* wash out. So my mother had the whole floor boarded over.

"The bedroom next to it had a door which always opened of its own accord at night. You could bolt it, lock it and even stick a chest of drawers against it—it was still open in the morning! So my parents took the wall down and put the door upstairs in another room."

I asked Lady Granville what was the truth of the alleged haunting of the Queen Mother's bathroom. It was once a small bedroom or dressing-room opening off the Queen Mother's main bedroom. It now holds a large, white boxed-in bath.

"It was very creepy," she said. "People who slept there had the oddest sensations. I believe some of them felt the bed-clothes being pulled off the bed. So they turned it into a bathroom a few years ago. Now it's all right."

Lord Strathmore added to the list: "There are legends of every sort of ghost here. A tongueless woman running across the park, pointing to her bleeding mouth. Jack the Runner who races wildly up the drive. A Mad Earl who walks about on the roof. Then there is the poor little ghost of the Black Boy. He sits on a little stone seat by the door into the Queen Mother's sitting-room. He's supposed to be a negro servant or page boy whom they treated unkindly 200 years ago or more. Oh, we've lots of 'em."

The most appalling legendary ghost of all is that of the Tongueless Woman. Many people, over the years, claim to have seen her pale, pleading face staring out of an iron-barred window in one of the turrets. One man, in particular, learned more of the macabre tale than just the face at the window. According to the late Sir David Bowes-Lyon, the Queen Mother's brother, who may have picked up the tale when he was a boy, this man was a guest who was taking a late stroll after dinner on a lawn, close under the castle walls, when he saw the girl gripping the window bars and staring into the night with a distracted look on her face. He was about to speak to her when she disappeared abruptly as though someone had pulled her away from the window. There came one appalling scream—then utter silence. It was one minute to midnight.

About five minutes later as he stood undecided on the lawn, he heard soft thuds down the winding staircase of the tower and the sound of heavy breathing. A moment later the tower door opened and a hideous old woman "with a fiendish face" staggered out with a large sack on her back. When she saw him she ran like a stag, in spite of the heavy sack, straight for the woods in the park. Her long black cloak flapped in the night wind and her black hair trailed behind her in the most approved witch-fashion. She looked the incarnation of evil. The guest felt certain that the girl, or her body, was bundled up in the sack, but he failed to explain why he did not chase the old woman.

The sequel to this tale, whether one can believe it or not, came years later when the same man was on holiday in Italy. He was caught by a blizzard high in the mountains. A rescue party of monks found him and gave him food and shelter in their monastery. During the evening they told him of a mysterious British woman living in a nearby nunnery. Her hands had been cut off and her tongue cut out. Apparently she had discovered some dreadful family secret in a house in Britain, been silenced barbarously and smuggled to the lonely nunnery.

The man pleaded with the monks to arrange for him to see the woman since he had an instinctive feeling that he knew the answer to her mystery. They took him to the nunnery. He saw the tongueless woman. She had the face which he had last seen imploring help at the window in Glamis.

This story may well be a lot of tarradiddle. Sir David Bowes-Lyon once remarked to me; "A frightful lot of rot was written about Glamis in Victorian days. Most of them seized on the Monster as a peg and then thought up the most unutterable bosh."

He did tell me, however, that Jack the Runner had been seen by more than one person running across the park. No one seems quite certain who Jack may have been.

There is an enduring legend that a woman servant in the castle, centuries ago, was a vampire who sucked the blood of the living as they lay asleep. Finally she was caught in the act, bundled into a secret room and left to die. Since vampires do not die it is a pretty thought that in her secret tomb she still lies, her eyes closed, but her flesh alive, her teeth sharp, her menace still potent.

The Room of Skulls is another and, possibly, a far truer, legend of Glamis. No one, indeed, seems to doubt its truth. Centuries ago when the neighbouring Lindsays and Ogilvies were constantly at each other's throats, raiding and counter-raiding, burning and murdering, a party of Ogilvies, on the run from the Lindsays, arrived panting and wounded at the outer gateway in the ring of fortified walls which then surrounded Glamis and begged the Lord of Glamis for sanctuary. He had little love for either family. However, he promised to put them in a secret room where no one would disturb them.

No one did disturb them. The door to the secret room remained locked for a century or more until a later Lord of Glamis opened it, shone a light into the black recesses of the room—and collapsed in a dead faint. The floor was littered with the grinning skulls and contorted skeletons of the Ogilvies who had starved to death. Some had eaten flesh off their own arms.

The room was bricked up and its location is now lost. Lord Strathmore, who does not doubt the truth of this story, told me: "There are probably half a dozen rooms bricked up in this place."

Another version of a Glamis haunting was given by a contributor to *All the Year Round* in 1880. The writer, who described himself as "an utter sceptic" to all supernatural happenings, none the less quoted the following two stories:

> A lady, very well known in London society, an artistic and social celebrity, wealthy, cultivated, clear-headed, and perhaps slightly matter-of-fact, went to stay at Glamis Castle for the first time. She was allotted very handsome apartments, just on the point of junction between the new buildings—perhaps a hundred or two hundred years old—and the very ancient part of the castle. The rooms were handsomely furnished; no gaunt carvings grinned from the walls; no tapestry swung to and fro, making strange figures look still stranger by the flickering fire-light; all was smooth, cosy and modern, and the guest retired to bed without a thought of the mysteries of Glamis.
>
> In the morning she appeared at the breakfast table quite cheerful and self-possessed. To the inquiry how she had slept, she replied: 'Well, thanks, very well, up to four o'clock in the morning. But

your Scottish carpenters seem to come to work very early. I suppose they put up their scaffolding quickly, though, for they are quiet now."

This speech produced a dead silence and she saw with astonishment that the faces of the members of the family were very pale. She was asked, as she valued the friendship of all there, never to speak to them on that subject again; there had been no carpenters at Glamis Castle for months past.

This fact, whatever it may be worth, is absolutely established, so far as the testimony of a single witness can establish anything. The lady was awakened by a loud knocking and hammering, as if somebody were putting up a scaffold, and the noise did not alarm her in the least. On the contrary, she took it for an accident, due to the presumed matutinal habits of the people. She knew, of course, that there were stories about Glamis, but had not the remotest idea that the hammering she had heard was connected with any story. she had regarded it simply as an annoyance, and was glad to get to sleep after an unrestful time; but had no notion of the noise being supernatural until informed of it at the breakfast table.

To what particular event in the stormy annals of the Lyon family the hammering is connected is quite unknown except to members of the family, but there is no lack of legends, possible and impossible, to account for any sights or sounds in the magnificent old feudal edifice.

Some years ago a house party of young guests made up their minds to find out if the secret room had a window. They waited till the late Lord Strathmore and the rest of the family were out shooting for the day, and then hung towels out of every possible window. Then they went into the garden to see which window was minus a towel.

Towels fluttered from every conceivable opening. Here and there a sheet or counterpane billowed in the breeze as a larger banner. Housemaid's dusters and butlers' glass-cloths flickered from the windows of pantries and landings. Rooks and jackdaws, the everyday familiars of the castle battlements, were on wing in wheeling fright, astounded at such levity. Carefully, the guests walked round the castle, scanning every wall, tower and turret for a window without its fluttering flag.

"Ah! Up there in the old tower!—Look at that window! Nothing showing." They peered up at the window. High up in the face of an old, square tower, part of the ancient fortress, there showed a dark window, blank of any drapery. They walked round the corner of the tower to place it more accurately. Another window without a towel and beyond that yet another! In short, the whole tower was devoid of napery. The trouble was that when they tried to get into the tower, they found the downstairs doors to it locked.

So, to this day, no one knows if the secret room is within the tower, or hidden, windowless, within the thickness of the walls elsewhere. All that emerged from that light-hearted attempt was a cold look from their host and a colder stare from their hostess when both returned home from shooting. One has a feeling that the guests were not asked again.

PART TWO

THE GLAMIS STORY

12

THE FOREST OF STONE

GLAMIS is the oldest inhabited and the most impressive castle in Scotland. From the hills it looks, bosomed in trees and green parks, like a forest of stone. Towers and battlements, roofs and turrets, walls and windows make a picture of stately strength and immutable age which is unforgettable. It is easy to believe every fantastic legend ever told about this ancient fortress of the kings of Scotland.

It stands splendid in the sun, history enshrined in stone. Here is no decaying fortalics of jackdaws and snoring owls. No roofless landmark from whose walls flowers grow and about whose ruins crows make mockery. Glamis is alive. There is no troop of retainers today, no forty servants as in the early days of this century. A few rooms only are lived in—but not a room is neglected, roofless or even damp. Somehow the Strathmores, crippled by death duties, hamstrung by taxation, have managed, by tightening their purse strings and denying themselves luxury, to keep this old place sure in its dignity. For that, history, and the nation, should be grateful.

Centuries ago four castles stood in the parish—Denoon, Cossins, Glen Ogilvy and Glamis.

No trace remains of the first three. Glamis, alone and splendid, survives from the rough, gilded past of Scotland.

The first castle on the site existed in the eleventh century or earlier. Whilst William of Normandy was conquering England and his successors were establishing feudal rule, the kings and courts of Scotland dwelt, from time to time, from the eleventh to the fourteenth century, in a castle of some sort at Glamis. It was probably a timber building surrounded by earthworks, a moat and palisade, since no castles of stone were built in Scotland until about the thirteenth century. Those which date from that period such as Kincardine, Kildrummly, Bothwell, Kinclaven, Castle Roy and Inverlochy were built in such a lasting and elaborate manner that had there been a similar castle at Glamis much of it would most certainly survive today.

Architectural experts agree that the oldest part of the present castle—the crypt and the lower part of the main central tower—date from about 1430. Mr. Sidney Toy in his masterly work *The Castles of Great Britain*, points out that whatever castle existed in 1376 was given in that year by King Robert II of Scotland to John Lyon, the first Lord Glamis, when he married the king's daughter and he adds: "Whatever may have been the character of the building he received it is clear that John Lyon at once began its complete reconstruction. The earliest part of the present castle, the rectangular tower with the short wing attached to it at the south-east corner, dates from his period; it occupies the central position round which the later buildings are grouped. Of the mediaeval outer defences all but two wall towers have disappeared."

A manuscript at Glamis, dated 1631, gives a definite clue to the building of the Castle. It says that the first Lady Glamis, "in her widdow-head finished the old house of Glams". Since her husband died in 1459 and she died in 1484 we can clearly infer that the Castle was built somewhere between their marriage in 1376 and Lady Glamis' death in 1484.

No description of the Castle in those days is extant, but it was obviously a great place, since the monarch and his court lived there on and off for many years.

Lady Glamis not only finished the Castle, but she built the beautiful fifteenth-century Gothic Chantry Chapel which is part of the church of Glamis.

One of the grimmest family tragedies was the burning alive of the beautiful Lady Glamis, widow of John, sixth Lord Glamis, who died in 1528. This tragedy is described by Lady Elphinstone, a sister of the Queen Mother, in her short descriptive booklet on the Castle:

In the first part of the sixteenth century the beautiful, widowed Lady Glamis, who before her marriage was Lady Jean Douglas, was imprisoned in Edinburgh Castle with her young son, Lord Glamis, and her second husband, a Campbell of Skipnish. She was accused of witchcraft and mixing of potions. Lady Glamis was condemned to death together with her young son. Campbell of Skipnish was killed trying to escape from the castle and Lord Glamis was reprieved until he came of age but was kept a close prisoner until the King's death. Lady Glamis's two Douglas brothers were hated by the King, James V.

Lady Glamis was found guilty of this trumped-up accusation and on 3rd December, 1540, was burnt alive as a witch on the Castle Hill of Edinburgh "with great commiseration of the people, being in the prime of her years, of a singular beauty, and suffering all, though a woman, with a manlike courage, all men conceiving that it was not this fact [witchcraft] but the hatred which the King carried to her brothers."

During her imprisonment the King, James V, and his Queen, Marie of Lorraine, held Court at Glamis and ransacked it of most of its valuable furnishings and silver. In the Exchequer Rolls of 1513–40 there is a note: "Twelve great silver flaggons melted down for the mint, each of seven pounds weight." While here, the "King of Commons" would seem to have lost his reputation for justice and fair play. During his visits to Glamis many royal documents and charters were dated from the castle between 1513 and 1546.

Not until the King's death was the young Lord Glamis restored to his nearly empty castle and ruined lands. One version of the story related that another Campbell wished to marry Lady Glamis and told the King tales of potions and witchcraft and that on his death-bed he confessed to the falsehoods and so Lord Glamis was restored to his possessions.

In the drawing-room there is a portrait by the French artist Clouet of this young Lord Glamis, with his secretary on the back panel. The secretary, whose name was George Boswell, has his ink-horn in his hand and his quill. The youth holding the inkwell has left us his loyal feelings to his master written in Gothic letters at the side of his picture:

My Lord I am at your command
As was my father's will
That I suld be ane trew servand

And yat I will fulfill
Quhat you command me eik
I sall do my devoir
God grant me have sic skill
As haid my father before
MCCCCC LXXXIII

The Exchequer Rolls record James' expenses for hawks, dogs, horses, and their attendants, and payments to surgeons, bards, shepherds, fishermen, and gardeners, for, even four centuries ago the gardens of Glamis were famous.

King James stayed at Glamis for the Feast of St. Andrew in 1538, in January and September of the following year, again in 1540, in the autumn of 1541 and in the spring of 1542. The expenses and dates of some of his visits are interesting. For example, Dr. Stirton shows that the King stayed at Glamis Castle on 22nd September, 16th and 20th October, and 17th to 20th December, 1537 (*Liber Emptorum*, fols. 21, 35, and 36). The expense of his visit in September and October was £43 8s. 1d. over and above 54 capons, 90 poultry, and 24 geese of the Kain of Glamis. He spent St. Andrew's Day at Glamis in 1538, for the Exchequer Rolls (XVII, p. 256) contain a note of fodder supplied for his horses.

He was back again in September 1539, and also in the same month of 1540 (Treasurer's Accounts, VII, pp. 201–62) and between September 1540 and March 1541. Evidently the Queen (Mary of Lorraine) and he were constantly at Glamis during 1540–1. The Register of the Great Seal shows that charters were granted at Glamis, on 15th September, by the King, and 14th October, 1540, 26th October, 1541, 11th and 26th February, 1541–2; and the Register of the Privy Seal shows that on 22nd October, 1537, 11th March, 1537–8, 28th November, 1538, 15th and 24th September and 14th October, 1540, 3rd and 26th October, 10th and 18th December, 1541, 9th, 10th, 11th, 16th, and 26th February, 1541–2, Writs passed under that Seal at Glamis Castle.

When at Glamis James V, as was his custom, frequently paid

visits in disguise to Kirriemuir and the neighbourhood, mingling with the townspeople, and so earning the title "King of the Commons". He had several adventures and hairbreadth escapes similar to the one recorded of him at Cramond Brig, near Edinburgh, when he was rescued by John Howieson of Braehead.

James died at Falkland Palace on 14th December, 1542, soon after his disastrous defeat at Solway Moss. His daughter, that enchanting woman, Mary, Queen of Scots, came to Glamis in 1562 on her way to quell Huntly's rebellion. The weather was filthy, the roads were nearly axle-deep in mud, it was bitterly cold, yet, says Randolph who accompanied the Queen: "I never saw her merrier, never dismayed." She exclaimed to him that she longed to be a man, "to lie all night in the fields, or to walk upon the causeway with a pack or knapschall (head-piece), a Glasgow buckler, and a broadsword."

Mary's retinue included her half-brother, James Stewart, whom she created Earl of Moray, and the Four Maries. They all dined and slept at Glamis. The English Ambassador was one of the party. The menu, written by the Queen's French secretary, is still in existence. Queen Mary issued a number of Royal documents under the Privy Seal from Glamis.

The entries in the *Despences de la Maison Royale*, written by the Queen's secretary, as as follows: "Samedy XXIIme. jour a' aoust mil VcLXIJ. la Royne et partie de son train disner a Coupres et coucher a Glames." "Dymanche XXIJJme. jour d'aoust mil VcLXIJ. la Royne et partie de son train disner a Glames soupper et coucher a Guelles [Edzell]."

During her visit the Queen presented a watch in a gold case ornamented with filigree bearing the maker's name, Etienne Hubert of Rouen, to the Lady Margaret Lyon. She was the daughter of the seventh Lord Glamis and sister of the eighth Lord Glamis, who was Chancellor of Scotland and Queen Mary's host. Lady Margaret married, first, Lord Cassilis and, secondly, the Marquess of Hamilton.

Dr. Stirton says that this watch was preserved in the Hamilton family until the Duchess of Hamilton, wife of William, second Duke, great-grandson of the Marchioness gave it to her daughter,

Lady Margaret Hamilton, on her marriage with William Blair. It remained in the possession of the Blairs until the marriage of Janet Blair with Mr. Tait, Clerk of Session, in Edinburgh. It was given by her to her niece, Catherine Sinclair of Murkle, from whom it was obtained and given to the Reverend John Hamilton Gray by his relative Mrs. Maddrop of Dalmarnock.

The Castle, as Mary, Queen of Scots knew it, consisted of a main keep surrounded by a great wall, battlemented, fortified by towers and containing a medley of stables and outbuildings. It was four storeys high, the three lower ones being vaulted. A corbelled parapet ran round the top of the walls. Some of the corbels can be seen in the west gable. The outer walls were surrounded by a moat, with ditches and mounds, some of which can be traced. The main Castle today, is an L-shaped block, 71 feet by 38 feet with a wing 29 feet 6 inches by 21 feet. The walls are 15 feet thick.

The first "improver" of Glamis was Patrick, the ninth Lord, who was created first Earl of Kinghorne and is referred to at Glamis to this day as Earl Patrick. He is one of the dominating men of the family. It is probable that he employed Inigo Jones to draw up the plans for the restoration of the Castle. He is said to have met Inigo Jones when he attended the Court of James VI in London. James VI often visited Glamis. Indeed, he arranged the marriage of the young Earl to Dame Anna Murray, daughter of the first Earl of Tullibardine. Their monogram can be seen above the window of the banqueting hall and on various walls of the Castle.

Earl Patrick largely remodelled the keep between 1600 and 1606 when he put in the great stone newelled staircase of 143 steps which sweeps up from the front door to the interior of the central tower.

The main door is most commanding. When I first rang the bell it greeted one like a challenge. It is at the foot of the main keep. This tower carries a great clock just under the battlements.

The doorway is supported by Corinthian pillars. Above, in a niche, a bust of the first Earl looks down upon the visitor. The Royal Arms sculptured in stone are displayed above the door.

A vast iron door-knocker is dated 1689, the year in which the grandson of the first Earl Patrick finished his work of restoration.

When you bang the knocker the great door swings open. But you cannot walk in. There confronts you an immense iron gate or "yett" heavily grated. It is 6 feet 8 inches high and 4 feet 8 inches wide. The Society of Antiquaries made a special study of this iron yett. It is four and a half inches behind the oaken door, of which the wood is modern but the iron ancient, including the hinges, bars, and square-headed nails. A single hole in the wall shows that strengthening bars may have been in use formerly. Clearly no door for a gate-crasher.

The stairway winds upward round a large, hollow, stone newel. The long cords and weights of the great clock at the head of the turret pass down the inside of this stone newel. The rumbling of the weights when the clock strikes, in the dead of night, might account for some of the ghostly noises which have frightened visitors out of their wits.

The roofs are ornamented with beautifully wrought ridges of foliated iron, with finials in the form of thistles, roses and fleur-de-lys. Two wings are set at diagonally opposite corners of the main keep. The west wing was added by Earl Patrick and rebuilt about 1800. The east wing also dates largely from the seventeenth century but its lower part incorporates walls and the great stone fireplace of a much earlier period. The residential quarters east of the tower are mainly late nineteenth century.

Earl Patrick enlarged windows and remodelled many rooms, but fortunately many original features of the early Castle remain and blocked doorways in the walls make it perfectly easy to follow the early plans of the rooms.

The first storey of the keep contained a kitchen and store room. It still has a deep well, the pipe of which went up the second storey. The second storey contains a large rectangular room with stone window-seats. There was a latrine in the north-east corner which has been altered. The original entrance to the Castle was on this second floor near the west end of the south wall. It is now converted into a window. The window is flanked by a small guardroom on each side. The door was reached by outside steps which could be pulled up in a siege. There is a straight flight of steps from the second floor down to the basement and remains of a spiral staircase to the upper floor. The plan of this floor is very like the original entrance floor of the keep at Cawdor Castle.

The Great Hall is on the third floor in the main part of the tower, a noble room, 54 feet long and 21 feet 6 inches wide. Earl Patrick embellished it in the seventeenth century. The dais was originally at the western end of the Great Hall and there was a large fireplace in the west wall. A spiral staircase led from the dais to rooms on the fourth floor. Originally a mural chamber and a latrine were on either side of the west window. The chamber is still there but the latrine is now a passage. The private spiral staircase was blocked up in the seventeenth century but has been re-opened. The old west-end fireplace was also bricked up. A large new fireplace with an elaborate overmantel was put in on the south wall and a plaster ribbed ceiling with pendants was erected over the barrel vault. The Chapel with seventeenth-century decoration opens off the Great Hall.

Earl Patrick's son, the second Earl of Kinghorne, carried on the remodelling. His monogram and that of his Countess are on the ceiling of the banqueting hall, dated 1621. It is remarkable that both Earl Patrick and his son, Earl John, should have carried out this highly expensive work of rebuilding when the country was in a state of wars and unrest.

The Glamis *Book of Record* says, flatly, that both Earls had to raise money for "the exigencies of war, by borrowing upon the security of their real estate, and every available piece of ground, even to the very Mains of Glamis, was mortgaged or pledged in some form to numerous creditors throughout the land." It was hard on those who came after them, but we applaud the lasting results of their work today.

Young Earl Patrick, son of Earl John and grandson of the "Great Earl" Patrick, was four years old when he inherited the Castle and estates. During his long minority Cromwell levied fines on the estates and the young Earl's stepfather, Lord Linlithgow, milked the estates of every penny he could squeeze out of them.

A troop of Cromwell's soldiers was billeted in the Castle in 1653. They played hell with the place and left it in a shocking state. The bakers of Forfar had to provide the troops with "fower dussen of wheate breade" daily, and the butchers had to provide "beefe, mutton, or lambe each Monday and Wednesday".

The garrison was hated and local men cut the saddlery of the horses to pieces. Long after they had gone hatred of the English smouldered fiercely.

When the young Earl Patrick and his Countess Helen returned to Glamis in 1670 the place was pretty well empty. There was no furniture worth speaking of and no furnishings. They had been living at Castle Lyon, near Longforgan, since they married. What little furniture had been at Glamis had been taken to Castle Lyon. When Earl Patrick returned to Glamis the Castle was in a shocking state. The estates were loaded with debt. Doggedly he set to work to renovate the Castle and put the policies in good order. In his *Book of Record* he records the difficulties:

> Tho it be an old house and consequentlie was the more difficult to reduce the place to any uniformity, yet I did covet extremely to order my building so as the frontispiece might have a resemblance on both syds, and my great hall haveing no following was also a great inducement to me for reering up that quarter upon the west syde wch now is, so having first founded it, I built my walls according to my draught and form'd my entrie wch I behooved to draw a little about from the west, else it had run directly thorrow the great victual house att the barns wch my father built, and I was verie loath to destroy it: verie few will discover the throw in my entrie wch I made as unsensible as possible I could. Others more observing have challenged me for it, but were satisfied when I told them the cause, others perhaps more reserved take notice of it and doe not tell me, and conclude it to be an error of ignorance, but they are mistaken.
>
> There be now an entrie from the four severall airths and my house invyroned with a regular planting, the ground on both sydes being of a like bigness, and the figure the same with a way upon either syd of the utter court to the back court where the offices are att the north gate; the gardener's house is upon the one side and the washing

and bleatching house on the other, with a fair green lyin thereto to bleatch upon, and a walk there is planted wch goes round the whole intake, wherein when you are walking you'll behold the watter running in both syds of the planting.

And upon the west syd where the river is to make the way accessible from the west, I have built a bridge and have cast down a little hill of sand wch I caused carrie to such places as were weat and marish. The utter court is a spacious green, and forenent the middle thereof is the principle entrie to the south with a gate and a gate-house besyde two rounds on upon each corner, the on is appointed for a Dayrie house and the other for a Still house, and the gate-house consists of on roume to the gardine and another to the bouling green, the walls are lined, the roof plaistered, the floor lay'd with black and are whyte stone, and verie convenient and refreshful roumes to goe in to from the gardine and bouling green.

In the end the young Earl turned down-at-heel Glamis into a splendid seat. Local craftsmen played a great part. Andrew Wright, the local joiner, was one. John Walker, the village blacksmith, made the beautiful wrought iron railings at the top of the main tower. The masons of Glamis village, the bricklayers, the painters, the carpenters, were all employed. Foreigners were engaged for the more ornate work.

Jacob de Wet, a Dutch artist, and Jan Van Santvoort, who had both come to do work at Holyrood Palace, were engaged to do the painting and carving. The Glamis *Book of Record* says that Santvoort in all probability made the carved chimneypieces, a number of the picture frames, the stone carving of the Royal Arms, and the bust of Patrick, first Earl of Kinghorne over the main doorway. The sum of £394 was paid to Santvoort in 1684. He probably also carved the gladiators, lions, and satyrs on the gateways. De Wet and Santvoort came to this country in 1674. The work at Holyrood was completed in 1686. Lord Strathmore made a contract with De Wet on 18th January, 1688, employing him to make a number of paintings. De Wet proved to be slippery and a law plea ensued.

Earl Patrick built the present Chapel and commissioned De Wet to paint the highly individual panels, which include Christ in a Cavalier's hat, from designs in an old bible in the Castle. He also built extensive walls round the Castle, put up several stone gateways, planted a vast number of trees, built various domestic buildings and furnished and decorated the rooms in the Castle. It was an enormous scheme carried out with meticulous care. The work began in 1671 and was finished in 1689. When it was complete Glamis was one of the finest castles in Britain. A picture in the drawing-room shows the Earl surrounded by his family and pointing, with justifiable pride, to the Castle he had brought to life.

Another Dutchman, John Slezer, who came to Scotland in 1669 and was made a Burgess of Dundee on 19th April, 1678, went over to have a look at Glamis and met Earl Patrick. Slezer was a draughtsman of outstanding quality. Earl Patrick, therefore, paid him to make a sketch of the Castle.

An old engraving in the Castle gives one a good idea of what it looked like at that time. It carries this inscription: "The frontispiece of the Castle of Glamis, given by King Robert, the first of the Stewarts, in 1376, with his daughter, to John Lyon, Lord Glamis, Chancellor of Scotland, as it is now reformed by Patrick, Earl of Strathmore, his lineall heir and successor. *Ano dom.* 1686. R. White, sculptor." R. White, who signs the drawing, was employed as an engraver by Slezer. The view does not show the courts and walls which then existed in front of the Castle.

Few alterations, if any, were made structurally during the next century. The outstanding event was that sad day in 1715 when the young Earl of Strathmore was killed fighting for the House of Stewart at the Battle of Sheriffmuir. His men deserted him as the tide of battle turned. He seized the colours and, surrounded by fourteen of his own men of Glamis, fought like a young lion until a musket bullet took him in the body. As he staggered, a dragoon slashed him hideously with his sabre. That was the end.

Elizabeth, the widowed Countess of Strathmore, wrote in her Household Book, still preserved at the Castle, these pathetic entries: "I sent my Chaplain, Mr. Balvaird, to see my son [the Earl who was killed at Sheriffmuir]," and later, "I sent to ——— for my son's equipment", and again, "I paid for my son's coffin and the journey of his body to Glamis."

A few months later, in 1716, the glens rang to the haunting music of the pipes. The towers and battlements of Glamis echoed with the tramp of horses, the jingle of bits and harness, the clang of swords on armour. The cheers of thousands scattered the crows from the rocks, the jackdaws from the turrets.

Prince James, son of King James VII and known as the Chevalier de St. George, arrived at Glamis accompanied by the Earl of Mar and a long train of gentlemen and soldiers. He stayed the night in the ancient castle of kings. He said that it was one of the finest palaces he had ever seen.

For a long time the bed on which the Prince slept used to be shown at the Castle, with his sword which bears the inscription: "God save King James VIII, prosperitie to Scotland and No Union."

He also left his silver watch under his pillow. A maidservant, who made his bed, found the watch and pocketed it. Years later it was restored to the Lyon family by her great-grand-daughter.

The Chevalier, who visited the Castle two months after Lord Strathmore had been killed in battle, was entertained by the new Earl, a charming boy of sixteen. He described the Chevalier later in these words: "He was a very cheerful, fine young gentleman and a lover of dancing; also of great and uncommon understanding, punctual to his word, very religious, modest and chaste".

Father Lewis Innes, Principal of the Scots College, Paris, who had been almoner to the Chevalier's mother, Queen Mary of Modena, accompanied the Prince as confessor and private chaplain. Historians relate that the Prince strictly banished all religious service by Protestants from his household, which resounded with the paternosters and aves of his confessor, Father Innes. Even the Protestant bishops, whom he had created himself, were not allowed to say so much as a grace. The *Book of Devotions*, used by Father Innes when officiating before the Chevalier, during his visits to Kinnaird, Glamis, and Scone, was in the possession of the late Dr. John Stirton. That night Glamis had to provide eighty-eight beds for the officers and gentlemen who attended the Chevalier.

The Duchess of York and Princess Margaret Rose
(*The Mansell Collection*)

The arms of the Earl of Strathmore over the simple entrance to the Castle
(*The Mansell Collection*)

Glamis Castle Chapel

Whilst at the Castle the Chevalier "touched" for the "King's Evil" (scrofula) and "all the patients recovered". The ceremony was carried out in the Chapel and one of the silver "touch pieces" which the Chevalier gave to each patient is still in existence. On the obverse St. Michael and the Dragon are displayed and the inscription *Soli Deo Gloria.* On the reverse there is a three-masted ship, in full sail, with surrounding inscriptions, "Jaco—III—D.G.M.B.—F.R. et Hi—Rex". All the Stuart sovereigns "touched" for the "King's evil". This type of touch-piece similar to the coin once known as an angel was hung by the Sovereign round the necks of the people whom he "touched". The Chevalier was described upon it as "Jacobus III" or, to suit his Scottish "subjects", as "Jacobus VIII".

It was probably made by Ottoni Hamerani, medallist to the Papal Court. He did a lot of work for Prince James. The medal is of much finer workmanship than the English equivalent used by King James II. The ship engraved upon the reverse was given a different "voyage" to suit the change in the family fortunes. If the prospects for the Stewart cause were good the ship was engraved on a quiet sea. If things were going wrong the ship was shown tossed in a storm.

Father Lewis Innes wrote an account of the "touching" in his shaky hand. It was for long in the possession of the late Mrs. Maria Frances Chisholm who lived at Glassburn House, Strathglass. Mrs. Chisholm was the last descendant of the Innes family of Balnacraig and Ballogie. Unfortunately the original document in Father Innes' handwriting was lost soon after Mrs. Chisholm died in 1912. Dr. Stirton fortunately took a copy of it. It ran thus:

> The King (!) knelt upon a cushion, and the assistants, as well as those who were to be "touched", knelt upon the floor of the chapel. The King's Confessor [Father Innes], wearing cotta and stole, recited certain prayers to which His Majesty responded. The priest then read the Gospel of Christ's ordering his disciples to go and teach all nations and afterwards using the words "*Super egros manus imponent et bene habebunt*".
>
> When these words were being said one of the King's aides-de-camp led the patients, some of them being children, one by one to

> His Majesty, who was now seated, and who laid his hands upon each, the priest meanwhile repeating "*Super egros*", etc.
>
> The King then knelt and recited certain prayers, after which, resuming his seat he hung a silver medal, bearing S. Michael on one side and a three-masted ship on the other, round the neck of each patient. The King performed the ceremony in a saintly manner, with great devoutness and recollection of mind. The office used was that of King Henry VII, revived by King James II.

Prince James also "touched for the evil" in Perth before his intended coronation.

Dr. Stirton adds that when Prince Charles "touched" at Holyrood, the act was unpremeditated and rather unwillingly performed. It is, therefore, not likely that the Prince was armed with his father's touch-pieces, and no mention of a special medal is made in the report given by Robert Chambers of this extraordinary occasion.

Chambers says that the Prince was first approached at Perth but "excused himself, pleading want of time". However, a little seven-year-old girl, "dreadfully afflicted with the disease ever since her infancy", was brought to him at Holyrood, where he was in the picture gallery, which served as his audience chamber, surrounded by his principal officers and many ladies.

He caused a circle to be made within which the child was admitted, together with her attendants, and a clergyman in canonicals. The patient was then stripped naked and placed upon her knees in the centre of the circle.

The clergyman having pronounced an appropriate prayer, probably the office for the ceremony, Charles approached the kneeling girl, and, with great apparent solemnity, touched the sores occasioned by the disease, pronouncing at every application the words, "I touch, but God heal".

The ceremony was concluded by another prayer from the clergyman, and the patient being again dressed was carried round the circle and presented with little sums of money by all present. The historian says the child recovered. Charles used the French and not the English words in healing.

King James II "touched" for the evil a great deal. He spent

£3,000 a year on his touch-pieces, of gold when he was in England, and of silver when he was an exile.

With his strong religious feeling, says Dr. Stirton, the King firmly believed that a special power was granted to him from above in virtue of his Divine Right as sovereign to effect a cure upon all afflicted by this disease.

We get a good picture of Glamis as it was when the Chevalier visited it, from *A Tour Through Great Britain*, published in 1723. The author was almost certainly Defoe. He says:

> It was one of the finest old built palaces in Scotland, and by far the largest, that when seen at a distance the piles of turrets and lofty buildings, spires and towers, made it look like a town. The palace, as you approach it, strikes you with awe and admiration by the many turrets and gilded balustrades at the top. The outer court has a statue on each side of the top of the gate, as big as life. On the great gate of the inner court are balustrades of stone finely adorned with statues; and in the court are four brazen statues bigger than the life on pedestals; the one of James VI and I of England in his stole; the other of Charles I in his boots, spurs, and sword, as he is sometimes painted by Vandyke; Charles II is in Roman dress, as on the Exchange in London; and James II in the same as he is in Whitehall.

From this description the changes wrought by the two Earls Patrick can be easily recognized.

Five years later, on 11th May, 1728, Charles, sixth Earl of Strathmore, was killed in a most disgraceful brawl in the streets of Forfar. A neighbouring laird, James Carnegie of Finavon, for no apparent reason ran him through and through with his sword. John Lyon of Brigton, a cadet of the Strathmore family, was involved, but not apparently to blame.

Lady Nairne, writing from Glamis on 15th May, four days after the murder, to Mrs. Oliphant of Gask, gives a living picture of the effect this frightful affair had on the family at Glamis. She says:

> I know, dear Amelia, just now it would take a volume to describe

the melancholy condition of the family from the highest to the lowest, but no words could express poor Lady Strathmore's sorrow nor can any but such unfortunately as I comprehend it. The state of her health is bad enough, she has a violent cough . . . you may be sure no care in my power will be neglected, but I have some influence with her by the unhappy sympathy in our conditions, so that often we cry together—then I endeavour to amuse her with idle stories, for I know by dear-bought experience in vain weak reason would command when love had led the way.

I thank you for the kind intention . . . but they have employment enough here. Katy is with Lady Kathy and Lady Strathmore often, but Mary is her principal favourite, her Lord was so fond of her . . . (on Tuesday senight, he told me he would wade up to the neck in watter to serve Miss Mary). Charlotte is all the housewife. We have to make tea in the drawing-room, for Lady Mary Lyon is so ill she keeps her bed.

You have heard the dismal story very wrong, for Brigton I believe would as soon hurt himself as Lord Strathmore, and so he thought and to the last was very fond of him. It was Finavon, who, without any previous warning ran throw and throw the body (and no sword drawn but his own) as he was walking on the street in Forfar after a burrial he had been at, whether it was premeditated malice or mad fury I know not. I shall make your compliments.

Robert Mercer, writing to his mother, Lady Nairne, from Aldie, on the same event says: "His friendship for which he was so conspicuous, for a more sincere friend never was, must, alas, have a hand in his exit, for by what I can understand had he had less of humanity to his murtherer and less friendship to his relative we might still have had the dear Strathmore."

After 1746 Glamis suffered neither from wars nor murders. Poets and writers were its welcome guests. Gray, the poet, a friend of John, ninth Earl of Strathmore, stayed at Glamis in 1765. He gives a charming picture of it in a letter to his friend, Dr. Wharton. He describes the Castle thus:

. . . rising proudly out of what seems a great and thick wood of tall trees, with a cluster of hanging towers on the top; the house from the height of it, the greatness of its mass, the many towers

> atop, and the spread of its wings has really a very singular and striking appearance like nothing I ever saw: adding, you will comprehend something of its shape from the plan of the second floor which I enclose. You descend to the Castle gradually from the south through a double and triple avenue of Scotch firs, sixty or seventy feet high, under the gateways. This approach is full a mile long, and when you have passed the second gate the firs change to limes and another oblique avenue goes off on either hand towards the offices. The third gate delivers you into a court with a broad pavement and grass plots, adorned with statues of the four Stewart Kings, bordered with old silver firs and yew trees alternately, and opening with an iron palisade on either side, and two square old-fashioned parterres surrounded by stone fruit walls.

It will be seen from this description that the Castle then was a fully fortified place, surrounded by outer and inner walls, guarded by gatehouses and thoroughly defensible. That is how it should have been left.

Alas, destruction in the name of fashion was on the way. "Capability" Brown, who improved many English parks and ruined a few others, influenced the country gentlemen of his day. One of his school went north to Glamis. Down came the encircling walls. The gatehouses and gateways were scattered to the wind, although two of the antique gateways were rebuilt at the north and south entrances to the present park. Two other flanking towers in front of the Castle stand naked and lonely today in the middle of lawns. All the grass parks were thrown into one park which is called the Angles Park, from the "angular shape of the rows of trees along them".

The stone bridge which spans the River Dean was fortunately left intact. On the parapet a coronet appears with the monograms of Earl John and Countess Elizabeth and the date 1697. Earl John was the fourth Earl of Strathmore and Kinghorne, being the son of Earl Patrick.

Those sweeping "improvements" are bitterly regretted by many members of the Bowes-Lyon family today.

Sir Walter Scott, who first stayed at Glamis in 1793 when he was about twenty-two was almost overwhelmed by the sense of history and of boding mystery which was the aura of the place in its old form. Later he had scathing things to say of the "improvements". He described his first visit thus:

> The night I spent at Glammis was one of the two periods distant from each other at which I could recollect experiencing that degree of superstitious awe which my countrymen call eerie. . . . The heavy pile contains much in its appearance, and in the tradition connected with it, impressive to the imagination. It was the scene of the murder of a Scottish King of great antiquity not indeed the gracious Duncan, with whom the name naturally associates itself, but Malcolm II.
>
> The extreme antiquity of the building is vouched by the thickness of the walls and the wild straggling arrangement of the accommodation within doors. As the late Earl seldom resided at Glammis, it was, when I was there, but half furnished, and that with moveables of great antiquity, which, with the pieces of chivalric armour hanging on the walls, greatly contributed to the general effect of the whole.
>
> Peter Proctor, seneschal of the Castle, conducted me to my apartments in a distant part of the building. I must own that when I heard door after door shut, after my conductor had retired, I began to consider myself as too far from the living, and somewhat too near the dead. We had passed through what is called the King's Room, a vaulted apartment garnished with stags' antlers and other trophies of the chase, and said by tradition to be the spot of Malcolm's murder, and I had an idea of the vicinity of the Castle Chapel.
>
> In spite of the truth of history, the whole night scene in Macbeth's Castle rushed at once upon me and struck my mind more forcibly than even when I have seen its terrors represented by John Kemble and his inimitable sister. In a word I experienced sensations which, though not remarkable for timidity or superstition, did not fail to affect me to the point of being disagreeable, while they were mingled at the same time with a strange and indescribable sort of pleasure, the recollection of which affords me gratification at this moment.

Whilst at Glamis Scott drank a pint of wine to the health of the absent Earl from the famous "Lion of Glammis". This is a splendid silver gilt beaker nine inches high. It was made at Augsburg early in the seventeenth century and is stamped with the letter "E".

There is no doubt that Scott had this beaker in mind as the prototype of the *"Pocolum Potatorium"* of the Baron of Bradwardine in *Waverley*, the Blessed Bear. He said himself that he "ought perhaps to be ashamed of recording that he had the honour of swallowing the contents of the Lion; and the recollection of the feat served to suggest the story of the "Bear of Bradwardine".

Glamis made the most profound impression on Scott. It influenced much of his later writing. Glenallen House in *The Antiquary* is undoubtedly his re-creation of Glamis.

After Capability Brown's disciples had done their damndest to reduce a splendid old fortress to the level of an eighteenth-century pattern of uniformity, Scott had his excoriating say. In his *Essay on Landscape Gardening* he talks of the proper ornaments of the Castle Pleasaunce and says of the Brown Barbarians:

> . . . down went many a trophy of old magnificence, courtyard, ornamented enclosure, fosse, avenue, barbican, and every external muniment of battled wall and flanking tower, out of the midst of which the ancient dome, rising high above all its characteristic accompaniments, and seemingly girt round by its appropriate defences, which again circled each other in their different gradations, looked as it should, the queen and mistress of the surrounding country. It was thus that the huge old tower of Glammis once showed its lordly head above seven circles (if I remember aright) of defensive boundaries, through which the friendly guest was admitted, and at each of which a suspicious person was unquestionably put to his answer. A disciple of Kent had the cruelty to render this splendid old mansion (the more modern part of which was the work of Inigo Jones) more parkish as he was pleased to call it; to raze all those exterior defences, and bring his mean and paltry gravel walk up to the very door from which, deluded by the name, one might have imagined Lady Macbeth (with the form and features of Siddons) issuing forth to receive King Duncan.
>
> It is thirty years and upwards since I have seen Glammis, but I have not yet forgotten or forgiven the atrocity which under pretence

of improvement deprived that lordly place of its appropriate accompaniments, "leaving an ancient dome and towers like these, beggared and outraged."

Today the Castle contains many interesting relics including the family jester's cap and bells, a great chestful of period costumes at one end of the crypt and the sword and bullet-proof coat of John Graham of Claverhouse ("Bonnie Dundee") who served under Montrose. His estate is now merged with that of Glamis. There is much good armour, weapons, fine china and furniture, more than a few splendid pictures, mainly Old Masters, a superb carved stone chimneypiece from Gibside in the billiards room, another splendid fireplace in the drawing-room which, like one or two other rooms, has a very beautiful decorated plaster ceiling.

The so-called crypt, which was the original main hall or dining-hall, displays outstanding big game trophies and a lot of good period furniture. The dungeon beneath the floor is now a wine cellar. The Queen Mother's sitting-room and King Malcolm's Room both contain good examples of rather heavy furniture, particularly chests and cupboards, whilst in a small bedroom which Lord Strathmore used when he was a bachelor there is an immensely stately four-poster which was the bed of the first Earl of Kinghorne.

A lot of good furniture was sold "for next to nothing", as Lord Strathmore told me, some years ago when about fifty rooms were cleared and most of the splendid library also went to help pay taxes. Among interesting books which remain are some Cromwellian folio volumes which bear the watermark of a jester's head and shoulders with cap and bells—hence foolscap paper.

The story is that when the paper-makers asked Cromwell what watermark they were to use he replied, "You had better go on using the old fool's cap", meaning the Royal Crown. They took him literally—hence the jester's cap and bells on folio sheets of the time.

The gardens are notable. The sunk garden was made about sixty years ago by the Queen Mother's great-grandparents. When it was being dug out workmen's pickaxes struck on the arched roof of an underground passage. As they uncovered it the tunnelling collapsed here and there. It was full of poisonous gases so they closed it up without exploring it. Lord and Lady Strathmore were abroad, otherwise more might have been discovered.

The imposing sundial in the middle of the lawn, with facets for each month of the year, was put there by Earl Patrick between 1671 and 1680 on a spot calculated to be three degrees west of the Meridian of Greenwich. It is twenty-one feet high, supported by four lions and surmounted by the Earl's coronet.

Beond the sunk garden is a small formal garden on the left and a larger garden on the right, both made by Cecilia, Lady Strathmore, about fifty years ago. Lord Strathmore does his best to keep them up.

Local craftsmen carved the stone flowerpots and seats on the terrace and summerhouses in a seventeenth-century style and one can see their names carved on the back of the seats in the right-hand summerhouse of the long walk. Thus, today, Glamis continues its traditions of improvement and maintenance by the craftsmen of its own villages.

13

GLAMIS AND THE JACOBITE RISINGS

THE Lyons of Glamis, their retainers and tenants, were strong supporters of the Stewart Cause. John, fifth Earl of Strathmore and his uncle, the Honourable Patrick Lyon of Auchterhouse took a prominent part in "The Rising of the Fifteen". Patrick Lyon, with his kinsman, the Earl of Aboyne, marched on the Braes of Mar on that heroic day of 9th September, 1715, at the head of the Panmure Highlanders when the standard of King James VIII blew royally in the breeze.

The Earl of Mar led the Rising. When he marched into Perth at the head of his own men and supporting clansmen, the young Earl of Strathmore, bold and splendid, marched at the head of a battalion of Foot known as the Strathmore Regiment. This body of men had been raised in the straths and glens around Glamis by young Strathmore and trained by him. He was young but a born soldier. He was brave and inspired loyalty. His three hundred men of Glamis adored him. They were divided into four Companies of whom the officers were:

William Douglas, Capt.
William Miller, Capt.
John Scremger, Capt.
John Balfewer, Capt.
William Lyon, Lieut.
Alexander Murray, Lieut.
Alexander Orrack, Lieut.
John Burnes, Lieut.
Patrick Douglas, Ensign.
Hugh Kerr, Ensign.
Alex. Magiven, Ensign.
Andrew Ramsay, Ensign.
Henry Ogilvey, Ensign.
Will. Henderson, Quar. Ma.

Lord Mar sent the Strathmore Regiment to join the forces of Lord Kenmure and the Earl of Nithsdale in the South of Scotland.

MacIntosh of Borlum, who commanded the lot, wanted to cross the Firth of Forth which was blockaded by English ships. He therefore left a few troops at Burntisland to make a pretence at crossing the Firth. Meanwhile he marched the main body along the coast of Fife and embarked them at various points. Most of his men crossed the Firth safely before the English ships realized that they had lost their chance of stopping them. Four companies of the Strathmore Regiment were involved in this.

These Strathmore companies attacked the remainder of the English flotilla. They had little luck. About 200 Jacobites, Lord Strathmore among them, had to take refuge on the Isle of May. They escaped to the mainland after a few days and returned to Perth.

Then, on 13th November, 1715, came the disastrous battle of Sheriffmuir in which so many of the flower of the Scottish clans were killed. Lord Strathmore marched at the head of Lord Tullibardine's Regiment on the left wing of the Stewart army. He was killed. So was his uncle, the Hon. Patrick Lyon. Strathmore's death was heroic. It was well described by the Master of Sinclair in his memoirs of the Rising:

> On our left the brave younge Strathmore was killed after being wounded and taken. . . . When he found all turning their backs, he seized the colours, and persuaded fourteen or some such number to stand by him for some time, which drew upon him the ennemie's fire, by which he was wounded, and goeing off was takne and murder'd by a dragoon, and it may be said in his fate that a mill-stone crusht a brilliant. He was the younge man of all I ever saw who approached the nearest to perfection . . . and his least qualitie was that he was of a noble, ancient family, and a man of qualitie.

Next day Argyll and his aide de camps rode over the battle-field. They saw a clansman guarding a dead officer. It was the body of the young Earl of Strathmore. The soldier was an old retainer of Glamis. "Wha's that man there?" demanded an aide de camp. "He *was* a man yesterday," said the man of Glamis.

Two months later, as I have said, the Chevalier de St. George himself, the "Richtfu' lawfu' King", arrived at Glamis. The wings of death beat about the towers and turrets of the old stronghold. The young Lord was slain, his uncle a bloody corpse. It was no time for joy. The Earl of Mar, however, sent out a circular letter from Glamis to extol the Prince, to chiefs and clansmen alike and arouse men to fight for him. It ran thus:

> Glames, 5th Jan. 1716. I met the King at Fetteresso, on Tuesday Sen'night, where we staid till Friday, from thence we came to Briechin, then to Kinnaird, and yesterday here. The King design'd to have gone to Dundee to Day, but there is such a fall of snow, that he is forced to put it off till to-morrow, if it be practicable then; and from thence he designs to go to Scoon. There was no haste in his being there sooner, for nothing can be done this season, else he had not been so long by the way.
>
> People everywhere, as we have come along, are excessively fond to see him, and express that Duty they ought, without any compliments to him, and to do him nothing but justice, set aside his being a Prince, he is really the finest Gentlemen I ever knew. He has a very good Presence, and resembles King Charles a great deal. His Presence, however, is not the best of him; He has fine Parts, and dispatches all his Business himself with the greatest exactness. I never saw anybody write so finely. He is affable to a great degree, without losing that Majesty he ought to have, and has the sweetest temper in the world.
>
> In a word, he is every way fitted to make us a happy people, were his subjects worthy of him. To have him peaceably settled on his Throne is what these Kingdoms do not deserve; but he deserves it so much that I hope there's a good Fate attending him. I am sure there is nothing wanting to make the rest of his subjects as fond of him as we are, but their knowing him as we do, and it will be odd, if his Presence among us, after his running so many hazards to compass it, do not turn the hearts, even of the most obstinate. It is not fit to tell all the particulars, but I assure you he has left nothing undone, that well could be, to gain everybody, and I hope God will touch their Hearts. I have reason to hope we shall very quickly see a new Face of Affairs abroad in the King's Favour, which is all I dare commit to paper.—*Mar*.

The Rising of the Forty-Five provoked a more idealistic

fervour of loyalty in Scotland than either of the two previous rebellions. Prince Charles Edward had that mysterious charm and kingly manner which the Stewarts possessed to an ineffable degree. The same mystic blend of "divine royalty" had captured the shrewd Yorkshire head and heart of Thomas Wentworth, first Earl of Strafford, the "Great Earl" of Charles I's reign, who began as a critic of the King and ended on the headsman's block as the most fervent martyr of the Stewart cause.

This aura of near-divinity which surrounded the House of Stewart divided the aristocracy and country gentlemen of England into two bitter factions of Civil War and later swept Charles II back to the throne in 1660 on a tidal wave of almost idolatrous joy.

It was something which the pudding-faced Hanoverian princelings who later ascended the English throne could never evoke. They were dynastic make-shifts, guttural compromises—but never the bright flame of true royalty.

This Stewart image, to use that overworked word, lingered strongly in the Highlands long after England had agreed, in her squirearchial heart, to accept the paunchy German princelings, and get on with the serious business of farming and fox-hunting, trade and seafaring, without a glance over the shoulder at the Court in London.

Things were very different in the lonely glens, the dark corries and on the misty moors and green straths of Scotland. The ancient splendour of the Scottish kings, men of the sword who never flinched to fight the English invader, was a very real thing. Loyalties to clan and chief were rooted deep. The whole country, with the exception of "the false Campbells" and a few other opportunistic Lowland lords, was fiercely devoted to the Stewart cause. It was of their blood and bone. It meant all that Scotland had ever been or could dream to be.

The Prince stepped ashore from the French ship *Doutelle* in lonely Loch Nanumah near Arisaig at the head of the Sound of Sleat on 23rd July, 1745, and marched overland to Loch Shiel. He was rowed up that narrow shining water in a state barge or beorlinn and landed at Glenfinnan where he set up his standard amid the clans who had marched to meet him.

The news rang like a silver trumpet-note from ben to saddle, from peak to corrie, from lochan to strath, from the primeval pine forests of Rothiemurchus to the grey-pink towers of Glamis, lordly beneath the stark beauty of the Grampians.

Alas, there could be no great uprising at Glamis. "The Bloody Butcher" Cumberland, that cold-hearted German master of ruthless war, marched there with his army on his way north. Cumberland slept in the Castle. One can imagine the irony of this visit, the icy contempt with which the Lord of Glamis received his visitor. When the Duke had gone Glamis gave orders that his bed was to be broken up.

Many a man of Glamis took to the hills to fight for the Prince. They were away with targe and claymore, flintlock pistol and muzzle-loading musket on

> . . . the ridge of hinds, the steep of the sloping glen,
> The wood of cuckoos at its foot,
> The blue height of a thousand pines,
> Of wolves, and roes and elks.

At nearby Cortachy, that splendid young chieftain, the twenty-year-old Lord Ogilvy, raised a regiment to fight for the Prince. Many a man of Glamis flocked to his banner. Lord Ogilvy was the beau-ideal of that type of young, soldierly aristocrat of which Britain seems to produce a rare and inexhaustible supply in all her wars. They are born leaders with that quality of being at one with their men which the jack-booted Prussian has never possessed. Ogilvy had the knightly graces. For a long time his sword was preserved at Cortachy. On the blade were engraved these words: "The man who feels no delight in a gallant steed, a bright sword and a fair ladye, has not in his breast the heart of a soldier." The quality of the man shines in those few words. The man who led the men of Glamis in the "last burst of chivalry".

David, Lord Ogilvy was born in 1725, the son of the fourth Earl of Airlie, and raised the Ogilvy Regiment when he was only twenty years of age. Alexander MacIntosh, the historian, gives a fair picture of Ogilvy, his regiment and his bold, pathetic attempt to fight for his Prince:

On the arrival of Prince Charles at Perth on his southward march, Lord Ogilvy, with all the Jacobite fervour of his race, waited upon His Royal Highness to pay his respects and offer his assistance. The Prince received him very graciously, and appointed him Lord-Lieutenant of Forfarshire, when he returned home to raise troops and money. Although his Lordship's father did not take an active part, he encouraged his son, and tradition has it that he even sold the silver plate and family jewels to support the Cause.

Having raised a body of fully 300 men, Lord Ogilvy proceeded with them to join the Prince at Edinburgh, arriving there on Thursday, 3rd October, twelve days after the battle of Gladsmuir. His Lordship having received from His Royal Highness a Lieutenant-Colonelcy for Sir James Kinloch, despatched him back to Forfarshire to raise a second battalion.

Prince Charles appears to have immediately held Lord Ogilvy in high respect, as, on forming his Privy Council before leaving Edinburgh, his Lordship was appointed a member, and during the subsequent campaign His Royal Highness often attached himself to the Angus Regiment. On the 1st November the Highland Army left Edinburgh on its march into England, and reached Moffat on the 6th, where it rested for one day.

Lord Ogilvy accompanied the Army into England, assisting in the siege and capture of Carlisle, and was among those of the Prince's Council who, on reaching Derby, fully realized that they had been misled as to the promised English support, and consequent futility of the incursion, and therefore successfully advocated returning to Scotland. In the retreat, Lord Ogilvy and his Regiment arrived at Stirling on the 8th January 1746, where he was joined by the Second Battalion of 400 men, under Sir James Kinloch. With the completed Regiment, His Lordship shared in the victory at Falkirk, being placed second on the right in the second column.

It being determined to retire beyond the Grampians, his Lordship and his men left Stirling on the 1st February, and on arriving at Perth took the route through Forfarshire, where he rested from the 4th till the 11th, in order to allow the men to visit their homes, and raise recruits. He then marched across the hills by Braemar, and rejoined Lord George Murray's forces on the 18th February. Lord Ogilvy and his Regiment took part in the attempted surprise on the Duke of Cumberland at Nairn on the 15th April, and next day in the defeat at Culloden.

According to Lord Elcho, who was present, the Angus Regiment was placed on the right of the Second Division, and immediately behind the Atholl and Cameron men. Here was the main attack, the onslaught of these regiments being terrible. In the words of Mr. Chalmers, the historian:

> Notwithstanding that the three files of the front line of English poured forth their incessant fire of musketry—notwithstanding that the cannon, now loaded with grapeshot, swept the field as with a hailstorm—notwithstanding the flank fire of Wolfe's Regiment—onward, onward, went the headlong Highlanders, flinging themselves into, rather than rushing upon the lines of the enemy, which indeed they did not see for smoke, till involved amid their weapons. All that courage, all that despair could do, was done.

At this moment Lord Ogilvy ordered his Regiment to advance, gallantly leading it, but after delivering a well-directed volley which told, noticing the other regiments giving way, and realizing the day was lost, his Lordship, wisely counselling his men to stick together for defence, marched them off the field. Unquestionably this movement saved many lives, the enemy not daring to pursue such a compact body: the loss sustained, so far as known, being only nine killed, two wounded, and forty-three prisoners.

A large proportion of the retreating force made for the Bridge of Failie, Upper Strathnairn, where, after parting with the Prince, the Forfarshire Regiment proceeded to Ruthven in Badenoch, where His Royal Highness had given orders to assemble and wait instructions. Here, after staying for a day or two, the Prince sent word that he intended going to France, and for every one to "seek the means of escape as best he can". During his stay Lord and Lady Ogilvy (for her ladyship accompanied her husband) resided at the house of Mr. Gordon of Killihuntly, near by.

There being now nothing but dispersion, his Lordship, again advising his men to remain together until they reached home, marched them across the mountains between the shires of Inverness and Aberdeen to Balmoral, where they rested for one night, then up to Glenmuick, and over the Capel into Clova. This place they reached on the evening of the 20th April 1746, or four days after Culloden, and next day his Lordship dismissed them with many sad good-byes.

Glamis Castle (*Radio Times Hulton Picture Library*)

Castle of Mey

Escape from capture being now the sole object, Lord Ogilvy arranged to keep in touch with several of his co-patriot neighbours until a way of escape could be secured. This was soon accomplished by Alexander Stewart, merchant, Dundee, who, although not in arms, zealously aided the Insurgents. Stewart secretly engaged and victualled a vessel owned and commanded by Captain Wemyss, of Broughty Ferry, near which it was lying, and three weeks after Culloden, his Lordship, along with the following gentlemen, embarked overnight, and in safety reached Bergen, Norway, viz.: Thomas Blair of Glasclune; Alexander Blair, writer, Edinburgh; Robert Fletcher, jun., Balinshoe; David Fotheringham, merchant, Dundee; James Grahame of Duntrune; David Hunter of Brunside; Alexander Johnstone, silversmith, Dundee; John Ogilvy of Inshewan; David Ogilvy, merchant, Coul; Thomas Ogilvy, Inverquharity; Henry Patullo, merchant, Dundee; and Sandilands, jun., merchant, Bordeaux, France. For this kindly act Captain Wemyss and his crew were arrested and imprisoned on their return to Dundee.

On landing at Bergen they were immediately seized, and confined in the castle there, at the instigation of the English Government, but after a short time were liberated, and made their way to France. There they received a kindly welcome, Louis XV honouring Lord Ogilvy with a commission to raise a regiment of his refugee countrymen for the French Service, thus providing a living for many of the distressed. This regiment was named after his Lordship, and consisted of twelve companies. Besides thus giving employment, the French King very kindly bestowed handsome gratuities upon many of the exiles, Lord Ogilvy included.

On the death of his father, the Earl of Airlie, in 1761, Lord Ogilvy succeeded to the title. His Lordship remained in the service of France until 1778, having risen to the rank of Lieutenant-General, and created a Knight of St. Lewis by the French King. In that year King George III granted the Earl a free pardon, and the restoration of his estates when he returned to Scotland, and again occupied the ancestral home of Cortachy Castle. Although known as the Fighting Laird, his Lordship quietly spent the remainder of his life in peace, interesting himself in improving his estates, bringing the knowledge acquired in France into requisition, and seeing to the well-being of his tenantry.

Lord Ogilvy's wife was taken prisoner and shut up in Edinburgh Castle. She managed to escape. Mr. Archibald Hart, an Edinburgh merchant, smuggled a suit of men's clothes into her apartments in the Castle. She dressed herself in them and posing as "a sick gentleman going away for his health" she walked out of the Castle, joined Mr. Hart in his chaise in the street and was driven by him to London. Which seems to argue that a good many people in Edinburgh Castle turned a blind eye. Lady Ogilvy joined her husband in France in 1748 and died there, nine years later, at the age of only thirty-three.

Dr. Stirton possessed a highly interesting autographed letter of Archibald Hart which throws such an unaffected personal light on the way in which the Rising affected the ordinary Scottish gentleman at that time that I take leave to quote it:

> Dr. Willie—Fortune I believe has resolved that I never am you to see. London afairs at present are so situated that I cannot venture to move. Saturday last we were alarmed that the young chevalier was at Perth that night tho we have heard since that he was at the Blair of Athole Friday last. I believe he may be at Perth this day. Things are at present here in disorder and no such thing as money paid, and its believed when he draws a little nigher the banks will retire to the Castel, therefor altho these bills that I drew on you last be presented don't accept them till further orders because if this be the case that the banks retires I'll not can remitt you which might put you into some difficulties which I would not willingly doe, but I am to write these gentlemen to this purpose, so I suppose they will not present them till further orders. I don't know what the event of this may be but it does not look well at present. Mrs. Hart and all friends join in there love to you,—and I am, Dr. Sir, your most affectionate Brother, and very humble servant, Archibald Hart. Edinburgh, Septe. 3rd, 1745. P.S.—My uncle Mr. Cambell told me that he was to pay you on my accot £27; odd money, which please put him in mind of; tell him also that I have got a Commission for my brother Daniel in Sir. Rt. Monroe's Regt.—To Mr. William Innes, Merchant, London.

James Arrat, a strict Roman Catholic and fervid Jacobite, who owned the small estate of Fafferty near Glamis was an ensign in the Ogilvy Regiment. He seized horses, arms and equipment from a number of people locally to help equip the Regiment. When Sir John Wedderburn of Blackness was a prisoner in London waiting trial for complicity in the Rising, one of his strong pleas in defence was that "there will be no difficulty in proving Fafferty seizing his horses and threatening more".

Arrat disappeared after the disaster at Culloden but turned up years later so utterly impoverished that he had to sell his little estate to the Earl of Strathmore in 1758. A Catholic Chapel and a priest's house had stood on the property for many years, but these were both burnt down by a party of dragoons after Culloden.

Another Roman Catholic family with strong local roots who paid a terrible price for their loyalty to the Stewarts was that of Alexander Bower of Methie and Kincaldrum, Inverarity. Alexander MacIntosh in his work *Forfarshire or Lord Ogilvy's Regiment* says that Alexander Bower

> . . . as Lieutenant, was in the same Company as Arrat, was also a Catholic, and was travelling on the Continent when the news reached him of the arrival of Prince Charles Edward in Scotland. He immediately returned home, and, raising his tenantry, joined the Forfarshire Insurgents, being appointed a Lieutenant in Lord Ogilvy's Regiment.
>
> After the war was over, and the disbandment at Clova, Lieutenant Bower, in company with his cousin, Colonel Kerr of Graden, Roxburgh, returned to Kincaldrum, where Mrs. Bower and her boy was. During the day-time the refugees took to hiding in the neighbouring hills, and at night returned to Kincaldrum House for food and shelter.
>
> One night after supper a party of Hessian Dragoons in search of fugitives surrounded the house, and while part remained outside, the officer and others entered. At this time all the lower part of the house had iron stanchioned windows, so, on hearing the noise, Colonel Kerr made for one of these, which he knew had a loose bar, through which he went, only to find himself in the hands of two of the enemy, who took him prisoner.

Lieutenant Bower sought refuge in a secret closet off a bedroom, the aperture to same being covered by an old cabinet. In their search the soldiers removed this article and discovered Bower. He gallantly attempted to defend himself, it is said with a poker, and knocked some of the enemy down, but, after being severely wounded, was captured.

He was removed first to Dundee, and then to Perth; and in a narrative written by the Lieutenant's grandson, Mr. Graham Bower, it is stated that, "having a fine head of hair, the Dragoons knotted it to one of their horse's tails", and dragged him in this way for about two miles, to a place called Cothiewards (Cuttywards), near Findrick, where a poor man, of the name of Saunders Kinear, was holling (digging up) broom, who, on his bended knees, interceded for his master, saying: "If you will only put the gentleman on a horse, I will gi'e you a' the siller I hae", which amounted to ten Pounds. The relief seems to have come too late, however. He was then mounted behind a trooper, carried to Dundee, from there to Perth Prison, where it soon pleased God to relieve him from his tormentors, having expired from the brutal treatment he had received.

Mrs. Bower, although in poor health, followed her husband to Perth, where learning that the Duke of Cumberland was at Stirling Castle, she went thither and interceded for her husband's life. At last the Duke consented to grant it, on condition that he would leave the country and never return; and he gave her passes for her husband, herself, and their only child, a boy about six years of age.

Mrs. Bower immediately returned to Perth, to find her husband had died of his wounds and cruel treatment. The sight of the dead body so terribly shocked her that she fell forward over the corpse and expired. The two bodies were placed in one coffin and brought to Kincaldrum House, where they lay some days previous to interment.

A strange story is told in connection with this part of the tragedy. James Bower, a relative, being anxious to secure the property of the deceased insurgent, bribed the soldiers stationed in the district to kill the infant son, he being then the next-of-kin; but the nurse, when she heard them coming, hid the boy in the coffin containing his dead parents, covering him with the pall, and so escaped detection.

The bodies were buried in the Chapel-yard on the farm of Easter

Meathie, which then belonged to the Bowers of Kincaldrum.

Lieutenant Bower married in 1736 Margaret St. Clair of Rosslyn, the last of the real St. Clairs of that estate near Edinburgh, and their only child and heir was Alexander St. Clair Bower, who so narrowly escaped. For better safety he was sent to France in the custody of Miss St. Clair, an aunt, where, on the advice and influence of Lord Ogilvy, he was placed in the Scots College in Paris.

Robert Fletcher the younger of Ballinshoe, was another officer in the Ogilvy Regiment:

He was a descendant of Sir Alexander Fletcher of Innerpeffer. The property was acquired in 1633. Fletcher shared in all the vicissitudes of Lord Ogilvy in France, and died in 1782. He was a grandson of Elizabeth Lyon of Wester-Ogil, and he married a Lyon of the same famous cadet family of Glamis. Patrick Lyon of Ogil, another cadet of the Glamis family, was a Lieutenant in the Ogilvy Regiment, and the Reverend Robert Lyon, A.M. of the same family, who was an Episcopal clergyman in Perth, joined the adventure, under a strong religious sense of duty, and bore all his own expenses. He was tried, condemned, and executed at Penrith on 28th October, 1746.

Before starting for the place of execution Mr. Lyon administered the Sacrament to his fellow-sufferers. On the scaffold he conducted divine service, and read a long speech setting forth his reasons for joining the Rising, and declaring his unswerving attachment to the Jacobite Cause. He is said to have been the author of the following lines:

God bless the King, I mean the Faith's Defender;
God bless—there is no harm in blessing the Pretender;
But Who Pretender is, and Who is King—
God bless us all! that is quite another thing.

Patrick Lyon, mentioned above, paid a fugitive visit to his home after Culloden, and left the famous sword—which bears the following inscription—in the castle of Coul from which the Deuchars recovered it: "Da Denquhyre his swerde at Bannockburn. I served the Brus of quhilk the Inglis had . . . naryss."

A pathetic relic at Glamis today is the prayer book of Miss Stewart Rose, daughter of Bishop Rose of Edinburgh, who was engaged to be married to the Reverend Robert Lyon of the Ogilvy Regiment who was executed at Penrith on the 28th October, 1746. This prayer book bears her signature. With it is a copy of the Rev. Robert Lyon's last speech on the scaffold.

Today, if you take the road up the strath into the bleak Grampians "the grey, gaunt heights . . . and the rampart of rocks, stark naked" and look down on the ancient fortress, think of that verse of Christine Orr:

> The Road it runs through Badenoch, and still, and on it rings
> With the riding of the clansmen and a hundred echoings;
> Oh, some they rode for vengeance and some for gear and gain,
> But some for Bonnie Charlie rode and came not home again.

The splendour and the pity of it all was put simply by my old friend, Frank Wallace, that Master of Deer, in his book *Hunting and Stalking the Deer* in which he said of another place:

> Many, many years later the last of the Stewarts with his little band of faithful followers wandered over the hills near by. I like to think that afterwards, when all the glamour and romance had gone, leaving only a worn, broken old man, the skirl of the pipes and the memory of those blue hills had power to kindle a flame that was almost dead and light an eye from which the sparkle had for ever flown. Let that at least be remembered of him!
>
> Still winding about the lonely places you may see paths, now used only by sure-footed ponies and an occasional stalker, which the red-coated soldiery employed to hunt him down and harry his men.
>
> "Ah!" said Willie, as we climbed a slope, "there was a different kind of stalking then!"

14

THE "BOOK OF RECORD"

PATRICK, first Earl of Strathmore and third Earl of Kinghorne was, in his quiet, forceful way, one of the most remarkable men Scotland has produced. As a youth he succeeded to one of the largest estates in Scotland, burdened with debts of no less than £400,000. By modern standards that could represent £4 million or more today. By shrewd finance and rigid economy he reduced this debt to £175,400. The interest upon this in 1684 meant an annual charge upon the Estate, at 6 per cent, of £10,524.

When we remember that most of his rents were paid in kind, in barley, meal and other farm products, all of which had to be sold in the open market to raise ready money, it is clear that he must have been a first-class agriculturalist with a keen sense of values and a shrewd financier.

The tasks he surmounted were truly formidable. For example, between 1678 and 1684 he paid off debts of £99,866 13s. 4d.—when he was heavily engaged rebuilding two castles, Castle Lyon and Glamis.

He kept a careful account to the minutest detail with shrewd observation upon the people with whom he dealt whether they were humble stone-masons, bricklayers, carpenters, farmers, or noblemen or Princes of the Realm. All this he set down in his *Book of Record* from 1684–9. The original is at Glamis and I am indebted to the present Lord Strathmore for permission to quote from it.

The diary shows in detail that Lord Strathmore was obliged to borrow heavily. Bills and bonds were then the only substitute for paper currency. This system often hit the original debtor hard.

The man who granted the bond might agree not to press the holder of that bond for payment within a certain time. But if the holder became hard-up he could assign the bond to a third party who could demand instant payment. If a bond got into the hands of an enemy it could be a deadly weapon.

Before we go into the details of Lord Strathmore's diary consider the man himself. He came into his estates in 1660 when only seventeen years of age. He had finished his studies at St. Andrew's. His father and grandfather had beggared the estate to raise money for war. Glamis was almost empty of furniture whilst Castle Lyon, in the Carse of Gowrie, was uninhabitable. It seemed hopeless to try to pull the estates round.

To make matters worse in 1650, when he was only eight, his mother married for a second time. Her husband, the Earl of Linlithgow, treated his stepson with cruelty and unconscionable extortion. It was not a happy childhood for the boy.

When he came home from the university there was not a bed in Castle Lyon for him to sleep on. He had to borrow a bedstead from the Minister of Longforgan and set it up in the cold, stone-floored, echoing waste of his uninhabited Castle with only the owls to welcome him. He waited for his humble student's furniture to arrive from St. Andrew's. Young Patrick Lyon could have become embittered or he could have funked the issue. Instead, he determined to pull the estates out of the mess, rebuild his two castles and re-establish his family. To his undying credit he did all these things. He records those hard days thus:

> I had a verie small and a verie hard begining and if I had not done so great and good things as I might or willingly would have done I desyre that my posteritie whom God has bless'd me with may excuse these my endeavours from the reasone before mentioned.

It would be hard to find in fiction a more pathetic picture of a young nobleman, reduced practically to stark poverty, than is given by his own simple description of his early days at Castle Lyon.

Mr. A. D. Millar, F.S.A., the distinguished antiquary of

Aberdeen, writing in 1890 in his introduction to the Glamis *Book of Record* said:

> The heir of a name that had been famous in Scottish history for centuries was reduced to a condition of extreme privation through no fault of his own but through the crushing weight of circumstances over which he had no control.
>
> His barns, his byres, and his stables at Castle Lyon were alike tenantless, and, as he quaintly puts it, "att that time I was not worth a four-footed beast, safe on little dog that I keeped att and brought with me from St. Andrews." The empty chambers within the prison-like Castle were bare of furniture, and it was here that he and his only sister, Lady Elizabeth Lyon, began their first attempt at housekeeping on a most parsimonious scale.
>
> For his sister he seems ever to have had profound respect and affection, and she worked for him in this matter of furnishing with unselfish devotion. Having scrambled together from the deserted Castle of Glamis "some old potts and pans qch were verie usefull," and collected odd furniture which plenished two rooms in an incoherent fashion, he and his sister began to decorate with their own hands their lonely dwelling-place, and to make it, in appearance at least, fit for habitation.
>
> Looking back upon this period of his life twenty-five years afterwards, Lord Strathmore was as keenly impressed by the sisterly affection of Lady Elizabeth during this trying period, as he had been at the time of its occurrence. "Her companie," he writes, "was of great comfort to me, so young as were both we consulted together, and partlie by our owne conclusions and partlie by advice, in two years time I gott togither as much of cours furniture as in a verie mean and sober way filled all the rowms of my house, some on way some another." With his sister he remained until his marriage, which took place in 1662.

Patrick Lyon was a man of strict integrity, with a tremendous sense of responsibility to posterity. He was just without being mean. He was thrifty without being penurious. He was generous, but a shrewd judge of men. He was affectionate with his family and "tender and true" to his friends and relatives. He was a canny farmer, with that sharp sense of values which springs from the soil, but he had the sensitive nature of an artist. His love of beauty, space, proportion and tradition is reflected in the splendour and dignity of the Castle today.

There are two pictures of him at Glamis and a marble bust. They show a mild, amiable man who would have made a good courtier, a wise political administrator, but not, unless pressed to it, a warrior. He was no coward but he knew when discretion was the better part of valour. Wars had nearly ruined his family. He determined to take as little part as possible in the intrigues of dynasties.

He was utterly sincere, grateful to God for the health and ability which enabled him to weather the hard storms of his youth, the oppressive cruelty of his stepfather and the claims of his creditors, and to emerge with his two ruined homes and his almost utterly ruined Estates re-established. He could hold his head high.

When he wrote his diary, communing with himself with no idea that he was laying bare his mind for unborn generations to read, he gave a rare insight into his own character:

> By Divine providence, which I may rather ascrive it to then out of any choice of my owne, being then so young and of no experience, I did then begin, and still have continued, with just and equall dealings to all men. I never defrauded the poor, nor had I ever any favour or ease from those who were powerfull, allwayes acknowledging my father's bonds when I saw them. And I hope, by the mercie of God, founding againe my familie upon the pillar of justice, I shall be able to transmitt a good pairt of my estate with much less of incumbrance and debt then I found att my entrie thereto.

His wife was a tower of strength, a fount of inspiration. She was Lady Helen Middleton, second daughter of John, first Earl of Middleton and of his first wife, Grizel, daughter of Sir James Durham of Pitkerro and Luffness. He found her not only a masterly manager of domestic affairs, but a wise adviser in times of crisis. A devoted mother, she reared her family with love and gentle discipline.

They were married at the Abbey of Holyrood by Archbishop Sharpe on 3rd August, 1662. They spent the first winter in Edinburgh. Earl Patrick gives a charming sketch of the surprise he prepared for her when he took her to her bridal chamber: "I caused bring home a verie fin cabinet, the better was not in the Kingdome in these days, which I never told my wyfe of till her comeing home, and upon her first comeing into her owne chamber I presented her with the keyes of the cabinet".

At this time they had practically no furniture. She was going to two bare, empty homes with only the carrion crows to welcome them from the battlements. It was typical of the man with his delicate sense of beauty that his first thought was to present his young bride with a piece of fine furniture.

In March 1663 they set out for Castle Lyon. They crossed the Forth to Aberdour where the bride's sister, the Countess of Morton, was living, and spent the night at Cupar where many friends were waiting. Next morning they went to Dundee and were given a welcome in state by the Provost and magistrates. When that was over they went straight to Castle Lyon. There they lived for seven years. Their eldest son, John, afterwards second Earl of Strathmore, was born there on 8th May, 1663.

Some of the Castle Lyon estate had been owned by the Lyons for ages, but the Castle with the remainder of the Mains and Kirktown had been bought from Lord Gray by Patrick, first Earl of Kinghorne. The Castle was still a rough, feudal stronghold. It did not satisfy the cultivated taste of the young Patrick. He set to work to repair and furnish it. He and his bride decided to live there until they could afford to put Glamis into habitable order.

Glamis was in such a state that it depressed him unutterably. He says in his diary:

> For the first three years of my life, wch I only reckon since the year 1660, I could not endure allmost to come near to or see it [Glamis] when the verie Mains was possessed by a wedsetter, so, when my wyfe after the end of the first seven years considered that nothing contributs so much to the distruction and utter ruine of furniture than the transporting of it, I was induced by her to make

my constant abode att Castle Lyon for some time longer till she gott togither some things necessary to be had before we could think of comeing to Glammiss, wch she provyded with so much care as that for our first comeing to Glammiss where I proposed to live for some time as rereteedly as I did att first when I took up house at Castle Lyon having scarce a spare rowme furnished to lodge a stranger in.

It was not until 1670 that the Earl and Countess found themselves in a position to remove to Glamis, and in the following year he began those alterations which transformed it into one of the noblest castles in Scotland.

The Earl began the rebuilding and furnishing of Glamis in 1671 and finished in 1689. It was a hard uphill fight. He was constantly paying off creditors, raising funds, saving money and forging ahead. Many odd things happened to him during this period.

Mr. Millar, the antiquary, records that:

His grandfather had been created Earl of Kinghorne in 1606, with strict limitation to his heirs-male. On 30th May, 1672 Patrick, third Earl of Kinghorne, obtained a new charter enabling him to nominate a successor in default of male issue. Five years afterwards he procured another charter, dated 1st July, 1677, ordaining that his heirs and successors in tailzie should be designated in all time coming Earls of Strathmore and Kinghorne, Viscounts Lyon, Barons Glamis, Tannadyce, Sidlaw, and Strathdichtie, and this is the full style and title of his descendant, the present Earl of Strathmore.

On 10th January, 1682 he was sworn of the Privy Council, and on 27th March, 1686 he was appointed an Extraordinary Lord of Session.

When Argyll's rebellion broke out in 1685 he was appointed to provide the stores for the army, and was commissioned to bring the prisoners and spoil from Clydesdale to Edinburgh, and the artillery from Glasgow and Stirling. By his commissariat transaction he lost a considerable sum of money, as a much larger quantity of provision was ordered from him than was required and this fact indicates that the government anticipated that Argyll's rebellion would be much more formidable than it really was. His connection with this rebellion proved disastrous for him. He obtained a portion of Argyll's lands in Kintyre, and, as the king desired to resume these lands and annex them to the Crown, a proposal was made whereby Lord Strathmore and the Earl of Errol were to obtain an equivalent from the town of Edinburgh.

The description of this curious transaction is somewhat confusing, though the following passage from a memorial presented to the Earl of Melville, then Secretary for Scotland, by the town of Edinburgh, renders the matter more intelligible. This memorial is quoted in the *Leven and Melville Papers*. The town of Edinburgh was in debt to the extend of 150,000 merks in 1633. Betwixt that date and 1654, the coronation of Charles I, the building of the Parliament House and of several churches, the besieging of the Castle, and other public affairs had raised the debt to 1,200,000 merks.

Cromwell granted an imposition of a plack on the pint of ale to assist in clearing off the debt, and this tax was continued till his death. At the Restoration this imposition was restricted to two pennies on the pint, and this was continued til 1682. In 1683, Sir George Drummond, Provost of Edinburgh, undertook the watching and warding of the city, which had been previously accomplished by train bands, and, acting upon his authority, the debts of the town were further increased. The tax upon ale had been farmed during its continuance to various parties, and in 1680 Charles II made a new gift of the imposition for twenty-one years.

Shortly before his abdication, James II (apparently in 1686) entered into a contract with the Earls of Strathmore and of Errol, whereby he granted a portion of the tax to them in exchange for the lands of Kintyre. "The two Earles parts of the contract was, to dispone to the King some lands in Argylleshire, out of which they had their relieff, the Earles of Errol and Strathmore being cautioners in a bond to Heriot's hospitall of tuentie thousand pounds scottis of principall of Argylle. The Town's part of the contract was to undertake the said debt dew to the hospitall, which of principall and annual rents amounts to near 5000 lib. sterling, for which the Town has given bond to the hospitall; but it's hoped the Parliament will reduce this transaction as done to the grosse and palpable lesion of the Town."

According to Lord Strathmore's account of the business, he could not obtain a just settlement of his claim against the town when he made application to James II at London, and in consequence of the loss he sustained he was made an Extraordinary

Lord of Session on 27th March, 1686, with a pension of £300 sterling. The arrangement of the "tripartite contract" between the King and the two Earls was ultimately accomplished in the beginning of 1688, and thus Lord Strathmore got rid of one of the onerous charges bequeathed to him by his father.

The part which Lord Strathmore took in the Revolution of 1688 is interesting. There can be little doubt that his first intention was to resist the Prince of Orange, and to join the leading Jacobite noblemen in the restoration of James II to the throne. He implicated himself with the Earls of Southesk, Callender, and Breadalbane, and endeavoured to assemble in arms such militia as he had control over. He was present as a member of the Privy Council when intelligence of the proposed invasion by the Prince was received. "This was the time", he writes, "of the first surprysing news of the Dutch invasion, and of the P. of Orange's designe of landing in England, wch he did afterwards wt wonderful success. It was then scarce when harvest was done that the militia was draw'ne togither, and by one detachment after another thes expeditions dwynled into nothing, as everything else did wch concerned the king's service, all succeeding wt the Prince to a miracle." Finding it hopeless to resist the progress of the revolution, as King James had gone beyond the seas, Strathmore deemed it prudent to make his peace with the Prince of Orange.

Life was by no means easy. He had plenty of setbacks. Immense liabilities to meet. A few enemies. Had he allowed his loyalty to the Stewart cause to overshadow all else he would undoubtedly have been ruined, probably imprisoned and executed. He chose to paddle his canoe in calmer waters. Thus he survived.

This instinct for caution was impressed upon him firstly by his father's connections with the Presbyterian party and with Montrose, which cost the estate dearly and, secondly, the cruel extortions of his stepfather, Linlithgow.

He has written one passage in the *Book of Record* which is highly interesting since it throws a sharp light on the Covenanters. His father, Lord Kinghorne, held a commission under Montrose at the Battle of the Bridge of Dee. A contemporary ballad ran thus:

God bless our Covenanters in Fyffe and Lothean,
In Angus and the Mearnis quho did us first begin
With muskit and with carabin, with money, speare, and shield,
To take the toune of Aberdeen and make our Marques yield.

God bliss Montrois our General,
The stout Earl of Kinghorne,
That we may long live and rejoyce
That ever they were borne.

His father's connection with the Presbyterians reaped the whirlwind for the son. There is something pathetic in the judgement which young Strathmore pronounced upon the career of his father, whom he dearly loved, although he suffered from the punishment which his father brought upon him. Young Strathmore was an out-and-out Royalist and Episcopalian. Thus he had little sympathy with the Presbyterians. He denounces their dealings with the martyred King. But in the *Book of Record* he seems to exonerate his father to some extent for the path he took, unwillingly, in the doings of the Presbyterian army. He suggests that his father did this to please his first wife, Lady Margaret Erskine (who was a daughter of the Earl of Mar), and his younger brother, James Lyon of Aldbarr. This is what he says:

But of all the actions of my father's life there was on which I am sorrie to mention since he is so inexcusable for it, but that the fault was truly more his brother's, The Laird of Aldbarr, then his, who was in his owne nature a man of a noble dispositione and feared no ill designe from any man, because he had none himselfe, only it was his misfortune to be easie to be intreated, and it was painfull for him to refuse to relieve his freind when in distress, not considering the hazard of the event, for indeed he was a man not fitted for the time he lived in, fraud and deceit rageing in the transactions of privat busines, and the purpose of rebellion in the publick.

All which prov'd too true by the ruin of many good families in their privat fortune and the murder of the best of Kings, but my father was preveen'd by death and did not behold this Tragedie, but was sufficiently convinced of the error of the times—tho. att the beginning he was carried away by the speat and by the influence of his first Lady and his brother Aldbarr, two mightie Covenanters, was induced to goe on too far, and was ingaged in persone with his regiment of Angus to march four severall times and companyed with many of his friends to the North, which expeditions and the buying of arms I have seen by the reall accompts thereof stood him no less then Fourtie thousand merks.

This and the lyke advancements for the propagating the good cause (for the rebellious covenant was so called at that time) were thought meritorious, and no less then heaven was the purchase, tho. it was the Divill in Masquerad, and my father's wyfe, who was the E. of Marr's daughter, dyeing and his brother Aldbarr soon after did discover the wicked designs against King and Kingdome which were carried on under the pretence of Religione, and in the parliament sometime before his owne death declared no less, and opposed as much as in him lay the preventing partie at that time, and when his countrie-men (an unpardonable sin in those who received the pryce qch will certainly prove a snare and a curse to their posteritie and does remain an everlasting reproach to the natione, tho. many there was in it honest and blamless) sold there King and voted in Parliament to delyver him up to the Inglish att Newcastle, and not only past his vote against it, and there was but a feu in Parliament did so, but entered his protestatione thereupon boldlie enough but honestlie done att that time.

There is no doubt that the second Earl of Kinghorne was far too easy-going and much too obliging to his friends. It landed him in political trouble. It plunged his family deep into debt. Throughout the *Book of Record* the son refers to many instances of "this over-obliging disposition" on the part of his father. He blamed him severely for incurring debts and granting bonds solely to oblige his friends. The father died of the plague when Patrick was only four years old. Therefore he had no personal memories of his father. Even so he felt deep filial affection for him.

Just as the sins of the fathers are visited on the children, so the unwise military activities of the second Earl rebounded upon the son. Oliver Cromwell slapped a fine of £1,000 upon the estate merely to punish the infant for his father's crime. Later, when he wrote his *Book of Record*, Patrick hit out:

> It was my misfortune being a child at that time not to be in that capacitie to act against him [Cromwell] wch had I been a man I would have done to my utmost hazard.

In another entry, harking back to those hard, early days, he writes, as I said earlier:

> I had a verie small and a verie hard begining and if I had not done so great and good things as I might or willingly would have done I desyre that my posteritie whom God has bless'd me with may excuse these my endeavours for the reasone before mentioned.

It was doubly hard that having, from the earliest days, tasted the bitter fruit of his father's and grandfather's misplaced loyalties, he should then be plagued by a stepfather with the instincts of a money-lender.

Mr. A. H. Millar summed it up seventy-five years ago in trenchant sentences thus:

> After the death of his father (Earl Patrick), his mother kept a strict note of all the money which she expended for him out of her own liferent, intending as he suggests, to claim for this money in the event of his dying without issue. She married the Earl of Linlithgow, however, and after her death, that nobleman, whose treatment of the young Earl was extremely cruel, compelled the repayment of all this money, and claimed upon the estate, though still under curators, for a debt to which he had only a secondary right.

Many other circumstances of the same kind will be found throughout the *Book of Record*. This method of assigning debts is shown to have brought about the ruin of many families. This aspect of the social life of the times has not received due attention from historians of Scotland. Millar says:

> The two principal methods then employed for raising money were the pledging of land as security, or the assigning of the value of so many ploughs for the liquidation of the principal sum and interest.

As an instance of the former, the transaction of Lord Strathmore with the Earl of Linlithgow, may be examined. When Lord Strathmore purchased some superiorities from the Earl of Crauford he borrowed £1,333 6s. 8d. from Lord Linlithgow.

Shortly afterwards, when Linlithgow married Lord Strathmore's mother, he preferred a claim for the money she had expended during her widowhood in the manner already referred to.

To meet this charge, which amounted to £14,666 13s. 4d., Lord Strathmore was compelled to pledge the lands of Cardean and the third part of Lenross, and thus run the risk of losing a large portion of the most valuable lands in his estate. Fortunately he was able to clear off the debt shortly afterwards; but the fact that he was necessitated to make such an arrangement shows how difficult it was to obtain money on any save heritable security.

It is interesting to notice that Lord Strathmore had frequent money transactions with Provost Coutts of Montrose, who was the direct ancestor of the late Thomas Coutts, the famous banker of London.

With very few exceptions, the whole rental of Lord Strathmore's estate was paid to him in kind, and the values of various farms were expressed more frequently under the form of their produce than in current coin. The Byreflat in Longforgan paid a rental of "ten bolls of bear, besyds the teind sheave drawne." The Templebank of Thorntoun paid an annual duty of 8 bolls bear, 8 bolls meal, and 12 poultry. These are examples of the yearly farm-rents exacted; but the entry-money had to be paid in coin.

The factors appointed for the administration of the different portions of the estate received the grain paid in name of rent, and stored it; and the proprietor paid his debts by giving an order to one of the factors to deliver grain to the value of the amount charged against him. In many cases this must have been a most inconvenient method of payment, as it threw the onus of selling the grain upon the creditor, and its frequent use shows in a remarkable way the great scarcity of ready money throughout the kingdom. In short, it was a survival of the old system of barter which was in vogue in very early times.

Tradesmen were paid in the same roundabout way simply because there was no real circulating money. Andrew Wright, the ingenious village joiner at Glamis who did so much splendid reconstruction work was paid partly in land. Lord Strathmore sold him the farm of Byreflat at an agreed price and Andrew was allowed, after having paid the deposit, to work out the rest of the cost of the farm through his own joinery work spread over so many years.

The masons and paviours worked by agreements which laid it down that they were to be paid so much in money and so much in meal. A memorandum in a bundle of Earl Patrick's accounts, now in the Charter Room at Glamis, shows the usual form of agreement. It also emphasizes the fact that there were layabouts, double-dealers, and men who skimped their work three centuries ago. We have no monopoly of them today. Earl Patrick was no fool, to be imposed upon. He writes:

> At Glamis the 15th of Aprile, 1685.—After communing with the four messons here at Glammis such is their shameless greed and unthankfulness albeit of all the work and employment they have had of me these many years past, in which they have gotten mony a pound and penie, I find that they demande for laying the walk about the inner court with stone upon edge verie exorbitant, it being no less than eight pounds and ane firlot of meall for the rood, which would come to a most extraordinar and exorbitant wage—but that I, considering that I have noe such thing to doe againe, have condescended to give them eight marks, and ane firlot of meall for each rood, but that if I fynd any part of it worse done then that is alredie, or that they presume soe much as on stone upon its back unless it be more than a foot thick, I'll withdraw at least the one half of the price, but if it be well done they shall be well paid—only this—since I give them so liberally there's a little peice of wall from the corner of the door which is to goe in to that eastmost gate house, which most be taken down and rebuld by them in bounty to me, for it is but a verie small matter if they had the good manners not to grudge when more than reason is offer'd—but that I observe there designe is upon task work to take it always soe as that they may have wages thereby and a third part more; and for to give them daily wages, that is a thing which I'll doe no more in all my life, for no master is able to subsist by soe doing, unless they resolve to build themselves out of doors.

On 1st July he records with a wry humour:

> I have payed Robert Stratone the apothecary his acct. of 123 lib. which is long owing and such accts are ridiculous, and I pray God help them who have ocassione to be much in there books, since ther drogs and pastiles are sett downe under such strange names and unknown marks that they cannot be weell controlled.

The average working day for masons and others from April to the middle of October began at 5 a.m. and ended at 7 p.m. with an hour off for breakfast, and hour and a half for midday dinner and half an hour from four to four-thirty for what was called "the four hours drink". In other words that hallowed festival of today, the tea-break.

Lord Strathmore was against it. He wrote:

> I chuse much rather to pay a very full and competent pryce to all kind of work men then to be in use of waisting meall and malt and allowing them morning drink and four-hours wch was the custom long ago: but that I have worn it out of use, finding too tho. it was much yet these kind of cattell being in use of it considered it very litle.

Modern wives who cannot get an allowance out of their husbands can quote Earl Patrick as the perfect husband. In order to prevent his wife being obliged to be continually asking him for money he arranged for £600 scots to be paid to her in four quarterly sums. An arrangement was also made for his eldest daughter to receive £100 a year, so that she might learn the value of money at an early age.

Though he dealt fairly with his workmen, Strathmore was sometimes imposed upon. The acute observations which he makes show his attitude towards work-people in his employment:

> Though I hold it as a rule to agree wt workmen so as not to have the trouble of feeding them, for in some cases if they know off no imployt elsewhere they prolong the work for the benefit of having ther meat bound to their mouth, yet such as thes painters and the

> more ingenious sort of craftsmen coming from places at a distance, there is a necessity of being liberall that way; and ev'ne of masons and wrights where a man has much adoe, it is expedient to have a headsman over the rest who must also have something of this nature done to them. Tho. ev'ne its frequently losed that is done that way, for they are apt enow to receive the favour wtout any rebatement of the pryce of ther work. And the only way not to be cheated is to have no work.

The ordinary work of the farm was done by oxen and horses. Though breeding was not so thoroughly understood as now, Strathmore was ahead of his contemporaries in this respect. His cattle account is a suggestive one. He had a hundred oxen, besides cows and young cattle, several oxen being utilized in the plough. Some idea of the price of horses is afforded by later entries in the *Book of Record*, which show that a dun gelding for riding cost £18, a saddle horse cost £2 sterling, and a cart horse £3 sterling.

During the years 1684 to 1689 he sold oats at from £3 to £4 per boll. Bear (barley) was sold at from £4 to £5 6s. 8d. per boll, the latter price being charged for home grain sold to the brewers at Glamis. In dealing with the Glamis brewers he had a peculiar custom difficult to account for which he refers to thus:

> I usually sell a quantity of bear more or less to my own brewars everie year at 13sh. 4d. of the boll att least more than the current rate. . . . the price accorded on with those in and about the toune of Glammiss is five pond six shill. eight pennies per boll, and those few of them who paid readiest money hes 13sh. 8d. of ease in the boll wch is yet six shilling eight pennies more then the current pryce in common mercats.

The price of meal does not vary throughout the period covered by the *Book of Record*, being quoted at £4 per boll. Wheat rules at £6 per boll, though after a scanty crop Strathmore sold 200 bolls in Glasgow at £8 6s. 8d. per boll. Taking these prices as the current rates in the markets of the time, we may easily calculate the stipend of the minister of Longforgan as detailed in the *Book of Record*. It was as follows: 5 bolls wheat, 46 bolls bear, and 44 bolls oats, which would amount in money value to nearly £350.

He gives an interesting sidelight on the value of property for taxation. His father seems to have left the management of his affairs very much in the hands of his servants. They, through vanity, thinking to increase the importance of their master, entered the valuation of his rental much above the real sum. The result was disastrous to Earl Patrick, for, as the taxes increased, and were exacted upon an overstated rental, he had to pay a sum out of proportion to that contributed by his neighbours.

Many curious items of information can be gathered from the *Book of Record.* In forestry, he was ahead of his time. He gives sound advice on the planting of new timber, both for amenity and as a source of income. He calculates that the timber planted in his time at Castle Lyon would come to be worth from £6 to £12 per tree, "but reckoning them all but att three pond the piece will aryse to a sowme exceeding the worth of the heretage of ane equal yearlie rent to it".

Alluding to the grounds at Glamis, he writes about "the old chattered and decayed trees wch surrounded the house, yet there were not many, and the most of these that were, were to the southward, a comon mistake of our ancestors, whereas reasonably any thickets or planting that are about any man's house ought rather to be upon the north, north-east, and north-west".

His re-planned plantations at Glamis did not meet with the approval of the "commons who have a naturall aversione to all maner of planting, and when young timber is sett be sure they doe not faill in the night time to cut even att the root the prettiest and straightest tree's for stav's or plough goads".

Among miscellaneous items of information the following may be referred to. A tun of French wine cost £312. Taking the tun as equal to four hogsheads, or 252 gallons, this would make the price of it a little over £1 4s. 8d. per gallon. On the marriage of his niece to the son of Lord Tarbat, Lord Strathmore paid £66 13s. 4d. for "a parsell of dry sweetmeats", which are distinguished from the "wet sweetmeatts" that Lady Strathmore had in her store-room.

Where Earl Patrick writes of his purchase of silver-plate that had belonged to the Earl of Perth he quotes the current value of silver at £3 4s. per ounce, to which he adds 6s. per ounce on condition that the Perth crest is removed and the Strathmore crest engraved in its place.

He also notes the price which he paid for a cabinet for his "fyne bed-chamber", a large looking-glass for the dining-room, a table, and two glasses, all of which cost £80 sterling. Wheels for stone-carts, which were strangely enough purchased in St. Andrews, cost £4 the set. For a hundred deals purchased from a Dundee timber merchant "for the use of the church" he paid £38, and thirty twelve-ell trees used for building purposes were charged £1 each. The price of coal brought by water to the Burnmouth of Invergowrie for the supply of Castle Lyon is quoted at £26 13s. 4d. per chalder, equal to £1 13s. 4d. per boll.

There is an interval in the diary in the first half of 1685 which he explains tersely:

> I am obleidged in this place to assigne some reasone why there should be so great an intervall of time of busines and the account thereof. And its shortlie this, that much about the time of the month of March mentioned before, I went to Edr [Edinburgh] and forgott my book behind me, it had been an easie matter to have supplyed this, but that about the time of returne the first appeerance of the rebellion wch thereafter happened broke out wherein every honest man was so concerned that for most pairt they did forgoe there owne private busines as indeed it took me up no less nor nyn or ten weeks, having carryed into the west countrey the militia regiment of Angus and continued their two full weeks longer then any militia of the Kingdome having it in charge to convoy to Edr the whole spoyll of the rebell Argyll—his stor's of ammunition and warlick provision and a great many prisoners from Glasgow, and the whole train of Artilery both from Glasgow and Stirlen.

The bitter fruits of his father's and grandfather's military adventures hit Earl Patrick's finances hard enough, but he had to suffer in less degree from his own experience of the backwash of war and rebellions. He records that at the first eruption of the rebellion great quantities of meal and oats were commissioned from him for the King's army. The grain was to be stored at Stirling but before many loads had been transported there the rebels had been routed. Although the Earl had made a bargain with the Treasurer the food was no longer required and he was forced to sell the meal and oats that were already at Stirling at a considerable loss.

In one entry he refers to his confidential servant, Thomas Crombie, who acted as his secretary and wrote the first part of the *Book of Record*:

> Immediatly before the march of my regiment into the west which happened in the beginning of June Alexr ffoster of Millhill payed in to me 333 lib. 6ss. 8d. in part payt of a greater soume wch he rests me upon which I gave him receite accordingly wch money and a greate dale more in the hands o on of my servants Thomas Crombie wretter of this book was expended in our western jorney conforme to his particular accompts thereof.

There is more than a hint of a scandal within the Castle household in this entry:

> My wyfe having made this present time the terme to on Isobell Atkinson her wardroper upon an offence done betwixt her and on John Tylor who is also put away which shall be nameless and the acct. being made of all that this woman can pretend to wch is resting unpayed the same does amount to 80 lib. which is payed to her every farthing.

One wonders if John Tylor was "put away" in one of the prison cells within the walls of Glamis.

After some preliminary entries for the cost of roofs and the east bell he remarks on the occasional lapses of the invaluable Andrew Wright:

> As for the flooring lyning and sylling wch the said Andrew hes placed so liberally and att randome in his acct. without considering the quantitie of the houses or the true availl of the thing itselfe in so

much that I wounder he is not ashamed, neither am I to have the ground storry floored as he hes supposed so that this article when reduced to 133 lib. 6ss. 8d. is too much.

The foregoing entries were written by Thomas Crombie in a crabbed, indistinct style. His spelling, which varied, is given faithfully. The succeeding pages are in Earl Patrick's own clear, bold handwriting. Crombie finished his entries in 1685 when he was sent to Paris in charge of Earl Patrick's second son. Three years passed before Earl Patrick found time from public affairs to put down his thoughts and business details.

Earl Patrick, as I observed earlier, would not tolerate fools or knaves. In the course of recording the payment of that formidable total of debts, £99,866 13s. 4d., the last entry records the payment to "Mr Cheesley att Edenburgh a bas uncivil raskel on thousand two hunder pond (£1,200)". Earlier, he records the payment to Sir George Lockhart of a debt of £2,000.

These two men, by an odd coincidence, were later the central figures of a murder which shook Scotland. Furthermore, the murderer, Chiesly, was sentenced to be tortured before being executed. There are various references to executions for different crimes in Earl Patrick's diary, but this is the only reference I can find to a man being sentenced to the torture chamber.

Sir George Lockhart, the second son of Sir James Lockhart of Lee, Lord Justice-Clerk, held office under Cromwell, Charles II, James II and William III as Lord President of the Court of Session. He was made a Privy Councillor and a Commissioner of Exchequer. He enemies called him a "trimmer". His supporters claimed that he was a patriot. Be that as it may he was murdered by John Chiesly of Dalry.

The latter, according to Millar, had been a litigant in the Court of Session, and a decree was pronounced against him by Sir George Lockhart and by Lord Kemnay, awarding aliment out of his estate to his wife and ten children. Chiesly was so incensed against the Lord President that he openly avowed his intention of assassinating him. He had the hardihood to say so to Sir James Stewart of Goodtrees six months previous to the deed, and Sir

James endeavoured to dissuade him. The Lord President was informed of Chiesly's purpose but paid no heed to the warnings.

On Easter Sunday, 31st March, 1689, Chiesly loaded two pistols and sat in the choir of St. Giles' church. When the service was over the Lord President, with two friends, took his way homewards to his mansion in Old Bank Close. As he was entering his own door Chiesly levelled his pistol and shot him in the back. The bullet passed through his body, and he died almost instantly. Chiesly was seized, though he made no effort to escape and boasted of his deed.

On the following day the Convention of Estates, which had adjourned on Friday preceding and was not appointed to meet until Tuesday, was hastily summoned. Owing to the enormity of the crime they passed an Act

> . . . granting power and warrand to the magistrates of Edinburgh anent the torturing of John Chiesly of Dalrye, the actor of the horrid and inhumane murder of Sir George Lockhart, and of William Calderwood, writer, as accessory therto. In regaird of the notoriety of the murder and the execrable and extraordinary circumstances therof, the Estates do appoynt and authorise the provost and two of the bailzies in Edinburgh, and lykewayes the Earle of Erroll, lord high constable, his deputs, if the said deputs shall pleas to concurr, not only to cognosce and judge the murder, but to proceed to torture John Chiesly of Dalry, for discovering if ther were any accomplices, advysers, or assisters to him in that horrid and most inhumane act. . . . And the Estates declair that albeit in this extraordinary case they have allowed torture, yet the samen shall be no preparative or warrand to proceed to torture at any tyme hereafter, nor homologatione of what hes bein done at any tyme bypast.

Chiesly did not try to evade punishment, and on the same day —Monday, 1st April, 1689—he was hurriedly tried before Sir Magnus Price, Lord Provost of Edinburgh, and condemned to death.

He was drawn on a hurdle to the Cross. There his right hand was struck off. He was then conveyed to Drumsheugh, where he was hung in chains with the pistol tied around his neck. (Hugo

Arnot states that the place of execution was at the Gallowlee, between Edinburgh and Leith). The right hand of the murderer was stuck up on to the West Port of Edinburgh, where it remained for months.

It is worth noting that although Chiesly was sentenced to be tortured the Act made it very clear that this was not to be taken as a legal precedent for sentence of torture to be passed on anyone else at a future time. Chiesly, by the standards of his time, deserved all he got.

Earl Patrick's activities in the years 1685–8 were later fully recorded in his diary. In 1685, after the rebellion of Argyll, the Earl attempted to negotiate an agreement with the King. He hoped to propose that the estate of Kintyre, forfeited to him by Argyll as a result of a former debt to the Earl should become the possession of the Crown in exchange for his own release from the debt to Heriot's Hospital in Edinburgh.

The Earl's first attempt to win the King's favour for this project failed because his friend the Treasurer, was at this time removed from office. It was difficult enough for Earl Patrick to expiate himself from the crime of standing by the former Treasurer and an attempt to further his own cause would have been, to say the least, ill-timed.

Eventually, after frequent written appeals to the Chancellor and the Secretary, the project was accepted, an agreement was concluded and the Earl was at last released from a debt which had burdened him for a long time.

This transaction with Heriot's Hospital is explained by Millar in the following note:

> George Heriot, the founder of Heriot's Hospital, is supposed to have been a descendant of the Heriots of Trabroun in East Lothian, and of Ramornie in Fifeshire. He was born in Edinburgh in June 1563, and was trained as a goldsmith in the workshop of his father. He began business in Edinburgh as a goldsmith and money-lender, and in 1601 was appointed jeweller to James VI.
>
> When the King went to London, Heriot followed in his train, and took up his residence in Cornhill, opposite the Exchange, following his double pursuit as goldsmith and money-lender. Here he was

married for the second time, his wife being a daughter of James Primrose, Clerk to the Privy Council, who was ancestor of the Earl of Rosebery, but she did not long survive this union, dying on 16th April 1612, and leaving him childless.

It was probably this latter circumstance that led him to conceive the idea of founding an hospital similar to Christ's Hospital in London, and by his will, dated 3rd September, 1623, six months before his death, he left the residue of his property, after the payment of several legacies, to the city of Edinburgh, "To found and Erect ane publick pios and charitable worke within the said Burgh of Edinburgh To the glorie of God ffor the publict weill and ornament of the said Burghe of Edinburgh And for the honour and dwe regaird Quhilk I have and beeres to my native soyle and mother Citie of Edinburgh forsaid And In Imitation of the publict pios and religious work foundat within the Citie of London, callit Chrystis Hospitall thair To be callit in all tyme coming . . . Hospitall and Seminarie of Orphans for educatione nursing and upbringing of Youth being puir Orphans and fatherles childrene of decayit Burgesses and freemen of the said Burgh destitut and left without means."

It is supposed that the sum left for this purpose amounted to not less than £50,000 sterling. With this money ground was acquired, and Heriot's Hospital was erected. The surplus money not required for the carrying on of the Hospital was lent at 6 per cent. interest, and it seems from the *Book of Record* that the Earl of Erroll and Lord Strathmore had become cautioners [guarantors] for a considerable sum to the trustees. The method taken to pay off the interest on the cautionery is fully explained.

Earl Patrick goes on to philosophize on debts, children and faith in God before proceeding to deal with the more mundane matters of rebuilding his houses, the peccadilloes of some of his workmen and the artistic worth of others including "two English women hous painters'.

He refers a little later in the *Book of Record* to "the glorious revolution of 1688" and the cost of his son's subsequent journey to London to attend upon the new king. Earl Patrick is determined to allow no dynastic upheavals to divert him from rebuilding his castles and estates. As he himself says about the events of the time: "I only hint at these extraordinary accidents in relation to my own private business".

He relates that he had to go to Edinburgh to attend a meeting of the Council there and that his stay cost him a great deal of money. Although he was appointed by the Council to attend the Prince of Orange in London, "the King having wtdrawn himself and gone beyond seas", he made an excuse not to go because the expedition would involve too much expense, "since I cannot in my humour easily refuse the temptation of buying". Instead the Council signed an address to the Prince and Earl Patrick's eldest son accompanied it to London. Money had to be borrowed to finance his trip but, the Earl remarks, "it may be hoped that it may be refounded again out of the treasury".

Earl Patrick goes on to expostulate on the uncertainty of the world and of human affairs. The Earl of Perth, Lord Chancellor, he says, from being the First Minister of State is now a prisoner in the Castle of Stirling "and his doers glad to convoy away the best of his goods, and dispose of them privatly".

After several entries relating to debts and payments and everyday affairs he gives a rare insight into his system of letting his farms and choosing his tenants, with engaging sidelights upon the characters of some such as "that infamous rascall, Mr. Thos. Wilson" or John Morris to whom he gives preference for a farm called "The Raws":

> This roume [farm] of Francis Grahams in the Raws I have sett to John Moreis a young man, and have accepted of ane hundreth merks of entry from him. I was the rather induced to be favourable to him because that his father, grandfather, and forbeirs have been ther since the memory of man, and Francis Graham had possession of it only as marrying his mother.

That business transactions were no less complicated in Lord Strathmore's time than they are today is evident from the following extract:

> When I sold the lands of Bakie to that infamous rascall Mr. Thos.

Wilson, I accepted of A debt due to him by one Capt. Wilson in the Grange of Aberbothrie and after some difficulty in't I attained to the possession of the roume wch continued so for divers years. Yet this thing was not to be coverted, so that I granted his son a reversion upon the payt of four thousand merks. Nether am I so nyce in the mater but accepts of partial payts. Some years ago he payed 666 lib. 13ss. 4d. yrof and yesternight eight hundreth pound so yt now ther remains unpaid only the soume of twelve hundreth pound scots. I continew in the possession of the roume and allows Wilson @ rent for the money he has made partiall payts of. My factor James Cuper must cleare accts. wt him about the @ rents of this four thousand merks wch were owent before I setled wt the son, and for wch the old fellow was put in prison.

Further on in the diary there is an interesting story about a former servant of the Earl's, one Francis Erskyne. It appears that this "infamous rascall", having been discharged from Strathmore's service, went around for over a year extracting money from people on the pretext of being in the Earl's employ, saying that "his money had fall'ne short". The Earl was obliged to imprison him in order to let everyone know that Erskyne was no longer his servant; but after a year in prison he broke out. By this time his elder brother had died and he had become heir to his father's (Lord Kirkbuddo's) money. Desirous to make his peace with Strathmore he went to an advocate trusted by the Earl, one Patrick Lyon, and gave a bond that he would pay back the money he owed. "And", says the Earl, "when the old man his father dyes [I] will persue him wtout mercy for it".

The diary continues with various mundane matters from the Countess's allowance and rent paid by the tenants to the following details:

I did ourreike two horse in Angus and one in Perthshyre for the levy of horse and had difficulty enow in pleasing the officers, wt ther ryders and arms.

I bought a dun gelding from Millfeild and 18 lib. for him to my son Pat.

I bought other two horses for service the one at 2 lib. ster. for the sadle and the other at 3 lib. for the cart from G. Henderson.

I gave a precept to Mr. Rankyne Catechist in Dundee for a years interest of 5000 merks, being 200 lib. scots, on John Nicholl Mossgreive.

Thus, on a humdrum note of buying horses and paying out monies, ends, on 1st June, 1689, one of the most revealing day-to-day diaries of life and work on a great Scottish estate, written by a man whose character shines with warm light down the aisles of Scottish history.

15

LIFE AT GLAMIS TODAY—AND YESTERDAY

"LIFE at Glamis is verra simple, the Family revolves as you might say round the Castle, the village and its people, the Church and then the farms and woods, rod and gun. Always good landlords. Always the friends of their ain people. There was never a bad Bowes-Lyon yet. I should know, I've watched 'em grow up and die for the last seventy years or more."

George Fairweather, the retired headkeeper, a tall, spare, steely-eyed man with a clipped moustache, sat back in his armchair by his cottage fire and delivered that pithy summing-up. It was not far short of the mark.

Outside, the rain lashed the windows of the Keepers Croft at Ballinshoe. A cloud of peewits and curlews wailed and whistled over a flooded ploughland. Far woods stood black against low hills dappled with snow. Up the road, bare and windowless to the winds, a ruined pele tower waited for the raiders who never come.

Fairweather spoke lovingly of old days with the gun when the world was young and famous men now dead were his companions on moor and bog, on the stubble and on the hill. There was that epic day, 18th October, 1936, when, at Colliedrum, Fairweather and his little army of beaters put a lot of partridges into a wild, rough place of bracken, broom and whins:

"We had six or seven drives", said he. "And, believe me, the guns got 550 partridges—our record bag. There was His Royal Highness the Duke of York, the late Lord Strathmore, Lord Glamis, Lord Granville, Lord Elphinstone, Admiral Leveson-Gower, Colonel Michael Bowes-Lyon and Mr. David Bowes-Lyon. A bright, brisk day it was, with quite a wind. I had about twenty beaters and nearly all the partridges we killed were English birds. I used to rear them under the Euston system.

"We've reared no pheasants for years, but I mind a rare day when we shot over 300 wild pheasants walking them up in wet bogs. Those birds, believe it or not, never roosted in a tree. In fact they never saw a tree. They roosted at night on the laid rushes on the bare bog. We got all sorts—Chinese, Black-necks, ringnecks, Melanistic and Mongolians. The best bag in my time, covert-shooting, was about 350 pheasants.

"But what Lord Strathmore liked and the Duke of York particularly loved was a rough day of hard walking with from two to four guns only.

"I mind the day on the Hayston beat on the 27th October, 1936, when four guns, Lord Dalhousie, Colonel Michael Bowes-Lyon, the Hon. James Stuart and Lord Granville, killed 191 head —a little of everything. That included forty-five pheasants, twenty-five partridges, twenty-two woodcock, seven grouse, one blackcock, sixteen hares, sixty rabbits, nine pigeons and half a dozen golden plover. Aye—that *was* a day!

"We never have killed a lot of grouse. There was a little moor then, less than 500 acres, near here at Ballinshoe, but now it's been reclaimed and all down to grass. Before they did that, I mind the day when King George VI and Lord Strathmore killed thirty-five brace between them from a couple of butts."

"What about duck and wild geese," I asked. "You must get a lot of them in the right weather."

"Aye, we do," he answered. "I mind one morning seeing the geese rise like thunder from the barley-stubble and they came over us darkenin' the air. Thousands of them. I said to Lord Strathmore: 'You'd be better off with a catapult, My Lord.'

"Then there was one morning, it would be about the winter of '34–'35, when Lord Glamis, Mr. Michael, Mr. David and Lord Elphinstone got up at three in the morning and I rowed them in a boat out to four reed-butts in the middle of the flight pond at Glamis. They were in their places before dawn. They got 95 duck between them at that morning flight—mallard, teal, goldeneye, widgeon and tufted duck. The greylag and pink-feet geese use the pond at night. They come into it to rest and wash and have a drink after feeding on the arable fields. I've known the present Lord Strathmore and a friend kill nine geese in an evening.

"This pond was made about 1929 by damming up a running ditch and flooding ten or twelve acres of low, marshy ground. Mr. Michael worked on that dam like a beaver. He used to go off early in the morning with a shovel on his shoulder, his lunch in his pocket, and work at it like a navvy all day and then come crawling home in the dusk, smothered in mud and dead-tired. He used to dry himself by the fire in the brushing-room and then brush himself down before he dare face his mother!

"After that morning when we got the 95 duck, we went up to Hayston Hill in the Sidlaws and got seventy-five brace of grouse. That'd be a fair average bag. It just topped up a grand day.

"We used to get a lot of snipe around the Forfar Loch before Lord Strathmore sold it to Forfar town. King George VI was mad on snipe. Many a time I took him out to shoot driven snipe on the sewage farm where he would get thirty brace in a day without much trouble.

"I mind one day when we were shooting the Loch. There were a'many snipe but they all flew straight for the road, fifty or sixty yards away. An old man stood there, gaping at us like a loon. I waved him to move on but he wudna. Then the Duke put down his gun, looked me straight in the eye and burst out laughing.

" 'Every time I put up my gun, Fairweather', he said, 'that old idiot is looking straight down the barrels at me. Go and drown the old b—— in the loch.'

"The next shooting season the Duke comes back to Glamis and is all for a day after snipe on the loch. So into the Land Rover we got and away to the loch. A dirty, wet, blowy day, but just fit for snipe. We shot all day round the loch, His Royal Highness killed sixteen brace of snipe and then when it got dusk we were away home to the Castle. Later that night I sent the game card up to Lord Strathmore. He studied it, looked a bit serious and then sent for Ralston, the factor, and said: 'Where did Fairweather take His Royal Highness today?'

"Ralston said that he thought we had been up the Forfar Loch. Lord Strathmore turned to the Duke and said: 'You've been poaching all day. I sold that bog-land months ago to Forfar.'

"He rang up the Provost of Forfar right away and apologized for the mistake as I had not been told that the place had been sold. 'His Royal Highness can come and shoot the loch any day he likes. We'll be only too honoured,' the Provost replied.

"After that the Duke always used to say to me, even when he was King: 'What about another day's poaching together, Fairweather?'

"The Queen Mother is a good shot with a gun or a rifle. Many a good stag she has to her credit at Balmoral and many is the time she has been out with the guns at Glamis. I mind the day when King George VI was at a Masonic meeting in Glamis. The Queen was in the Castle. A reporter comes nosing round to me and says: 'Did her Majesty accompany the King to the village?'

" 'No,' I said. I was always short with the Press.

" 'What is she doing then?' the nosey man asks me.

" 'Out shooting,' I told him.

" 'What did she shoot?'

" 'A splendid bag o' craws,' I told him.

"Next day, believe it or not, out comes the newspaper with a report which said just this: 'Her Majesty did not accompany the King, but went out with the gun and made a splendid bag of rooks on her own.' "

I asked about badgers, foxes, hares and capercaillie.

"Caper? Aye, we have them. Not a lot, eight in a day would be a good bag, but that minds me of a day at Drummond Castle when they shot thirty in a day. There had been a tinkers' camp in a glen and they had left a lot of crusts of bread, potato peelings and the like lyin' about. The caper came down into the glen in droves to feed on the garbage.

"Badgers—we have a few, but hundreds of foxes. Far too many of them. We killed 52 foxes in one season and 49 the next year. There are roe-deer in the woods, but none too many. I mind when the Italian prisoners were here during the Second World War, I found a wire noose dangling from a stiff wire which hung from a tree branch about three feet above the ground. There was a roe-deer dead in it. Those fellows would have anything.

"We used to ring a lot of woodcock in my time. They breed on the place. So every keeper was given a box of rings and told to fix them on the legs of the chicks when they found any. About ten per cent of them would be recovered from all over Scotland and England and, occasionally, away over in Europe.

"Aye, they were grand days," he sighed. "And we were all as happy as larks. Would you believe me if I tell you now, that after a day's shooting the King's yellow Labrador bitch, Joan, would always go into the boot room at the Castle, wet and muddy, dry herself by the fire and then stand there like a statue until the valet had brushed her down from head to foot. You believe me, now?" I assured him that I did.

"Aye! Well ye'know what they say to a liar in Glamis village when he tells a tall tale. They juist look him in the eye and say: 'Och, away to the Stone Men at the Castle gates, laddie, an' tell them your yarn. They'll no answer you or deny you."

I left the old keeper in the glow of dusk, sitting in his armchair with a bundle of letters from Princess Margaret clasped in his hands and pictures of the Royal Family and the Strathmores on the mantlepiece.

I got back to the Castle in the windy glow of a gold and scarlet sunset, with the wild geese clanging overhead and as I rounded the angle of the kitchen garden wall, a couple of woodcock flashed by like arrows and nearly took my hat off. That crowned the day.

That evening, poring over household papers in the Charter Room, I came across records of wages paid to maidservants a century or more ago. Jessie Robertson was paid £1 13s. 4d. for three months' work in 1854, whilst Mary Ann Piggott got £4 for half a year, Isabella Brown received £13 for half a year, but a little girl called Ann Gittens in 1851 received only £3 12s. 1½d. for her six months. It should be remembered, however, that they were fed, housed, clothed and well looked after whilst the pound was worth eight or ten times its present-day value. Generation after generation, village maids came to the Castle in their teens to learn cooking and housekeeping, butchering, mending and sewing, cleaning and polishing, how to lay a table, laundry work and the rest of the infinite tasks of a great household. Such tuition was worth a dozen modern courses in so-called domestic science. The result was that they made first-class wives. The competition in the village to get the rising generation "into service" at the Castle was terrific.

Today, as I have said elsewhere, the place is run on a shoe-string, with about four resident servants and a string of "dailies" on tap.

There are sixty tenanted farms on the estate, a lot of woodland, about four acres of kitchen garden and a good deal of house property. The total rent roll is about £20,000 a year from 20,000 acres of land. Most of that goes in upkeep, wages, estate repairs. When the Castle roof was repaired the year before I was there, it cost £8,000. The upkeep of the State Rooms which are open to the public is about £3,000 a year, just met by the 25,000 visitors who pay to see them. Rates on the enormous Castle are a mere £265 a year. Staff wages average £1,500 a year.

Mr. James Kemp, the factor, has a full-time job helping to administer the property. Farm rents, he told me, average about £2 an acre for good mixed farms which in England would command £6 to £8 an acre or more. Hill land is let at from 5s. an acre upwards according to quality. Farmers' shoots are held every year when the hares are given a good dusting. About 150 will be killed in a day on the Mains of Glamis.

Thus Glamis as an entity keeps its head above water—only just. There is little money to spare, but no cottage roof leaks and annually large sums are spent on modernizing them, as well as the farm-houses, buildings and field drains, fences and farm roads.

The great days of splendid entertainment have gone, probably for ever. Fairweather summed it up in a phrase:

"I've seen the big dining-room full at night with Royalty, the nobility and gentry, with the two pipers marching bravely round the table, piping the auld tunes. They were my eldest brother, William, then head-keeper, and Alec Craig, a forester who was the Pipe-major of the Glamis Pipe Band. Aye, a brave show it was and a'."

Today, many rooms in the Castle, especially those on the upper storeys, are unfurnished. "There was a sale some years ago", Lord Strathmore told me, "when a lot of furniture was sold. Any number of good things went dirt-cheap."

The parish church at Glamis is very much the spiritual heart and soul of the district. Its history begins in the mists of the eighth century when St. Fergus, who was a Bishop in Ireland, came to Perthshire and founded the three churches of Strogeth, Blackford and Dolpatrick. After that he went north to Caithness to try to convert the barbarous tribes of that land of flat moors, rolling hills and misty marshes. Then he visited Buchan where he built a basilica at Lungley which he dedicated to himself.

Glamis was his next stopping place. There he consecrated a tabernacle and died a shadowy, revered figure of glory. His bones were buried in a tomb of marble. His head was conveyed with great honour to the monastery of Scone "where many miracles were performed". At Glamis a cave and a well are named after him. In a little grotto in the rocky sides of the Den of Glamis, overhung with sedges and ferns, is a well of water. In it he baptized the first Christian converts in Strathmore. His cave-home, collapsed some years ago. The well of dew-clear water is a sparkling link with the ancient Celtic Church of Scotland. The Glamis Burn whispers over its rocky bed, singing the same quiet tunes of water which it sang twelve hundred years ago. From the bank above the well one can see the tower of the ancient church around which sleep many generations of the men and women of Strathmore.

There is a fascinating entry in the accounts of the Lord High Treasurer of Scotland more than five and a half centuries ago which throws light on the legend that the head of St. Fergus was taken to Scone and that King James IV paid for repairs to the silver box in which it was enshrined.

The King, accompanied by Pate Sinclair, the Squire of Cleish, Alexander Law and Willie Strang, falconers, the four Italian minstrels and the "More Taubroner", Andrew Stewart, the Duke of Albany's son, and others set out from Dunfermline upon his usual autumn pilgrimage to the shrine of St. Duthus at Tain, on

11th October, 1504. On reaching Perth (St. Johnstoun), the King made gifts of 11s. to the "Gray Freris of Sanct Johnestoun", of 13s. to the "preistis there", and of 28s. to the "Blak Freres and Quhit Freris there". He also got his hat mended in Perth and bought a new pair of gloves as witness—"Item, To Thomas Boswell to by taffeti to the Kingis hat in Sanct Johnstoun . . . xixs." "Item, to ane man brocht gluffis to the King in Sanct Johnestoun be the Kingis command . . . ixs." The King then visited Scone—"Item, to the masons of Scone, in drink silver be the Kingis command. . . ." At the same time he made an offering of 14s. for the repair of the silver case containing St. Fergus's head—"Item, to the Kingis offerand to Sanct Fergus hede, in Scone . . . xiiijs." Again in 1506 we find that on 28th September the King made a similar offering—"Item, the xxvij day of September, to the Kingis offerand to Sanct Fergus hede in Scone . . . xviijs [18s.]."

The Reverend John Stirton, Senior Minister of Crathie and a Chaplain to the late King George VI, who was an outstanding authority on the ecclesiastical history of Glamis cast academic doubt upon the legend of St. Fergus as it stands. In his book on Glamis he says:

> Reviewing the legend in the light of the contemporary evidence, we are forced to the conclusion that there were several saints of the name of Fergus, and that the life experiences of these various saints have been all mixed up and applied to the Fergus of Glamis, according to the fashion of the Roman Church, of a later time, and for reasons of her own.

A stone in front of the Manse of Glamis was raised in memory of St. Fergus some time after his death and, possibly, near the spot where he was buried. This stone shows all the lovely features of the Celtic stones of the ninth or early tenth century and embodies a beautiful Celtic cross. The three cusps at the junctions of the arms of the cross are unique. Various symbols embodying human beings, a centaur, animals, fish and a reptile are engraved on the stone.

The Glamis Stone once stood in the churchyard when the latter was much larger. Dr. Stirton believed that the present Manse stands on part of the graveyard since "relics of burials were found (in the 1930s) near the Manse gate and beneath the road that runs between the Manse and the Church".

Some years before Dr. Stirton went to Glamis part of an old Celtic stone was found in a grave in the old churchyard. Part of a Celtic cross of interlaced work was engraved on it. Dr. Stirton put the relic behind the mortuary chapel as part of the church possessions. Someone removed it.

Other stone fragments with Celtic work engraved on them were found on the church floor during renovation work in the 1930s. These fragments emphasize the fact that here in the churchyard of Glamis Christian worship has been held and communion celebrated for twelve hundred years, without stop, from the days of St. Fergus to the present time.

Dr. Stirton wrote:

> We can picture the saint in the long dress of the ecclesiastic, richly embroidered, in loose short boots, and carrying a crosier and book-satchel, as portrayed on the fragment of a Celtic stone of large size at St. Vigeans, with head tonsured after the Roman fashion. The tonsure of the Celtic Church was from ear to ear, in a semi-circle over the frontal portion of the head, and this was one of the points in which the Church of our forefathers differed from the prevailing custom of European Christendom. The Celtic Church, however, adopted the coronal tonsure of the European Church in the first half of the eighth century. No doubt the saint sent out many clerics besides St. Drosten to neighbouring glens and hills to impress Christian truth upon the minds of the simple dwellers, as Forfarshire or Angus is peculiarly rich in relics of that Celtic period.

No record exists to tell what the Church of Glamis as a building was like at that time, but it would be Celtic, with certain Romanesque features. This style of architecture was quite peculiar to the Celtic people. None of the buildings were large, though many were of great beauty and elegance. Their interest lies in their singularly local character and in their age, which probably extended from the fifth or sixth century to the eleventh century in Scotland. No church of this period is perhaps even sixty feet in length, and generally they are very much smaller, the most common dimensions being from twenty to forty feet. The favourite number for a complete ecclesiastical establishment was seven, as in Greece, this number being identical with that of the seven Apocalyptic Churches of Asia.

None of the earliest churches were Basilicas, being undivided into aisles, either by stone or wooden pillars, or possessing an apse, and no circular church has yet been found.

The Celtic Church in Glamis no doubt stood on the site of the present church, as it was the unfailing custom after the Norman Conquest to build new and more elaborate Norman buildings in the Romanesque style, and later still in the Gothic manner, on the same spot rendered sacred by the worship of former Celtic generations.

An edifice in the neighbourhood, of the period of St. Fergus and combining both Celtic and Romanesque features, probably gives an indication of what the early church of Glamis was like in appearance. At Restenneth, within six or seven miles of Glamis, a church was bult in the eighth century, contemporary with the lift of St. Fergus. All that remains of this ancient church—most probably the oldest in Scotland—is the lower portion of the tower which bears distinct evidence of its Celtic origin, as well as displaying some characteristics of the style known as Romanesque.

Restenneth was closely connected with Glamis in very early days. Glamis was then a Royal residence of the Kings of Scotland who granted many charters therefrom to Restenneth. These charters covered the period from King Malcolm Canmore to Robert the Bruce—whose son was bured at Restenneth—and David II. For centuries a number of twelfth-century charters concerning Restenneth and its mother church at Jedburgh were stored in the Charter Room at Glamis. They disappeared mysteriously some years ago. I searched the Charter Room thoroughly with the faint hope that an early charter might still be hidden among the mass of documents. I could find none.

The church at Glamis was appanage of the Abbey of Arbroath

from the twelfth century until the beginning of the Reformation. King Robert the Bruce when in residence in Forfar in 1322 confirmed by a charter the gift of "Glammis" to the Abbey of Arbroath.

The most interesting building in Glamis churchyard is the Aisle or Chantry Chapel. This Chapel was built by Isabella Ogilvy, wife of Patrick Lyon, the first Lord Glamis. He died in 1459 and she died in 1484. Both are buried in the Chapel. The family vault of the House of Strathmore is under the pavement of the Chapel. Many of the family have been buried there for the past 400 years.

The Chapel is fifteenth-century Gothic, just over 35 feet long, 26½ feet wide and 17 feet in height to the top of the arch. It is lit by one fifteenth-century Gothic window. A stone lion sits on the roof above the window holding a shield. Beneath it on the wall is a dial dated 1771. At the other end of the roof sits a stone griffin bearing a shield which displays a lion rampant. The Chapel is in good repair but is not used for services nowadays.

Patrick, first Lord Glamis, was, incidentally, one of the hostages sent to England as security for the ransom of James I of Scotland. In front of his tomb lies a stone slab, let into the floor. This is the tombstone of John, third Lord Glamis, who died on 1st April, 1497, and his wife Elizabeth Scrymgeour of Dudhope.

When one stands in silence in this small but beautiful Chapel Sir Walter Scott's description of Roslin Chapel comes eloquently to mind: "There are twenty Barons bold lie buried within this proud chapelle. . . . Each Baron for a sable shroud sheathed in his iron panoply; and each was buried there with Candle, with Book, and with Knell".

It is easy to imagine the early scenes of worship in this ancient chapel, the soft light glowing with the splendour of vestments. The swinging of censers, scent of incense and the solemn chanting seem to linger even today.

> Still in the Kirk the mass was sung
> With small bells ringing and censers swung,
> Still bowed the priest before the pyx,

The altar high and crucifix:
And still the grand old psalm
Pealed through the pillared calm.

For long the Abbots of Arbroath appointed a Chaplain to the church whilst they drew the revenues. The Lords of Glamis did not approve. From time to time they made various "mortifications" to endow the chaplains.

Finally, John, seventh Lord Glamis, bought the whole teinds of the parish from Cardinal Beaton, the perpetual commendator of the Abbey of Arbroath. Robert Boyd was the first minister to be appointed to the living of Glamis after the Reformation. That was in 1567 and his stipend was one hundred merks, otherwise £5 11s. 1½d. a year. His successor, John Nevay, was better off with a stipend of £8 6s. 8d. with the Kirk lands.

There followed a succession of ministers, most of them men of considerable academic qualifications. They were on close and friendly terms with the family at the Castle.

I like the entry in Earl Patrick's diary in which, speaking of John Lammie of Dunkennie, brother of the Reverend Silvester Lammie, who was presented to the living of Glamis in 1625, he says:

> There was on Lammie of Dunkennie good for telling of old stories, and a familiar friend in the house who I cannot tell how transported in the time, but made a shift to spend up his owne litle estate. My father still engaging for him till his debts exceeded the double of the worth of the estate. It was then sold, and what the estate did not pay of his debt, my father behooved to pay being ingaged for it; which did not serve, but my father also gratified him and his wyfe with a pension of fiftie bolls of victual. His brother was minister of Glammiss, which has not such a provisone as could inrich any man, but such were the advantages, these had, who were constantlie about my father, that he without any visible cause made a shift to purchase bonds of my father so as he obtained a wedsett for his money from my Tutor, Bridgton, to the value of Balnamoon, and sixth part of Drumgley, with which his son, I having redeemed these wedsetts, hes again made a purchase of his uncle's lands.

George Middleton, a seventeenth-century minister of Glamis, who preached his farewell sermon there in January 1685, died in 1686 at the age of eighty-two, having been minister for fifty-nine years. His widow, Janet, lived to be a hundred and one and had fourteen sons and four daughters.

The first volume of the register of Kirk Session which begins in 1677 gives pretty little insights into the life of the church, castle and village:

September 24, 1685.—Sermon by Mr. Thomas Small, moderator, upon the 13 Heb., 17 verse, which day Mr. John Balvaird was admitted to the ministry at Glammis with the unanimous consent of the whole congregation.

September 27, 1685.—Which day ye minister enquyred after the number of ye elders whose names are as follows:

Frederick Lyon.	James Cathro.
Thomas Abbot.	James Blair.
John Low.	James Horne.
Thomas Kinmont.	George Porter.
John Nicoll.	Andrew Chaplin.
John Smith.	John Philip.

October 11, 1685.—Which day the minister caused reckon ye money of the church box, and there was found in it ane guinea of gold with thirtie three shillings Scots.

July 22, 1689.—No sermon this day but reading, the minister being absent to assist the minister of Kirkden at his communion.

The second Earl Patrick, who stamped his strong personality on Glamis, was a deeply religious man. He took a close interest in the church. Like the castle it badly needed repair. This entry in the *Book of Record* speaks for itself:

Att the Church I have made a loft for my owne use, and built a little addition to my burial place both wch contribute extremelie to the adornment of the Church, besydes three other lofts that I made therein, yet the Church stands uncompleit for the time by reasone of the Laird of Claveres [Claverhouse] interest in the parish, who does not contribut his help for makeing other two lofts betwixt the pillars on the southsyd as well as it is done upon the north.

Relics belonging to the Church date from this period to restoration. The old Poores Box, 1688; the Pulpit Bible, bought for £16 Scots in 1689; and the Communion Chalices, 1676.

The Session Register contains entries of payments made for work done at the Church.

The following list is interesting:

November 15, 1685.—Given by Frederick Lyon, in Arnafoull, for his wyffe's burial place in ye Church, 06-13-04.

January 3, 1686.—Given to John ———, measone, for fixing a knock in the back door of ye Church, 2/8.

February 2, 1686.—Given for a new Sessione Book, 4/8.

March 14, 1686.—To Catherine Hill for soap to wash ye communion table cloaths, 4/8.

Apryll 4, 1686.—Given to James Tylor, measone, for pavementing of the Church floore, being a week's work, three pounds, sax shillings, eight pennies.

Given to the Church Officer for serveing the measone, 12/8.

Given to ye Glaisior for mending ye church windows, 3/8.

Apryll 13, 1686.—Given for timber for the communion tables, 7/8.

May 2, 1686.—Given for aill to the wrights who erected ye communion tables, two pounds.

December 21, 1689.—Given to my Lord's Chamberlain for a chest to keep the mortcloath in, £1, Scots.

Apryll 10, 1692.—Given to Andrew Wright for leather to the pulpit, £2-3-8, which he is obliged to pay to the merchant. Given to Apolonea Kirkheis for colouring the pulpit, £4-4-8.

Item for nails to the pulpit, £2-18-8.

May 15, 1692.—Given by my Lady of Glammis ane guinea of gold, it being her first entrie to ye Church.

June 19, 1692.—Given to Thomas Spalding for furnishing silk and buttons to the velvet mortcloath, and for his workmanship, 10/8.

December 11, 1692.—Given to William Johnston for mending the west window of the Church, 6/8.

May 27, 1694.—Given for a new tow to the bell, 14/8.

Given to William Johnston for making up the great window on the west end of the Church, £8-13-8.

Andrew Wright, the local joiner, did most of the alterations to the Church. When he sent in his bill he charged for the rectification of one of his own mistakes. Lord Strathmore, who employed him to do the work, wrote opposite the entry: "Because he made the reeders seat *wrong*, it is just to give him nothing for making it *right*."

Earl Patrick was a friend of the poor. No man or woman went hungry on his land. There is in existence a deed drawn up about 1693 in draft form which for some reason was never put into practice. In this draft he set out his wish to build four almshouses near the Kirktoun of Glamis "for the use of four aged men of his own surname if they could be found, and failing them, to such decayed tenants as had been reduced to want not through their own faults", to each of whom he intended to mortify yearly four bolls of oatmeal and twenty-five merks, Scots money, with "a new whyt coloured wid cloath coat lyned with blue serge once every three years".

He desired that these four men should attend the parish church and "wait always at the Church door when we goe there, and at their own dores whenever we shall have occasion to pass by, if they be not employed abroad . . . and that they shall be holden (if sickness and infirmity do not hinder) to repair everie day once at the twalt hour of the day to our buriall place (whereof a key shall be given to each incomer), and a form of prayer to be read by them by turns by such of then as can read, and if they cannot read, that they learn the same by heart." Earl Patrick wished to form this little institution as a mark of gratitude to Providence for blessings and mercies received.

In 1695 the Church was seated with fixed pews. Hitherto stools or "creepies", as they were called, had been used by the worshippers, although many came without them and had to stand during the service. Pews were seldom seen in Scottish churches until the eighteenth century. Glamis must have been one of the earliest to adopt them. Andrew Wright, the joiner, who had already proved his skill, was commissioned to carry out the work:

> Apryll 19, 1695.—Given to Andrew Wright twentie pound Scots, which with four-score pounds he received before, made up in hoill ane hundred pounds Scots, which compleets his hoill payment for the new pews in the Church with there back pannels, and repairing the Stooll of Repentance with the end of the west loft, the pews being formed as follows: Forasmuch as the Church Session att Glammiss have at there charge erected several new seats in the said Church, and that it is just and equitable that this advancement should not only be refounded but improven to some advantage by making out some constant rent to return yearly to the publick box.

Seat rents thus instituted were imposed for a long period in Glamis. The custom is no longer followed.

The "Stooll of Repentance" throws a bright light on the habits of the young men and maidens of Glamis. Few remained maidens for long. Many a babe was "got in the heather". Dr. Stirton blandly remarks:

> At that time immorality was very common in the parish, and a constant and watchful vigilance was exercised by the church over all offenders, who had to pay fines graded according to the seriousness of the offence, the lowest being £4 Scots. The guilty had to stand at the pillory, which was a raised wooden platform in front of the pulpit, and clothed in sackcloth they were thereupon publicly rebuked and exhorted to penitence by the minister. Sometimes the "Stooll of Repentance" was requisitioned for the same purpose. To stand on the Stool was a sign of penitence, and immediately afterwards the offenders received the rebuke, and, if regarded necessary "the wee sermon" or exhortation.
>
> There are many notices in the session records of delinquents appearing "on the pillory" and "in sackcloth" at the Church, and being obliged to pay heavy fines for their offences.

Churchgoing in those days was a dreary business. It was not only a pilgrimage but a penance. At ten o'clock on Sunday morning the people of Castle and village were roused by the ringing of the "first bell". The "second bell" rang when the congregation were assembling in the Church. The reader then gave out a psalm. The congregation stood up and sang it. Then the "third bell" began to ring. The minister, hat on head, climbed into his pulpit.

He made a low bow to the Earl in his loft. If any other members of the family were present he bowed to them also. The Earl and his family then stood up and bowed elaborately to the minister. After that the service began.

The men in the congregation took their caps or bonnets off for the first part of the service, but put them on when the sermon or "lecture" began. The church service consisted of a prayer, a lecture or a Bible subject, a second prayer, then a sermon of intolerable length, followed by a third prayer, the singing of a psalm and, finally, the benediction.

The Earl and his family remained in their loft where a meal was served to them in the interval between the morning service and the afternoon service.

The rest of the congregation went home to their cottages, if they lived in the village, for a little cheese and beer. No food could be cooked on a Sunday. Others who came from far glens and moorland crofts either went to the change-house or sat it out in church, eating the victuals they had brought with them.

The schoolmaster led the singing of the psalms and chanted over each line of each psalm for the benefit of those who could not read.

Dr. Stirton gives an enchanting picture of a typical congregation of farmers, ploughmen, artisans and estate workers with their families:

> The men wore bonnets and plaids of rough homespun, with knee breeches, hose and brogues, the women were attired in mutches, plain gowns of home-spun, and woollen shawls or plaids of bright colours which sometimes were drawn over their heads. The noble proprietor and the other lairds would be conspicuous by the elegance of dress then fashionable among gentlemen of quality. Their full-bottomed wigs and three-cornered hats, coats of rich

material and braided with gold, swords by their sides, long jack-boots and gold-headed canes, all would form a marked contrast to the simple attire of the homely villagers.

The ladies, too, were not behind their lords, but rather surpassed them in the gaiety of their costume. The Countess of Strathmore in a superb dress of green and gold with two pages bearing her train was a sufficiently impressive and awe-inspiring figure herself, not to speak of the others in their bright scarlet silken plaids, wonderful lofty head-dresses, hoops and powder. No wonder that a traveller of the period who made a journey through Scotland then said that a "Scots Church was like a parterre of flowers".

Many entries in the church register naturally refer to the family from the Castle:

July 12, 1699.—Which day the Right Honourable the Earl of Strathmore presented his son to baptism, and named him Charles, witnesses, the Rt. Hon. the Laird of Auchterhouse, Mr. Alex. Maitland, brother German to the Earle of Lauderdale, the Laird of Powrie, with many other honourable witnesses. Ye noble chyld was born the night immediately preceding, about eight of the clock.

Apryle 29, 1701.—Which day Alexander and Margaret Lyon, twins, lawful children to John Lyon, Factor to ye Earle of Strathmore, baptised, witnesses, John Hood in Little Cossins, and Patrick Lyon, unquil to the children.

November 7, 1703.—After sermon in the Castle by the minister there was collected 14 pounds Scots for the poor.

November 19, 1704.—After sermon in the Castle there was collected 14 pounds Scots for the poor again.

Apryle 24, 1707.—Pews payed, John Lyon, late Factor to the late Earl of Strathmore, two pews lying upon north side of church of Glammiss. Catherine Lyon, lawful daughter to John, Earle of Strathmore baptised upon the 17th day of this month. Witnesses, Rt. Hon. the Laird of Auchterhouse, the Laird of Powrie, with many other honourable witnesses.

May 1, 1712.—The which day the Laird of Kaim, having spoke unto the minister concerning a seat in the church of Glammiss for himself, his familie, and tennants, and having claimed the whole loft on the north side of the Church, next adjacent to the Earle of

Strathmore his loft, as his proper seat belonging to him as portioner of Denoon Easter, the minister having imparted the same to the foresaid Earle to whom the other half of the foresaid lands of Denoon Easter belonged, and likewise to the Church Sessione of Glammiss anent the foresaid claim. The Earle and Church Sessione after consideration do allow the foresaid Laird of Kaim, for his interest in Dennon Easter, being the half of the fors'd lands, the first seat in the foresaid loft and the third falling in number behind it, and therefore it is hereby declared that onlie the first proportion of the above-mentioned loft belongs to the said Laird of Kaim, and the rest of the loft to the Earle of Strathmore as heretor and possessor of the other half of the fors'd lands. This enacted in the Church Sessione of Glammiss by the Earle's allowance insert in the sessione book.

December 14, 1712.—Payd by Robert Mitchell for trees growing in the Church yard of Glammiss, which he bought by roup £22-20/. Paid by George Maxwell for his pew 12 shillings, also by Patrick Lyon for his pew in the Church of Glammiss, also by Agnes Brown for her pew there 10 shillings, also by Patrick Mitchell for his pew there 6 shillings, also by Alexander Skene for his pew there 12 shill. Scots, which pays all byegones to them preceding Whit-sunday in the present year 1712, and accordingly they all received their discharge.

May 24, 1713.—For the new velvet mortcloath out off the Paroch, £2.

June 16, 1714.—After prayer at the Castle, collected for the poor, £00-13-6.

December 5, 1714.—After sermon at the Castle, collected, for ye poor there, 17.shill. Scots.

The Jacobite Rising of "the Fifteen" had its repercussions in Glamis Church. For three years, 1716–19, there were no elders of the Kirk. The records give no reason. The best guess is that the elders had gone out in the Strathmore Company to fight for the Stewart cause. The Church of Scotland was strictly Hanoverian so the elders probably resigned office before shouldering their muskets.

The rising of the "Forty-five" had sterner results in the church life of Glamis. The Church decided rigorously to stamp out any possible outbreak on behalf of Prince Charles Edward. After rebellion broke out the Presbytery of Forfar issued this set of questions which all ministers had to put to the members of their Kirk sessions:

October 5, 1746.—The Session being met and constituted by prayer, the minister represented yt an act of ye General Assembly having been laid before the Presbytery of Forfar at their last meeting enjoining the several members to enquire into the part of different members of ye several kirk-sessions, that having aided during ye late unnatural rebellion, the Presbytery in obedience unto this order agreed upon a set of questions to be put to ye members of ye severall kirk-sessions, and appointed their anwers to be recorded, and for that purpose appointed their several members to hold a meeting of their several sessions betwixt it and next Presbytery day, and to be ready to give in their deposition at that time. The minister, therefore, signified that he had called a meeting of the session this day for the end aforesaid, and having read over the questions agreed upon by the Presbytery, the same were put to each of the members, and are with their answers as follows accordingly, George Doig being first interrogated.

1 Was you concerned in ye Rebellion by bearing arms in service of the Pretender? Answer, No.

2 Did you contribute men or moe to ye rebels and on what inducement? Answer, I was forced by William Ogilvy, one of ye rebel captains who was in ye town with a party at ye time to do so.

3 Did you in your conversation or talking with your neighbours say anything to encourage ye Rebellion, or against His Majesty and ye great establishment? Answer, No.

4 Did you attend a non-juring meeting-house during ye time of ye Rebellion? Answer, No, but always attended on ordinances dispensed by the minister of this church.

The same questions were put to Tho. Ogilvie and Patrick Gillies, and they returned the same answers, signed George Doig, Tho. Ogilvie, Pat. Gillies. John Wright, being asked ye same questions, gave ye same answer as did ye other elders, only he acknowledged "yt ye rebels forced him by fire and sword to go through ye parish and summon'd ye tenants to bring carts for carrying their arms to Coupar of Angus," and this is consistent with ye knowledge of ye people in ye town, yet, I am ready to prove if required, signed,

> John Wright. The same question being put to Mr. Robert Smith, schoolmaster and session clk., he returned ye same answers excepting yt he had neither contributed men nor moe for ye rebellion, yt that he was not qualify'd to the government it never being appointed of him, only he had signed ye confessione of faith and formula, signed, Robert Smith (he is qualifyed since). The above questions being put at John Allardice, officer, he answered all of them in ye negative, sign'd, John Allardice.

From the above examination it would seem that the elders had taken some little part in the Rising.

Dr. James Lyon, who was ordained minister of Glamis on 14th September, 1780, gave some account of the state of the old church in his statistical account of the parish. It was then "old and in very bad condition" but was obviously a building of great beauty. The pity is that it was not restored. This elegant church which enshrined much medieval beauty was pulled down in 1792 when the present church was built on the same site. Fragments of the old building are still occasionally found when graves are dug near the church.

Dr. Lyon was the son of the Reverend George Lyon of Wester-Ogil. Born on 29th March, 1759, he was presented to the living of Glamis by the tutors of John, Earl of Strathmore in 1780. He received the degree of Doctor of Divinity from Aberdeen University in 1823 and died in 1838 in his eightieth year. His wife, a daughter of John Ramsay L'amy of Dunkenny, was a poetess of some note. Many of her verses are in Roger's *Modern Scottish Minstrel*. She composed the words to Neil Gow's "Farewell to Whisky" in the Manse of Glamis.

Glamis Church has a number of interesting relics. Four old communion cups, a pulpit Bible, a Poores Box dated 1688, an old "mortcloath" of fringed black velvet, a baptismal basin of pewter, two pewter collection plates and some communion tokens dated 1783.

The two oldest communion cups are of beaten silver with the arms of Earl Patrick engraved upon them. They are dated 1676 and bear the mongram P.E.K. (Patrick, Earl of Kinghorne). He was created Earl of Strathmore in the following year 1677 and there seems little doubt that he gave them to the Church. These cups were missing for some years, probably between 1688 and 1750. The Pulpit Bible is bound in calf and was printed in 1679. The Poores Box, like the communion cups, was lost for many years, but was found in the cellar under the Session House. It is a smallish oaken box, panelled, black with age, contains four drawers and has a double lock to which there were two keys, each held by a different elder, both of whom had to be present before the box was opened. This box held the money and valuable papers of the Kirk Session.

Castle, Church and village today are a living microcosm of history. Kings and Saints, Queens and Nobles, legend and fantasy, wars and feuds, farmers and shepherds, foresters and gamekeepers, the blacksmith and the stone mason, the gardeners and stockmen and a host of humble men and women from cottage and moorland croft, sure in their native Scots dignity, are the warm colours in this living picture of more than a thousand years of history, humanity and beauty.

Glamis is like an ancient jewel glowing with the inner lights of uncounted suns—precious and irreplaceable. An unique heritage, part of the soul and blood of Britain.

The Queen Mother goes seldom or never to Glamis today. For her it is not only the place of happy childhood memories, but of infinitely tenderer memories of the days when she and her young husband and their children, the present Queen and Princess Margaret, made it their other home.

Those near to the Queen Mother have told me that when King George VI died her grief was so deep that, like a wounded creature, she wanted to hide herself in a secret place of her own, far from the rest of this world.

That, perhaps, is why she chose to buy for herself the Castle of Mey: a house which lies alone in a strange, other-worldly land of legend and austere beauty—a land where old men still tell of the last witches, and the great Water-Horse who snorts fire as his hooves churn the waters of Loch Calder. There, just within living memory, "Sandy of the Second Sight", the wizard of Houstry, raised the last Teine-Eiginn or need-fire in the North to propitiate the fairies. They believe in these things over the peat fires in the croft houses of Caithness. It is a land of sharp winds, high skies and dun, flat moorlands with bright barley fields to lighten the scene. To the south the blue mountains of Ben Hope, Ben Hee, Ben Loyal and others stand against the sky like barriers to shut out the outer world. The Atlantic beats its everlasting roll of drums against the towering cliffs of Handa, the isle of wheeling seabirds, of Scourie and Cape Wrath. To the north the sharp tides of the Pentland Firth race by Thurso Bay, Dunnett Head and Duncansby Head, whilst to the east the North Sea glitters lonely. In this bleak land the Queen Mother has chosen to live in her rare moments of privacy.

The Castle stands on the lonely northern shore of Caithness, almost the most northerly point of Britain. From the back windows you look across the racing tides of the Pentland Firth to the grey-green loom of the Orkneys. The cliffs of Stroma rise from the wine-dark sea, gold and purple in the sun. Along the shore at the foot of that brief strip of rough grass which flows from the Castle walls to the tideline, oyster-catchers, brilliant in black, cream and scarlet, trip like ballet dancers, go scything over the waves, flinging their wild whistle to the lonely sky.

In the dawn, from the bedroom windows of the Castle, you can see the grey geese, fresh from the Arctic, marching like soldiers over the grass pastures where black Aberdeen Angus cattle move in stately manner.

You will not see many ships bucketing through the sharp tides of these northern seas. The Orkney ferry steamer "takes it green" as she plunges her bows into the tide-race and flings the spray mast-high. The motor fishing smacks from Thurso, high-prowed, with splendid names, *Golden Harvest* and *Ocean Treasure*, go hull down on the skyline. They earn a hard living from the fierce tides, the spume and spindrift and stinging sleet. Sometimes a coaster passes, its black plume of smoke low down on the sea-horizon. When northerly gales roar down from the Arctic and the Great Skuas, those huge pirate gulls ride the blast like Valkyries, this old Castle of Mey, the private house of the Queen Mother, is crusted with salt spray.

Landward the Castle faces up a long farm road, through barley fields and potato haulms, to the bleak moors of Caithness and the far blue loom of the mountains of Sutherland.

It is not a grand castle. No stately pile like Dunrobin, or feudal stronghold like Blair. It is small, ancient, compact and cosy. That is, as cosy as you can be with all the winds of the world to beat about your ears. It sits there, as it has sat for centuries, half encircled by two little protecting woods of wind-twisted oak, ash and elm, bent awry by sea-gales. Black-muzzled cannon on wooden carriages grin defiance to the south. No red-hot cannon ball or whiff of grapeshot will ever mow down the foe.

I doubt if there are more than half a score of bedrooms in the Castle. The Queen Mother's own bedroom, like the windows of her study, look down a garden walk of lilies and roses and flowers aflame to a gate which leads to the little wood on the east. The wood which, in spring, is alight with primroses, daffodils and violets. A wood of the fairies if ever I saw one.

On the other side of the gravelled sweep at the front door lies a two-acre walled garden. It is the nearest thing to paradise on your way to the Arctic Circle. A garden bright with flowers, ripe with fruit, enchanted with roses and nostalgic with herbs, marjoram and mint, rosemary and rue, basil and fennel, thyme and parsley. And, of course, potatoes, carrots, beans, currants, beetroot, apples and pears.

An enchantment to the eye when I saw it bloom in the autumn sun, but when winter gales roar down from the Faeroes it is, as the head gardener remarked, "A verra whirlpool o' the winds." The Castle of Mey is no home for a weakling.

This miniature castle which was once the home of the Earls of Caithness, who called it Barrogill Castle and owned tens of thousands of acres of bleak moors, wind-bitten farms and mountains of the deer, is the heart of no great estate today. It sits snugly in a mere twenty-five acres of field, wood, gardens and lawns, with an off-farm of seventy acres a short walk across the fields. Here Alex Swanson, who looks as though he has Viking blood in him, was when I saw him, harvesting the barley with a "sailer reaper" of the type that went out of use in England thirty years ago or more. He is now dead.

There is no great garrison in the Castle of Mey—merely a charming couple, June and Sandy Webster, who with their children hold the fort when the Queen Mother is away. Mr. Webster is head gardener.

If the last of the Vikings were to come alive and ground their raven-beaked galley on the beach on a wild night of winds, and storm ashore, swords in hand, with that bloodcurdling war-cry "Yuch! Hey! Saa-saa!" going before them on the gale, the ghost of Alec Swanson, "the Son of Sweyne", like enough a descendant of one of Forkbeard's men, would be waiting for them. They would know the cut of each others' jibs at first sight. This is Viking country. A fit place for a Lyon of Glamis.

16

THE CASTLE OF MEY TODAY

NOW let us consider the Castle of Mey as it is in this year of 1978, more than twenty years since I last saw it. It has undergone a few modernizations but none which spoil the architecture or atmosphere of the place. The Castle of Mey, like other castles in Scotland (and elsewhere) grew out of the country's history, its development reflecting changing conditions over the years. It is splendidly sited, at times dramatic and remote.

The castle is situated in the Parish of Canisbay, in the County of Caithness, about fifteen miles to the East of Thurso. It stands on rising ground, about four hundred yards from the sea-shore, overlooking the Pentland Firth and the Orkney Islands.

The earliest castles to be found in Caithness date from the fourteenth century. They were built of necessity when defence was very important, during the lean years, beginning with the Wars of Independence.

The original structures were rudely built with thick stone walls forming small, rectangular keeps. The windows were narrow and few in number. The castles were sited in positions of great natural advantage on rocky promontories rising sheer out of the sea, with a deep trench cut across the neck of the promontory, making them easily defended from the landward side. The Castle of Old Wick and Forse are examples of this type of construction.

As the need grew for less primitive accommodation and with firearms coming into use, so castle design changed. A wing was added at right-angles to the main rectangular keep, enabling the frontage of the main building to be covered by fire from the wing, and vice versa. This became known as an "L" plan castle. At the same time, a court-yard was added which contained out-buildings and this construction was typical of the period from 1400 to 1542. Bucholie and Girnigie Castles are typical examples of this period. Castle development continued and the 'Z' Plan was introduced during the last half of the sixteenth century and the beginning of the seventeenth century. Another wing, or "jamb" was added diagonally opposite the first one, which afforded all round protection and increased the accommodation. The whole building was extended upwards, the upper floors being used for sleeping accommodation, with the wings often ending in turrets at the same height as the main building.

The Castle of Mey is an example of a "Z" plan Castle.

The "Z" plan of the Castle indicates that it was built between 1566 and 1572, and, despite various changes over the years, the original outline can still be seen.

The main entrance used to be on the sea-side of the Castle, through the court-yard, at the base of the North-west Tower in which was the original staircase. This is evident from the vaulted roof above the stair-landing on the first floor, and, at that level, another stairway goes up at an angle into a turret which leads to the next floor.

There is a vaulted passage on the ground floor, leading to the cellars and the original kitchen, which is situated at the East end of the building. The kitchen required a very large fireplace, 12 feet 6 inches (3.8 metres) in width and 6 feet (1.83 metres) in depth. It was built outwards to project 6 feet (1.83 metres) from the building line, which explains this slight deviation from the usual "Z" plan. To the south of the kitchen is another circular stone stairway which winds upwards, serving all the floors, to come out on to the roof of the main turret.

The first floor contained the great hall, 40 feet (12.2 metres) long by 18 feet (5.5 metres) wide, with a private room off it, which was over the kitchen, and another, smaller room with a vaulted ceiling in the South-east Tower at a slightly lower level.

The second and third floors contained the bedrooms and do so to this day.

Seen from a distance, the turreted aspect of the Castle is striking. The jutting towers and corbelled turrets are typical of the period of the sixteenth century subsequent to the Reformation, particularly the chequered character of the corbelling of the smaller turrets.

The parapet of the large turret is supported on winged cherub heads as corbels, similar to those on Canberry Tower, Midlothian.

Most of the windows have been enlarged.

There are numerous horizontal gun holds throughout the ground floor, several in the angles of the Tower and also on the first floor.

The round, arched entrance to the court-yard is unaltered and is very old.

Over the years, a number of modern additions were added, some of which were removed by Her Majesty Queen Elizabeth, the Queen Mother, who is anxious to preserve the Castle's original character.

The principal additions which remain are the porch-type structure, now the main entrance on the south side of the Castle, and, on the west end, a two storey addition containing the kitchen, at ground level, with the dining-room above. The accommodation to the west side of the court-yard has been improved to provide staff quarters.

The Castle was built by George, Fourth Earl of Caithness, who granted it to his second son, William Sinclair, who died at an early age. It was then granted to his next son, George, who founded the family of the Sinclairs of Mey. This family succeeded to the Earldom of Caithness in 1789 and the Castle became the seat of the Earldom for the next 100 years.

Originally, it was known as the Castle of Mey, but its name was changed to Barrogill Castle. The Castle and Estate changed hands several times, until the Estate had to be broken up in 1952. Her Majesty Queen Elizabeth, the Queen Mother, purchased the Castle and Policies in 1953, and gave the Castle back its original name. The farm of Longoe was added shortly afterwards and the property is farmed as a whole by Her Majesty who breeds Aberdeen-Angus cattle and North Country Cheviot sheep, which are often seen grazing the Castle Policies.

A woman's castle calls for a woman to describe it. This is the vivid picture drawn by Josephine King in the magazine *Woman* of August 9th, 1975, which permits me to quote thus:

> For eleven months of the year the Castle of Mey stands bleakly against the bitter winds that sweep in from the sea. Grey stone house and high-walled garden wait silently for the moment each August when the Queen Mother sets out for her private home on this most northerly coast of Britain, overlooking the islands of Orkney. Everything is carefully timed so that when she arrives the garden blazes with colour and the house with warmth to welcome its royal mistress. Here in this romantically lonely landscape, relaxed and with the minimum of fuss, she celebrates her birthday, with only a small household at hand, and a few friends to join her on a picnic and stroll along the beach.
>
> The only permanent residents at Mey are June and Sandy Webster, who act as housekeeper and caretaker, with their two children. Inside, the house, kept polished and aired by June, immediately beckons you with its light friendly interior.
>
> There's a hotch potch of comfortable chairs and a portable record player in the drawing room; an upright piano in the study with the songs of Jerome Kern lying on the top; a shelf full of the sort of books everyone likes to read on holiday. In the hall is a clutter of deckchairs and a croquet set; a beachcomber's trophies lie on a little antique table.
>
> It's very much a home, full of individual touches, some personal, some associated with Royal duties.
>
> In the dining-room, there's a dummy fireplace—as a back-cloth to it Sir Martin Charteris, the Queen's private secretary, designed and himself cast in bronze a screen depicting the Queen Mother's connections with Scotland; like the puffins on nearby Dunnet Head, and the Royal Yacht sailing through the Firth, for most years the Queen visits her mother at Mey when the Royal yacht anchors in these waters.
>
> On the opposite wall is a tapestry of the Queen Mother's coat-of-

arms; designed by Stephen Gooden, it took three girls three years to embroider it. In the drawing-room are beaded footstools bought in local antique shops, and all round the walls are local landscapes by local artists, the result of the Queen Mother's visits to the annual art exhibition in Thurso. Among her favourite artists is Alec Sutherland.

As we climbed the steep winding stairs of the tower we caught glimpses of chintzy bedrooms, gaily coloured bedspreads, a huge four-poster and a decor where the only continuous theme is the white-painted walls.

In the atmosphere of comfort and cosiness it's hard to imagine a ghost staying the course, with nothing of eeriness or gloom to encourage it but, needless to say, the tower is supposed to be haunted. If you look up from the outside you can count five windows, but however hard you try, the number inside won't tally. The story goes that Lady Fanny Sinclair, daughter of the thirteenth Earl of Caithiness, fell in love with an equerry—in those days a humble stable servant. He was sacked, but she followed him to London only to be brought back and locked in her room in the tower. In her despair she flung herself to her death on the cobbles below. Mrs. Webster says Royal guests are not given the haunted room—only servants sleep there, and whether they are told the story of the "Green Lady" or not depends on their toughness!

Ignoring the lift, the Queen Mother climbs the stairs often to watch the sun set over the Island of Hoy. Nearer to, the tower looks out over sloping fields to the beach awash with sea shells.

Days spent at Mey are for casual shopping in local towns, for shooting parties on the 2,000 acres of moorland on which she has the sporting rights, for angling for trout and salmon in the brown fast-flowing rivers of Caithness and Sutherland.

A policeman may stand at the gate to stave off eager sightseers, but anyone strolling on the beach may find themselves saying good-day to a member of the Royal family out for a walk.

While the whole estate is managed by Factor Mr. Martin Leslie, the head gardener, Mr. Jimmy Matheson,* is responsible for the grounds. Together with two helpers he tends the lawns, and the flagstone fences of red Caithness sandstone; avenues of ancient sycamores—the only trees capable of surviving what locals call the "blast"—blend to form a delicate archway from gate to castle door.

* Mr. Webster's predecessor as head gardener.

But Jimmy's special pride is his domain of about two acres hidden behind high walls. Here he has worked for twenty-seven years—the last three as head man—building and watching the garden flourish in defiance of the gales which sweep in laden with sleet, hail or just salt spray from one of the deadliest stretches of water in the kingdom.

The work starts in two small greenhouses crammed with seedlings: pansies, lobelia and marigolds, to join giant primulas in the herbaceous border: alyssum, verbena and borage for the Queen Mother's favourite herb garden, spanning almost the whole of the north wall—and late sowings of cauliflower, peas and cabbage. Here too in pots are petunias, begonias, fuchsia and a bank of another of the Queen Mother's favourites—lemon-scented geranium. Chrysanthemums too, with the buds nipped out to hold back the flowering. Throughout her stay there is a constant flow of brilliant colour from the little greenhouses to the main house to join cut flowers which are changed daily, and the bouquets which regularly greet her from all over the country on her birthday.

Jimmy Matheson uses only varieties that he knows are tried and tested against the northerly climate—southern plants he says are not acclimatised. Young vegetable seedlings are hardened off in cold frames before being planted out at the end of May in one of the squares that make up the central garden. Here, protected only by hedges of flowering currant, centuries old, and fed only with manure from Long-goe farm, the rich Caithness soil produces a crop of vegetables which is more than adequate for the needs of the Castle.

Beside the traditional root and green crops, the Queen Mother can feast on Jerusalem and globe artichokes, celery and leeks, and long after the South has had its fill, she can enjoy raspberries and strawberries, by the bowlful.

Every day of her stay the Queen Mother walks round the garden with Jimmy, discussing its progress, planning for future summers. This year there's a new rose to admire—it's called Glenfiddick and won't be on sale until 1976—and two more newcomers to Mey, the cold beauty of Iceberg and blood-red Europeana.

On two days in July and one in August the garden only is open to the public—in aid of the Lifeboat Institution—but, for the rest, the Castle and garden wait, wracked by wind, for the next visit of a queen.

17

THE QUEEN WITH HORSE SENSE

No Queen since Queen Anne, who founded Ascot, has made such an impact on racing history. The Queen Mother was born with an instinctive love for and judgement of horseflesh. Racing and breeding has dominated much of the leisure of her life. Her patronage was of immense value to the bloodstock industry after the War when racing was in the doldrums. Her presence on the race course cheered up the nation. The English people have always had an affection for a monarch who loves horses. The Stuart Kings made Newmarket. They had a wooden throne on a hillock overlooking the gallops on the Bury road. Charles II was a splendid horseman and a tireless walker, facts overshadowed by his harem of beauties. Edward VII was no great man in the saddle—good living and cigars did not help—but his appearance on the racecourse in the early years of this century caused scenes of unparalleled enthusiasm. No king had been so popular at Epsom as "good old Teddy". George V, whose *Life as a Sportsman* I was privileged to write, was very much the true horseman. He loved Newmarket and was never happier than when he was there, perhaps staying at the Jockey Club, and walking about on the turf, greeting his friends and looking over his horses. The late Cecil Leveson-Gower, who was kind enough to write a special chapter on George V's racing stable, summed it up neatly when he wrote

> Although he has not enjoyed the same measure of success as his father, King George won his first race as far back as 1911 at Newmarket, with a horse called Pintadeau, and thereafter the deeds of

London Cry, Friar Marcus, Knight of the Garter, Limelight, Scuttle, Fox-earth and the Royal Hunt Cup Winner Weathervane, have added fresh lustre to the Royal colours.

Her Majesty Queen Elizabeth the Queen Mother's ancestors on the Bowes side had owned racehorses with up-and-down luck in the past. The most successful was Mr. John Bowes who won the Derby four times; with Mündig in 1835, Cotherstone in 1843, Daniel O'Rourke in 1852 and with West Australian a year later. His first win was when he was only twenty-one and still at Cambridge. The vast income from the lead mines and other mineral rights on the estates in Durham cushioned his way. Gradually, as the mines were exhausted much of that income dried up.

The Second World War cut racing to the bone. Newmarket Heath became an aerodrome. It was feared that one day the German *Luftwaffe*, that deadly Air Force would choose it as a main landing ground for their threatened invasion of Britain. At that time the late Mr. Marriott was Agent to the Jockey Club. That made him the supreme figure of power and discipline on the Heath. His prestige was neatly pin-pointed when a newspaper man asked a local stable "boy" if the racing world did not fear an air invasion of the Heath.

"Not for one minute, Sir," the wizened little "boy" replied firmly. "Not bleeding likely. Mr. Marriott would never allow it."

It was widely feared that owing to the general stringency of economics and their tight schedule of official work, that the new King George VI and his lovely Scots wife, now the Queen Mother, would quite likely reduce the royal racing interest or drop them altogether for the time being. Far from it. He ascended the throne on 12th December, 1936. A few days later it was officially announced that he would "maintain the royal racing stable and stud on the same lines as his late father, King George V".

George VI and his wife paid a more or less unexpected visit to Newmarket in June, 1942. They were visiting reclaimed

Fenland a few miles away much of which, incidentally, belonged to me and was a remarkable duck shoot and wild life sanctuary combined. Alas the bureaucrats requisitioned it and my paradise vanished. Mechanical diggers clanked where the bittern had boomed. The reed beds went up in flames and smoke. Wild duck fled on whimpering wing. Marsh harriers took lordly flight and never returned. Instead the black ash-strewn bed of the old Fen mocked the sky. The King and Queen came in a Fenland barge to inspect this triumph of land reclamation.

The rumour reached Newmarket that they were in the neighbourhood but it was almost too much to hope that they would attend. Racing began at noon. There was a lot of peering through field-glasses to see if anything like a Royal party was approaching the Heath. It seemed too much to hope for. Suddenly, a small cavalcade of motor cars was spotted in the far distance. They were coming up the course from the Plantation with a police car leading. The motorcade was so very ordinary that few paid any attention to it. The procession stopped just short of the Silver Ring and lo!—out stepped the King and Queen. They walked slowly up the course escorted by the Stewards of the Jockey Club. The cheers from the astounded crowd rent the skies. The delight of the people was unbounded. Bombers were flying overhead either on their way to face hideous death in Germany or to give equally hideous revenge. The King and Queen daily faced the perils of war with their subjects in London or elsewhere and here they were, dropped out of the sky, so to speak, to join their subjects for a day's racing without fuss or pomp. It was typical of the Queen Mother that although she had worn stout shoes and warm tweeds for her visit to our bleak and windswept Fens, she managed to change into a very attractive mauve crepe dress, with a long coat to match, a mauve straw hat with a feather, complete with handbag. Not a lot of women would have taken the trouble to change thus simply to please their husbands. The Queen did it to please her people! They were having a day out. So would she. It was a rare touch of Royal courtesy. It was significant that the Queen Mother, another Scot, should in such a happy fashion help to revive the racing glories of Newmarket which her Stuart ancestors had founded. Since then she has created for herself a unique niche in English history.

When the Second World War was over and peace returned to a torn and tattered land, the Queen Mother's interest in horses and racing revived, like a flower that had been buried under winter snows. Her daughter, Princess Elizabeth, had clearly inherited her mother's love for horses. As a child she was a good little horsewoman. As she grew older, she became outstandingly good. Princess Anne today carries on that tradition of good horsemanship.

So it surprised no one when in September, 1949, the Queen Mother went into partnership with her daughter under National Hunt rules. She became a familiar figure at Newbury but not at Newmarket. Her love of steeplechasing was predominant. One's mind goes back to a frosty March morning when Platform One at Paddington was packed with race-goers. Horsey-looking men and women in checks and tweeds, bowler hats and cloth caps, ruddy-faced and crisp-voiced. The train which was the focus of attention, towed the royal coach, maroon, blazoned with the royal coat of arms. Then suddenly the tension of the waiting crowd stiffened a little. There was a bustle at the far end of the platform. The Queen, as she was then, appeared. She wore a frilly hat, long pastel-coloured coat, a scarf round her shoulders and her collar turned up. Ahead of her stalked the soldierly figure of her private secretary, Sir Martin Gilliat, preceded, as one journalist waggishly wrote, "by a magnificent pair of eyebrows". He gently edged a way through the crowd. He was an encyclopedia of racing. Just the man for the job. Behind the Queen Mother marched her private detective, carrying a couple of large umbrellas, fur-lined boots, a hat-box and a raincoat or two. It all had the atmosphere of a week-end family party off to the country. The Station Master greeted the little party with a magnificent sweep of his shiny silk top hat. That gave the final touch.

The charming thing about these race journeys was that the Queen Mother seemed to know pretty well everyone on that platform. She greeted them with the smile of an old friend. It could only have happened in England. In most European countries where monarchy still remains, there would have been a military guard and stiff decorum.

The Queen Mother stepped aboard the royal coach and the engine stopped hissing as if to order. A gentle jerk, the train glided forward and they were off. Paddington slipped back to normality and the aura of the stables dissolved.

Naturally enough the Queen Mother brought the old Strathmore colours to life again. They are blue jacket with buff stripes, blue sleeves and gold-tasselled black cap. The horse she shared with Princess Elizabeth was Monaveen, an eight-year-old Irish horse who only a couple of years before had fetched the ludicrous price of £35 at an auction in Ireland. Then the rumour went round that he had a chance of winning the Grand National. His price went up to seven thousand. The Queen Mother was naturally very proud of her first horse, or half a horse, but alas Monaveen fell and broke a leg at Hurst Park in December 1950 and had to be destroyed. He lies in a grave near the course.

The Queen Mother was very fond of that horse and although it never carried her colours to victory, she still has a tender memory for the gallant Monaveen. Better luck came with her next horse. Shortly before Monaveen died, Manicou, a five-year-old, won a race for her in November 1950 at Kempton Park. It was the first win for a Queen of England since the robust days of Queen Anne.

That started the chain of successes which have marked the Queen Mother's racing ever since. Most of her horses have been consistent steady goers. One cannot fail to be captured by the story of how the Queen Mother, when she was building up her string, asked for one horse to be sent to her for appraisal at Clarence House, St. James's. It arrived in a horse-box and was led into the garden. Thereby, it re-opened the stable doors of history for Clarence House was born out of the stables of old St. James's Palace. The horse, Super Fox, was led gently up and down. The Queen Mother ran a practised eye over him from nose to tail. She is a shrewd judge of a horse and has an instinctive sympathy for them and understanding of their moods. That is the inner mark of the true horse-lover—and horses know it. She took only a few minutes to size up Super Fox. She bought him. Probably the only racehorse ever to be bought in a royal garden in the heart of London. Super Fox rewarded her faith and judgement by winning fairly consistently.

She was cheered up in her racing career by Sir Winston Churchill, an old friend and admirer, who had a tremendous admiration for her naturalness, and her devotion to duty. He admired also her good sportsmanship and the fact that she took the rough with the smooth in racing with cheerful philosophy. Winston owned horses himself and had known the champagne taste of victory as well as the sharp whip of defeat.

She had a taste of both in dramatic fashion when another of her horses, Devon Loch, trained by Peter Cazalet, nearly won the Grand National at Aintree, Liverpool, in 1956. No one who was there on that day more than twenty years ago will ever forget the drama. The field, a tidal wave of colour and movement, was thundering up the course to the deafening roar of the onlookers. All the "sporting boys of the North" seemed to be lining the course—noblemen, gentlemen, miners, factory hands, farmers, shopkeepers and the rest of the motley throng to whom Aintree is the playground of the Gods, cheered the Queen Mother's horse. Devon Loch was striding ahead with what seemed unlimited reserves of power. He was almost certain to win. He was fifty yards from the post. Victory seemed absolutely certain. The cheers of the crowd rose to a thunderous crescendo. The Queen of England was going to win and set a unique stamp of glory on the noble role of National History. This would be the Day of Days.

The Queen Mother herself stood watching the race, her cine-camera glued to her eyes, her face tense with excitement. Suddenly her horse Devon Loch, ridden by that splendid jockey Dick Francis, spread-eagled not fifty yards from the winning post and came down with a muddy crash. Dick Francis was out of the saddle. The horse lay twitching. Heaven alone knew what hideous injuries both had suffered. The rest of the field thundered past, their galloping hooves threw a shower of mud over horse and jockey who had so gallantly led them only a few seconds before. Dick Francis, his face quivering and almost in tears, struggled to his feet, threw his whip away with a gesture of infinite despair, and helped Devon Loch gingerly to his feet. The horse strained and shook. How many bones were broken? That was the question on everyone's lips, especially those of the Queen Mother. The moment the horse fell, she put down her cine-camera, hurried from the royal box, and almost ran to the enclosure, into which horse and jockey limped.

"Are you hurt? Is the horse hurt? I am so terribly sorry for you all." The words of warm sympathy tumbled out.

"Yes ma'am, everyone's alright, no one's hurt," said Peter Cazalet, "but you should have won the race."

"There'll come another time," replied the Queen Mother. "After all, that's racing."

She talked to the disconsolate trainer, jockey and horse with a quick, warm understanding which cheered them all up. Her relief that no one was seriously hurt warmed the cold douche of defeat.

Devon Loch rewarded her selflessness seven months later at Nottingham. Half-way through he was lying well to the rear, seemingly without a hope of winning. Then he suddenly picked up, and with a superb burst of speed, crept up and then flashed past the leader, Northern King, to win by two lengths. He had shown the North what he could do when bad luck seemed dead against him.

A few months later, this gallant 'chaser met his Waterloo. He cracked up in the Mildmay Memorial 'Chase at Sandown Park in 1957, a year after that disastrous fall in the National. He went badly lame. Was it the result of that ghastly fall at Aintree when he crashed down in full gallop? We shall never know. He was sent to recuperate at stables in Berkshire. The Queen Mother, to whom horses are almost like human friends, made several special visits to see how her good old horse was doing. When it became clear that he would never be fit to race again, Devon Loch was sent off to Sandringham to spend the rest of his life there as an honoured member of the Royal family of horses. There, in peace and quiet, he died in 1962. The Queen Mother, when at home at Sandringham, never failed to go and look at her old hero and give him lumps of sugar which he nuzzled at in her coat pocket. He knew well that she would never visit him without them.

Devon Loch is a unique milestone in racing history. Had he won the Grand National of 1956 he would have been the first royal horse to do so since Ambush II won for the Prince of Wales in 1900. That indeed would have been the Day of Days.

People often ask why the Queen Mother is so deeply interested in National Hunt racing. The answer is that she was inspired by the courage and superb horsemanship of Lord Mildmay of Flete, the greatest steeplechaser of his day. Mildmay was typical of the older landed aristocracy who have produced so many men, leaders in statesmanship as well as sport, in agriculture as well as in war, colonial pro-consuls as well as foxhunters. Steadfast in loyalty and utterly fearless in physical courage. Mildmay and his horses had that mutual understanding which is the secret of all great horsemen. The Queen Mother has it too.

So, although she and the late King George VI, from the time the King succeeded to the throne until his death, took a very personal interest in racing as such, it was done partly as a sense of duty. The racing industry, as it is now officially called, represents many millions of pounds in exports and imports. It is no longer merely a sport but a great national money-spinner.

Mildmay was the supreme sportsman, the last of the Corinthians. He rose with grace and strength. His seat on a horse and his hands on the reins were a delight to the eye. His courage was little short of epic. The daredevil feats of this young man over "the sticks", which for a few years electrified the nation, set him on a pedestal far above the common ruck. He created a mystique. This captivated the Queen Mother who at first gingerly, and then wholeheartedly, took to "the sticks". Mildmay alas was drowned at sea whilst bathing on his private beach at Mothecombe in South Devon. That happened in May, 1950. He may well have had a muscular seizure while swimming which paralysed him. Two years before in 1948 he had ridden in the National and narrowly missed winning. He was coming up to the last three fences on Cromwell when an old spinal injury suddenly gripped him in excrutiating agony, but he gritted his teeth, and white with pain, finished the race. Twelve years before in 1936 he just missed winning another National. Now the sea claimed the brave heart.

I quote briefly the career of this classic rider because a well-known trainer, once said of the Queen Mother "She has done more for National Hunt racing than anybody since Lord Mildmay." That is a tribute which she will treasure all her life.

Her interest in racing grows each year. She studies the Form Book without missing a point. Her racing library and knowledge is quite astounding. She collects pictures of former great horses and has got together quite a notable gallery of them. Three quarters of her everyday life is devoted to her public duties and preparing for them. Nonetheless, she manages to keep level with most of the races in which her horses run. When she cannot attend a meeting she has it relayed to her at Clarence House on the "blower". This invaluable service relays to its subscribers everything they need to know about a particular race. It relays up-to-date information on the going, weights, weather, jockey changes, starting prices and so on. She misses little, but her interest grows all the time. She has less time for shooting, although she is a fair shot with both a game gun and stalking rifle and a good fly fisher with many good salmon and trout to her credit! Steeplechasing has taken the lead in her affections.

She does not bet. Her wins, however, have contributed more than usefully to the cost of her horses. After her first decade of racing it was estimated that to keep from a dozen to twenty horses in training cost her ten thousand pounds a year. As her judgement paid dividends, she expected to win nearly as much in prize money in years when she might reasonably expect to finish with a hundred or more wins to her credit. When she entered her nineteenth season in 1967–'68 she had more than a dozen horses training in Kent and had owned more than fifty others which had won her some £75,000 of prize money in 160 races.

She certainly does not race for the sake of money. Her love of racing is the very real love of horseflesh and the atmosphere of the racecourse itself. She is thoroughly at home with trainers, jockeys and racegoers alike. The atmosphere of stables and racecourse fascinates her. She is at home in it. Her most flamboyant racing acquaintance was that incredible tipster who called himself Prince Ras Monolulu. His real name, believe it or not, was Peter Carl McKay. When the Queen Mother was explaining the finer points of 'chasing to her son-in-law, Antony Armstrong Jones, at Newbury in March, 1960, the gigantic black man, clothed in brilliant swirling robes, wearing brightly coloured ostrich plumes, capered up shouting and cheering "Here they are—give them a cheer!" and cheer they did! The Queen Mother was amused and fascinated. She became a friend of the towering Ethiopian. Monolulu began his career as a tipster in 1920 when he gave a tip to his patrons which made little fortunes for some of them. He tipped Spion Kop to win the Derby and win it did. Fifteen years later he won £25,000 on the Derby and lost the lot the next day. Nothing daunted, he continued his ebullient career, and earned a smile and a nod from the Queen Mother whenever she saw him on the course. He died, beloved by many, at the age of eighty-four, in the Middlesex Hospital in 1964.

In the next year, 1961, the Queen Mother did remarkably well. The *London Evening News* said this: "The Queen Mother's enthusiasm for racing seems to be gaining impetus from her highly successful year. She was at Sandown Park again this afternoon for the second successive day. This made her third day's racing this week. . . . Surely the Sport of Kings should be renamed the Sport of Queens."

One of her greatest horses was Double Star who gave her more wins than any other horse. He won seventeen races before arthritis beat him. A wonderful horse. Gay Record, a temperamental, choosy horse, of highly individual character, was one of her favourites. She knew that horse as well as other people know a human friend. The Queen Mother once said "I wish they were all as honest as him." On 20th October, 1964, at Folkestone, this great horse won for the Queen Mother her one hundredth victory.

A month later three others of her horses, Arch Point, Super Fox and Gay Record did the hat trick for the Queen Mother. They won three separate races for her, again at Folkestone, that green and lovely course within the smell of the sea. The Queen Mother ran down the steps from the glass-fronted visitors' box to pat her horses and congratulate her jockeys. She beamed with joy. The crowd cheered like mad, and threw their hats in the air, and yelled "Well done, Ma'am!" One of the stewards said afterwards, "She was up and down those steps like a two-year-old." Her horses had won the hat trick once before at Lingfield in 1961 with Laffy, Double Star and The Rip.

The Rip was perhaps the Queen Mother's most personal horse. The story of how she bought him is almost a little romance in itself. She spotted the horse when he was grazing in a paddock near a pub called The Red Cat at Sandringham. A big powerful animal, beautifully built, with all the right points, he caught her eye immediately. She made enquiries. Lo! Who should the mystery horse be but the son of her own great horse Manicou, whom she had bought from Lord Mildmay. It was her first winner. And here was its son out of a mare called Easy Mare. She had the horse paraded in the pub yard. There among the crates and bottles she ran her expert eye over the son of her old favourite—and bought him on the spot. He won ten races for her and justified her faith and judgement so well that she decided to enter him in the 1965 Grand National. He was obviously a born steeplechaser, as cunning as a fox, a good jumper, and a consistent all-round performer. Sir Martin Gilliat summed it all up in a phrase when he said just before the race: "It seems almost too good to be true that a horse chosen entirely on the Queen Mother's own judgement and sired by her own stallion, should now be in this position."

The Queen Mother watched the race, all tension and attention, from Lord Derby's box. Her eyes followed every second of the great race. Her jockey Bill Rees, crouched on The Rip's back like a mouse on a pound of cheese, obviously did his best to win, but an American-owned horse, Jay Trump, kept up a relentless neck-and-neck race, and won. The Rip, alas, was seventh. The Queen

Mother, as usual, welcomed her horse and jockey warmly and without a trace of disappointment.

In the next year 1966, the dark shadow of destruction loomed over the Grand National course at Aintree. It was threatened by building development. That would mean an end of the National. Luckily it was saved for the moment and the great race was run again. The many thousands who adored the Queen Mother and almost regarded themselves as part owners of her horses, hoped that she would win—at last. Earlier in the year she hoped that she might win with Oedipe which had belonged previously to Prince Rajisingh of Rajpipla. Major Cazalet, however, decided that the horse was not up to the race and did not enter him.

The Grand National was run in March when the Queen Mother was on her third Australasian tour. The Australians were thrilled by her practical knowledge of racing and were even more so when she picked four horses in one week-end, three of which were winners but the fourth was a good second. They were Storm Queen in Sydney, Bowl King in Melbourne, Better Queen in Adelaide and the fourth which came second was Klim King. It seems she was influenced in her choice by the royal names of the horses. Then she went on to New Zealand. The sporting New Zealanders, more British than the British, greeted her with two new races in her honour—the Balmoral Steeplechase and the Glamis Stakes. A pretty compliment.

Despite her vast number of public duties and her devotion to racing, in her few spare moments the Queen Mother has still squeezed in occasional visits to her childhood home, Glamis, and the family estates in Durham. In 1975 there was a gala day at Holwich Hall in the Bowes-Moor country when the entire tenantry of the English estates gathered to give her a resounding welcome which she will never forget. It was a unique day.

INDEX